A SHORT HISTORY OF THE MIDDLE EAST

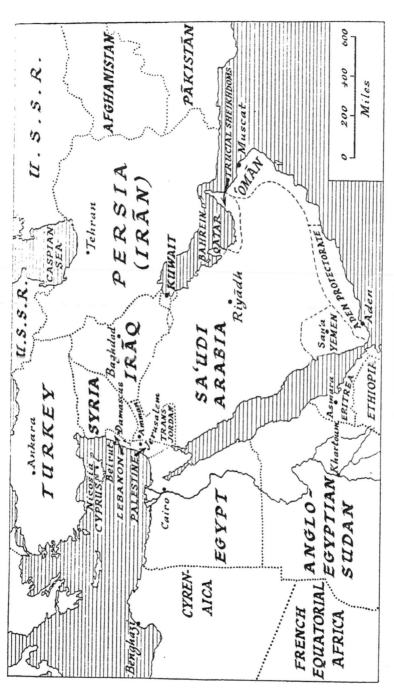

I. THE MIDDLE EAST

A SHORT HISTORY OF
THE MIDDLE EAST

from the Rise of Islam to Modern Times

by

GEORGE E. KIRK

M.A. (Cantab.)

sometime Sandys Classical Student

*"Universal history . . . is not a burden on the memory,
but an illumination of the soul."*   (LORD ACTON)

METHUEN & CO. LTD. LONDON
36 Essex Street, Strand, W.C.2

First published in 1948

CATALOGUE NO. 3788/U

THIS BOOK IS PRODUCED IN
COMPLETE CONFORMITY WITH THE
AUTHORIZED ECONOMY STANDARDS

TO MARGARET

'for the Resurrection of the dead,
and the life of the world to come.'

Contents

Maps

From drawings by S. O. Pritchard and N. S. Hyslop

Introduction

THE PRESENT volume has grown out of a course of lectures delivered since the War at the Middle East Centre for Arab Studies to British students who required a general grounding in Middle East history and current affairs to assist in fitting them for active careers in that region, but not to make them historical specialists. The views stated throughout are entirely personal, and are in no way to be taken to represent any official view presented to students at the Centre; nor has there been any access to unpublished official information. It is thought that the content of these lectures may interest a wider public whose attention has been drawn to the Middle East by current political questions, and for whom no general introduction to the subject exists.

What then do we mean by the 'Middle East'?

At the time of the First World War there was in general use a satisfactory terminology for the sub-divisions of Asia, south of Siberia, as viewed from Europe: the Far East comprised China and Japan, and the geographically dependent lands of South-East Asia; India-with-Burma, Afghanistan, and Persia formed the Middle East; and the Near East was understood to comprise the Ottoman Empire and the Arabian Peninsula.

For some reason which is not clear, this accepted terminology was upset at the outbreak of the Second World War, when the British forces based on Egypt were called the Middle East Command. There has been some criticism of this change of name; but in answer to a question in the House of Commons in April 1946 the Prime Minister stated, 'It has become the accepted practice to use the term "Middle East" to cover the Arab world and certain neighbouring countries. The practice seems to me convenient and I see no reason to change it.' American usage is still divided between 'Near East' and 'Middle East'.

In this work the Middle East is taken to comprise the Arabian Peninsula and the Arabic-speaking lands on its northern border; the Arabic-speaking lands of North East Africa (Egypt, the Anglo-

Egyptian Sudan, Cyrenaica, and Tripolitania); Asia Minor or Anatolia, which now forms the greater part of the Turkish Republic; and Persia or Iran. The Arabic-speaking lands form, both geographically and historically, the central core of this region, and it is with them mainly that this work is concerned; but they cannot be studied in isolation, either in the past or the present, from the linguistically-foreign lands of Anatolia and Persia which border them on the north.

CHAPTER I

A.D. 600—The Middle East in Disintegration

THE POSITION that the Middle East occupies in history is a unique one. It was there in all probability that Man, having lived for perhaps one million years in complete dependence on the wild vegetable and animal foods that he could acquire by gathering and hunting, learnt by laborious trial and error some 8,000 or so years ago to cultivate food-plants and to domesticate certain useful animals, and so for the first time became capable of advancing to a higher civilization. From between three and two thousand years ago, as the map of that higher civilization in the Middle East was beginning to burn lower, there sprang from it two beams of dazzling light, the moral-intellectual beam of Greek humanistic thought and the moral-spiritual beam of the Judaeo-Christian awareness of God's Presence, which have conjointly illuminated Western civilization down to the present time. There have been periods in which one of these twin lights has shone more brightly than the other; but without the two of them our own civilization could not have come into existence; and where either of them is extinguished, as some men have thought to extinguish them in the last thirty years, our witness is that the very tissue of civilization degenerates by rapid and dreadful processes into a malignant and swelling growth of barbarism.

Man's great step forward from food-gathering to agriculture, his Response to a great Challenge[1] presented by fundamental changes in his natural environment, has been well set forth by archaeologists in the last thirty years. So many learned and brilliant books have been written about the Greek genius, and about the origins and growth of our Christian Faith, that one would be perplexed where to advise the enquiring reader to turn first for enlightenment on these subjects. On the Silver Age of the Middle East also, the age of the Islamic or so-called Arab Civilization,

[1] cf. A. J. Toynbee, *A Study of History*, one vol. abridgement, part II, especially 68 ff.

there are numerous scholarly works; but for those, made aware by the daily paper that the Middle East is still of great significance in the modern world and desirous of orientating themselves in its recent history, there is no single guide. This book is an attempt to provide that guidance, though the course it has to follow is neither a clear nor a brilliant one. We cannot embark on our voyage at a nearer point than the eve of the rise of Islam; and already

>   'sands begin
> to hem his watery march, and dam his streams,
> and split his currents; that for many a league
> the shorn and parcell'd Oxus strains along
> through beds of sand and matted rushy isles—
> Oxus, forgetting the bright speed he had
> in his high mountain-cradle in Pamere,
> a foil'd circuitous wanderer—till at last
> the long'd for dash of waves is heard. . . .'[1]

To the pioneers of the Arab Awakening thirty years ago the 'luminous home of waters' did indeed appear to be 'opening wide'; but we are now proving all over the world that the nineteenth-century solutions, liberal-democracy and national self-determination, were at best palliatives, and at worst symptoms, of Man's primeval disease, his Original Sin of self-will;[2] that the twentieth-century totalitarianisms only foster that self-will in its most hideous form; and mankind will find no home

>   'bright
> and tranquil, from whose floor the new-bathed stars
> appear'

this side of the Civitas Dei.

★   ★   ★

Climatic changes covering thousands of years, which may be summarized in popular language as the recession of the last Ice Age, had by about 6000 b.c. reduced large tracts of the Middle East to the virtually rainless and desert conditions which still obtain in the Sahara, lying athwart Africa with a depth of 1000 miles from north

---

[1] Matthew Arnold, *Sohrab and Rustam*, end.
[2] cf. Reinhold Niebuhr, *The Children of Light and the Children of Darkness*, 16 f.

to south, and its extension, the Arabian Desert. To the north of this sterile belt, the mountain-ranges of Syria, Anatolia, and Persia receive an adequate winter rainfall from the Mediterranean; and this relatively well-watered region is flanked to west and east by the basins of two great river-systems, the Nile and the Euphrates-Tigris, to form a Fertile Crescent which was in all probability the home of the original Agricultural Civilization to which reference has been made above.[1]

The state of society in the Middle East in 600 A.D. was still the direct outcome of the expansion and development of this Agricultural Civilization. Agriculture had naturally not been possible in the vast desert regions, except in small oases isolated from one another, where subterranean water could be tapped by wells; but in the marginal steppe-lands one of the arts of this civilization, the taming of useful animals, had enabled man to gain a precarious footing and win a hard livelihood as nomad Bedouin with their herds of sheep and goats and camels. The more favoured lands produced abundant grain and fruits for consumption and export, while in the towns secondary manufactures were worked up, and there was eventually a lively commerce in luxury goods between India and the Mediterranean, and in objects of less value over shorter distances. The distribution of the products of labour was, however, so far from equitable that it had become a brake on material inventiveness and economic enterprise. While the precarious little communities of men in a 'food-gathering' state, before the discovery of agriculture, had probably practised a primitive communism of goods as the only way of ensuring their group-survival, the growth of the Agricultural Civilization with its rapid development of new techniques had (like the Industrial Revolution of the nineteenth century) temporarily caused the supply and variety of goods to outstrip the increase of population; and it was probably with general approval that those sections of the population deemed most instrumental in bringing about or maintaining this new abundance had acquired an unequal share of the goods. These privileged sections were the priesthoods, originally the repositories and guardians of the traditional science and other learning of each community, and the military leaders who protected the community's goods against the depredations of uncivilized raiders from

[1] For a study of the historical process, see C. F. C. Hawkes, *The Prehistoric Foundations of Europe*, 70.

the wastes or struggled with jealous neighbours over some debatable right. On successively lower levels came the small class of public servants, the merchants, the artisans, and, on the lowest level of all, the cultivators, close to the soil and scarcely reached by the higher material and intellectual gifts of successive periods of civilization. Such is the force of tradition that the individual's place in one of these social and occupational classes was generally determined by his parenthood and upbringing, though the Middle East never knew the rigidity of the Hindu caste-system and it was always possible for an exceptional man to improve his station.

Since a large section of the population, the artisans and peasants, received so small a share of manufactured goods, there was little incentive to expand their production, beyond the limit of what was consumed by the small privileged classes or exported, by the harnessing of power other than that supplied by human or animal effort. Consequently, although the motive power of steam had become known as a scientific curiosity, it was not applied to industry or transport, and both were restricted to the tempo furnished by muscular power. Thus circumscribed, technical inventiveness, which had been lively in the earlier stages of the Agricultural Civilization, had slackened, and the rate of material progress had tended to slow down.

In the realm of ideas, however, there was still plenty of activity on various planes. Politics had grown out of economic needs, a community's quest for materials not present in its own area, or the defence of its goods against a predatory neighbour. From this beginning war-leaders-become-kings had sought to bring ever larger areas under their domination in the will-o'-the-wisp pursuit of economic self-sufficiency or complete security. Successive empires had crossed the stage of history—Egyptians, Hittites, Assyrians, Babylonians, Persians, Alexander the Great and his generals, the Roman Empire—each uniting an ever larger area under their domination, but finding it continuously difficult to maintain that unity in view of local separatisms and the slowness of communications. While the earlier of these warlike peoples had done little more than impose their tax-collectors and impart some elements of their civilization to the conquered peoples, the unification that ensued under the later ones had gone deeper. The Persian Empire had a common coinage and a common everyday language of commerce; in the Hellenistic kingdoms that followed Alexander the Great's conquests in Egypt and Western Asia the Greek language and the elements of Greek intellectual civilization had spread over the urban middle-classes, and commerce extended almost to the limits of the Old World; and this process had been confirmed and intensified by the Roman Empire, which was the lineal heir of the Hellenistic civilization.

Nevertheless, in spite of the fact that the peoples of the Roman Empire enjoyed greater security and a higher general level of material, social, and intellectual civilization than had ever been known before, there were millions of peoples who were unhappy and dissatisfied and saw no prospect of improving their lot in existing circumstances, or who felt more profoundly that contentment did not lie in the acquisition of material goods. Many of these had, through captivity in war or through commerce, been displaced from their homes and flung together to form the proletariat of the great cities—Rome, Alexandria, Antioch—where their various traditions of thought and belief were fused in a cosmopolitan crucible, with the added flux of Greek philosophical speculation. Displacement from one's home meant losing contact with that normal type of religious cult that had fixed local associations, and had caused lonely men to turn for comfort and hope to the unlocalized mystery-religions that had found favour throughout the Mediterranean, offering in this world communion with the divine and the hope of a blessed hereafter.

One originally localized cult, that of the Hebrew god Yahweh, had itself suffered displacement when the Jewish people were taken away into exile. It had already acquired moral and spiritual overtones of exceptional richness through the teaching of prophets in protest against religious laxity or social injustice; and in the humiliation of the Exile it had survived only by its enlargement from being the national cult of a small people into a religion with a universal message in the teaching of the Second Isaiah. But the Return from the exile, giving the Yahweh-cult once more a local habitation in Jerusalem, had reversed this spiritual expansion, and the Jewish religion had become bound in those fetters of national exclusiveness and legalistic minutiæ from which it has never escaped. Individuals had however broken loose from time to time; and in His human aspect the Founder of Christianity had met the fate of such a rebel against Jewish authority. St. Paul, a Jew of

Greek education, and others had propagated their Master's Gospel of Love among the cities of the Levant, clothing it in philosophical terms which had made it more readily acceptable to men of Greek civilization.[1] Thus, among those drawn to Christianity by dissatisfaction with the cosmopolitan materialism of the Roman Empire there had been a continual influx of alert minds who had brought it to the forefront of the intellectual activity of the age. When therefore in A.D. 313, after two generations of military anarchy had brought the Roman Empire near to economic and political ruin, the emperor Constantine had sought some institution to take into partnership for the restoration of order and the preservation of civilization, he had found it in the Christian Church which, though still a minority in the Empire as a whole, had withstood the shock of the 'Time of Troubles' and gained adherents despite intermittent persecution, and now had no rival. Constantine's recognition of Christianity as the official religion of the Roman Empire, and the close association of Church and State in the highly institutional type of government that followed, had caused Christianity to spread rapidly throughout the settled lands of the Empire until only scattered pockets of paganism were left there, and it also spread beyond the Roman frontiers along the routes of commerce.

Nevertheless, the triumph of Christianity at this stage had not made the majority of men appreciably happier or fundamentally altered the springs of their conduct. The Church had become bound to the state-machine which, faced with the task of salvaging as much as possible from the third-century anarchy which had destroyed the middle-class liberalism of the self-governing cities of the earlier Roman Empire, had been forced to truss up the shattered body-politic in a harness of compulsory enactments that, while it averted total collapse, hindered free economic and social development and imposed a constant burden of heavy taxation. The unity conferred by the Greek language and culture and by the Christian religion was moreover only partial, since the former did not effectively descend beyond the urban middle-classes and barely reached the artisans or the large rural population who maintained their local languages and customs; and Christianity had come to these multitudes in

[1] cf. A. J. Toynbee, op. cit., 426.

LATE ROMAN
(BYZANTINE)
EMPIRE

Antioch

Palmyra

Damascus

Alexandria

Jerash

Jerusalem

BANI GHASSĀN

Babylon
(Old Cairo)

Petra

DESERT

DESERT

DESERT

SASSANIAN
PERSIAN
KINGDOM

Ctesiphon

STEPPE

AND

DESERT

Madina

Mecca

Approximate extent of
Christianity in the Fertile
Crescent and Nile Valley
early 7th. Century

Main trade-routes in Arabia,
and lines of Arab penetration

0   100   200   300
Miles

2.   THE MIDDLE EAST IN THE SEVENTH CENTURY

translations from its original Greek, and through the mouths of
men of their own stock, so that the masses without Greek culture
were not brought by Christianity very much closer to one
another. National particularism and the general resentment
for the heavy-handed, exacting, and corrupt bureaucracy through
which they were rules from Constantinople, having no outlet in politics, found expression in the dogmatic disputes to
which the Christian Church had become a prey when men
had brought the keen edge of Greek philosophical reasoning
to bear upon the difficult concept of the Triune Godhead.
In the Levant early in the fifth century a dispute between the
theologians, concerning the relative degrees to which our Lord's
Nature during His life on earth had been divine or human, was
taken up by the fanatical Egyptian monks and the ignorant populace of Alexandria, who made of the Monophysite doctrine of the
One Divine Nature a rallying-cry against Greek reasoning and
thought. A Council of the entire Church, held at Chalcedon
in A.D. 451, adopted a compromise formula which neither
emphasized the Humanity of Christ on earth to the extent
favoured by the followers of the patriarch Nestorius, nor
subordinated it to His Divinity as totally as did the extreme
Monophysites. The result was a violent Monophysite reaction: the Patriarch of Alexandria was murdered on Good
Friday in his own cathedral and his body dragged through
the streets by the mob. Despite harsh attempts by the imperial
government to repress the secession, the movement spread through
that majority of the population of Egypt and Syria that had never
effectively been reached by Greek civilization, and they broke
away to form two national churches, the Coptic Church of Egypt
and the Syrian or Jacobite Church, using in their respective litur-
gies, in place of the Greek which was the cultivated language of the
Eastern Mediterranean and the language of the Church throughout
that region, their native Coptic (the contemporary form of
Ancient Egyptian) and Syriac.[1]

[1] These churches, together with the followers of Nestorius, have survived to
the present day among those Oriental churches which are little known in
Western Europe: the Copts, despite thirteen centuries of Muslim rule, still
number over a million adherents in Egypt, and the national Church of Ethiopia
also derives from them; the Syrian Church has 150-200,000 followers in North
Mesopotamia, Syria, and Southern India; the Nestorians, after evangelizing a
large part of Central Asia during the Middle Ages, have shrunk to the few score
thousands of homeless 'Assyrians'.

Thus in the civilization of the Middle East at the beginning of the seventh century A.D. it was difficult to find a single unifying factor. Two great military empires, the Later Roman or Byzantine and the Persian, had contended for centuries for mastery over the region, the Byzantines holding the Levant lands but failing to make a lasting conquest of Mesopotamia, while during the sixth century the Persians had made several serious inroads into Syria, once destroying its capital of Antioch and in 614 capturing Jerusalem and burning its churches. Despite these wars, commerce and industry were far from inactive. There was a sufficient surplus of wealth to make possible the founding of many new churches, especially in the reign of Justinian (527-65), to whom we owe the rebuilding of Constantine's Church of the Nativity at Bethlehem, as well as Hagia Sophia at Constantinople. The towns, of which Jerash in Transjordan and Palmyra are the best extant examples, together with many lesser sites in Syria, presented a picture of busy life, though the archaeologist, looking below the surface, finds much of the apparent opulence to have been Ersatz.[1] While landed proprietors, the wealthy religious houses, and merchants prospered, the urban and rural masses were oppressed by heavy taxation and corrupt officials, and had no sense of loyalty to the régime. The Christian Church, in becoming an established institution, had itself become as stratified as official society; and while the monasteries did a valuable service for posterity in keeping alive some part of the tradition of Greek science and scholarship that would otherwise have been irreparably lost, there was no longer that sense of brotherhood in the Church which had characterized primitive Christianity as it was to characterize primitive Islam. Moreover the Church had ceased to be universal and undivided: but the nationalism betokened by the breaking away of the Monophysite churches was manifested only in opposition to the centralizing and Hellenizing tendency of the bureaucracy and the œcumenical church, it did not make a positive patriotic appeal to their adherents: there was nothing that could be called an Egyptian or Syrian nation, only a congeries of individuals at the mercy of any determined external force. Successive emperors after the Council of Chalcedon were fully aware of the political danger to the Empire of the estrangement of the Levant provinces, and sought to

[1] Lankester Harding, *Official Guide to Jerash* (Transjordan Dept. of Antiquities, 1944), 8.

reclaim them by doctrinal concessions to the Monophysites: but the latter were hard bargainers, and the emperors' freedom of negotiation was restricted by the watchfulness of the Popes who, while less concerned in Rome than the emperors in Constantinople with the political exigencies of the Levant, were insistent that orthodoxy should not be imperilled by excessive indulgence of the Monophysite heresy; and for thirty years they broke off relations with an over-accommodating emperor. The Monophysites for their part were not disposed to compromise with the hated Greeks, and periodically imperial conciliation was replaced by savage persecution. Thus the breach with the Levant provinces was never bridged ,and they were ripe to fall to any invader who would offer them greater freedom from imperial interference.

CHAPTER II

The Rise and Decline of the Muslim Civilization
(610–1517)

THE ARID climate of the Arabian Peninsula had caused its level of civilization to remain well below that reached in the Fertile Crescent, except for the Yemen with its monsoon rains, where the legend of the Queen of Sheba and archaeological evidence combine to indicate a more advanced culture founded on the profits of seafaring in the Red Sea and the Indian Ocean. The greater part of the Peninsula, however, was suitable only for the nomad tribes whose livelihood depended on the rearing of camels and small cattle, and whose characteristic social trait was the raiding of other tribes for plunder, for prestige, and in the pursuit of traditional feuds, and the celebration of these raids in heroic lays handed down from generation to generation. Such nomads, speaking a family of languages that has been termed Semitic, had from the beginnings of the Agricultural Civilization pressed upon the inner margins of the Fertile Crescent and at intervals broken in to pillage the cultivated lands and sometimes settled there. It was one such wave of invaders that brought the Hebrews into Palestine soon after 1400 B.C. Later, Arabic-speaking peoples had begun to appear in North Arabia, among the first of them the Nabataeans who from about 300 B.C. were settled in Southern Transjordan round their stronghold of Petra, and lived by agriculture based on highly-developed water-conservation and by the tolls they exacted from the profitable trade in incense and other luxuries that came up by caravan through their territories on their way from Southern Arabia to the Mediterranean coast and Syria. Early in the Christian era other Arab tribes had succeeded them, and in the sixth century the Beni Ghassan were enlisted by the Byzantine Emperors to protect the desert borders of Syria and Transjordan against the Persians and their Arab allies.

The land-route from Southern Arabia up through Western

Arabia to the Mediterranean remained commercially important after the decline of Petra; and among the goods which the Fertile Crescent exported in return were the elements of its higher civilizations, Christianity and Judaism: colonies of adherents of these faiths lived in the towns along this route, side-by-side with the Arabs who worshipped the manifold forces of nature through the medium of idols. The principal town in the sixth century A.D. was Mecca, where the road to the Mediterranean branched from another leading to Mesopotamia and the Persian Gulf; it had an important pagan cult centring round a meteoric Black Stone built into a sanctuary called the Ka'ba; and it was in this environment, culturally outlandish but impregnated by its commercial contacts with the higher civilization of the Fertile Crescent, that the Prophet Mohammed was born in 570.

When he began to undergo his religious experience about A.D. 610, he could have had no adequate first-hand knowledge of the Jewish or Christian scriptures, which had not been translated into Arabic while he knew no other language; but he had opportunities for conversations with Jews and Christians both on his caravan-journeys and in Mecca itself; and his religious experience, which took the form of an uncompromising monotheism in opposition to the polytheistic idol-worship of Mecca, was affected to a considerable degree by indirectly-acquired and imperfect notions of these two developed religions. At the time a dissatisfaction with the traditional polytheism was evidently stirring in the minds of other Arab thinkers, whose personalities have been obscured for posterity by the triumphant Muslim tradition.[1]

At the early stage of his ministry Mohammed evidently did not regard himself as the founder of a new religion, but merely as one whose mission it was to warn his fellow-townsmen of the impending Judgement Day revealed to Christians and Jews in their scriptures. Though his preaching made no great headway, it aroused the opposition of the leading merchant-tribe of Mecca, the Quraish (to a somewhat unimportant family of which Mohammed himself belonged): not only had he attacked their traditional beliefs, but he threatened the commercial profits which the town derived from the annual pilgrimage (hajj) which the inhabitants of the surrounding country paid to the Ka'ba. The menaces of the Quraish eventually constrained Mohammed to

[1] cf. *Encyclopaedia of Islam*, arts. Hanif and Musailima.

seek another home; and after receiving overtures from merchants of Madina (then called Yathrib), some 200 miles to the north of Mecca, where the presence of a substantial minority of the Jewish faith offered a more sympathetic milieu than conservative Mecca, he followed his three hundred adherents thither in A.D. 622. From this Flight (Hijra) the Muslim world dates the beginning of its era.

It was now that Mohammed first found it necessary to act as lawgiver for his little community of refugees from Mecca (Muhajirun), and for the converts that he made among the people of Madina (Ansar). He had hoped to receive cordial support from the Jewish community in Madina, since he regarded himself as the successor of the major Hebrew prophets, notably Abraham, and he adopted some Jewish forms of worship, including especially that of facing Jerusalem when at prayer. But it soon became obvious that the Jews of Madina had no use for this new revelation, and they ridiculed his misunderstanding of various Old Testament narratives and Jewish rituals. He retaliated by denouncing them as concealing or falsifying parts of the divine revelation given to them; and since he had already begun to regard current Christian doctrine as a perversion of the original teaching of Jesus, in so far as he had any clear idea of either of these two things, he underwent a sharp revulsion from the two religions which had hitherto inspired him, and instead proclaimed the true and uncorrupted revelation of God to himself as the 'seal of the prophets'; this revelation he termed Islam, resignation to the will of God. Reverting to his Meccan traditions, he transferred the direction of prayer to the Ka'ba and proclaimed the Hajj one of the obligations of the Muslim faith. He revived or invented a tradition that the Ka'ba and the rites connected with it, though since corrupted by polytheism and idol-worship, had been founded by none other than Abraham and his son Ishmael, the ancestor of the Arabs. It was his mission to restore this cult in its original purity.

From this time onwards it appears that Mohammed experienced little in the way of spiritual exaltation, and that the rest of his career was devoted to the more mundane tasks of regulating the public and private conduct of his devoted Muslim followers at Madina, and of asserting his supreme authority over the townsmen of Mecca who had rejected him. Faced by this striking change in the motivation of the Prophet's teaching, some European writers[1]

[1] Summarized by Tor Andrae: *Mohammed, the Man and his Faith*, ch. VII.

have in the past declared that he was never anything more than an ambitious politician who insincerely professed a new religion as a vehicle for attaining political power. But this cynical interpretation will not bear analysis: there are too many hazards in the preaching of a new religion to commend it to the politically ambitious. Mohammed himself had to endure twelve years of neglect, derision, and growing hostility before he attained political authority over the small band who followed him into exile. It is far more reasonable to suppose that his original religious experience was entirely genuine, but that when the call came to undertake the governance of the Muslim community at Madina, it opened up or confirmed in him a rich vein of practical authority which from now on superseded his spiritual powers. 'Had not God laid upon him the duty of conveying the revelation of God's truth to his fellow-men, and would he not be executing this duty if he embraced this heaven-sent opportunity of providing the new religion, whose path had been obstructed for ten years by human *force-majeure*, with a human political vehicle without which, as personal experience showed, Islam could make no further practical progress?'[1]

He now proclaimed a holy war (jihad) against the people of Mecca who had rejected his teaching and driven him out, and induced some of his followers to attack a Meccan caravan during the truce of a holy month. This was the prelude to a series of minor skirmishes with the Meccans (622–28), in most of which the Muslims gained the upper hand. During this period he expelled two of the Jewish tribes from Madina, and had the third tribe massacred on suspicion of treasonable correspondence with his enemies in Mecca. By this time an increasing number in Mecca had grown tired of the desultory warfare which interfered with the caravan-trade and was prepared to compromise with Mohammed, especially now that he had incorporated the Pilgrimage into the Muslim ritual. In 628 they agreed by the Pact of Hudaibiya to allow him to make the Pilgrimage in the following year, on which occasion some of the leading personalities of Mecca embraced the new faith. In 630 he advanced upon Mecca at the head of his armed forces and, meeting with resistance only from a few irreconcilables, received

[1] A. J. Toynbee, 'The Political Career of Mohammed', an appendix to Vol. III of *A Study of History*, 466 ff. For a modern Muslim commentary, see Abdul Latif Tibawi, in *Journal of the Middle East Society*, I, No. 3–4 (Jerusalem, 1947), 23 ff.

the submission to Islam of almost all the townspeople, and destroyed all the idols in and around Mecca. His triumph was complete, and the small Jewish and Christian communities of the Hijaz, and Arabs from as far away as Bahrein, Oman, and Southern Arabia recognized him as their overlord.[1]

His sudden death in 632 left the Muslim community in confusion, since he left no son and had not designated a successor. The very real danger of a breach between the diverse sections of the community was averted by the selection of the venerable and respected Abu Bakr as Khalifa (successor, hence our 'caliph') of Mohammed in his secular capacity as ruler and lawgiver only, but not in his spiritual role as prophet. In Abu Bakr's short reign of two years the whole of Arabia was brought under the dominion of Islam. Already in the lifetime of the Prophet the Muslim bands had essayed a raid across the borders of the Byzantine Empire into Southern Transjordan, but had met with a serious reverse. Now however, under the second elected caliph 'Umar able commanders led large raiding-parties into Palestine, Syria, Iraq, and Egypt, and met with astonishingly little effective resistance. What began as raids for booty after the customary Arab fashion thus developed imperceptibly into campaigns of permanent conquest. Muslim historians attribute the great successes of their ancestors to the inspiration of Islam but though it cannot be denied that the new religion played an important part in providing a social bond which held together for the time the fickle loyalties of the tribes, the main factor in the Arab conquests was the feebleness of the forces that opposed them. The Byzantine and Persian Empires were both exhausted by a generation of warfare; the Semitic majority of the inhabitants of Syria, Palestine, and Mesopotamia were more nearly akin to the Arabs, in race and sympathies, than to their Byzantine and Persian rulers, from whom they were further estranged by generations of excessive taxation and bureaucratic misrule; the Bani Ghassan, who should have taken the first shock of the invasion of the Byzantine Empire, had been alienated because the Emperor Heraclius, his treasury emptied by his victorious Persian expedition, had in 629 stopped his annual subsidy to them;

---

[1] The Muslim tradition that the whole of Arabia was converted in the Prophet's lifetime, and that he addressed to the rulers of the great Empires to the North demands that they also should accept Islam, is probably fabulous. Effectively, his political control did not extend beyond the Hijaz. (Fr. Buhl, in *Encyclopaedia of Islām*, Art. Muhammad, 653 ff.)

in Egypt the Patriarch of Alexandria had attempted to impose
a doctrinal compromise on the Monophysite Copts by force,
and in his complementary role of civil governor had been
ruthless in the collection of taxes, with the result that the Coptic
Bishop of Alexandria ordered his coreligionaries not to resist the
Arabs. The only effective resistance to them came therefore from
such centres of Greek civilization as Alexandria, Caesarea, and
Jerusalem; and by 660, one generation after Mohammed's death,
his green banner was flying over an empire which extended from
Persia in the east, through the Fertile Crescent, Egypt, and Libya,
to Tunisia in the west. Of these the only country to offer a determined resistance was Persia, which had been the seat of an empire
with a thousand-year-old tradition of proud domination. It is this
period of conquering puritanism, of the very essence of Islam, and
not the great age of cosmopolitan culture that was to follow, which
Muslims themselves have always regarded as their Golden Age,
the age of the rightly-guided (Rashidun) caliphs.[1]

The task of improvising an administrative system for the vast
Arab empire was taken up in the main by the second caliph 'Umar.
Authority in the provinces was placed in the hands of the Arab
military commanders who had conquered them. Arab garrisons
were established in newly-created cantonments in each of the conquered countries, of which Fustat, by Old Cairo, and Basra in
Lower Iraq, are examples. In order to maintain their separate
identity from the conquered peoples the Arabs were not at first
allowed to acquire land outside Arabia. Civil administration was
left in the hands in which the Arab conquerors found it—Christians
of Greek education in the lands of the Roman Empire, and non-
Muslims of Persian education in the lands of the former Persian
Empire. It is doubtful whether Arabs, in the stricter racial sense,
have ever acquired any taste, or much aptitude, for such prosaic
occupations.

For the Muslim conquerors themselves the Qur'an, the compilation of the divine revelations received by Mohammed throughout his ministry, provided the rudiments of a civil and criminal
code of laws, as enunciated by him in the ten years in which he
governed the Muslim community at Madina. This was supple-
mented where necessary by reference to what his Companions
could remember of his day-to-day habits, his Sunna or custom;

[1] Christopher Dawson, op. cit., 143.

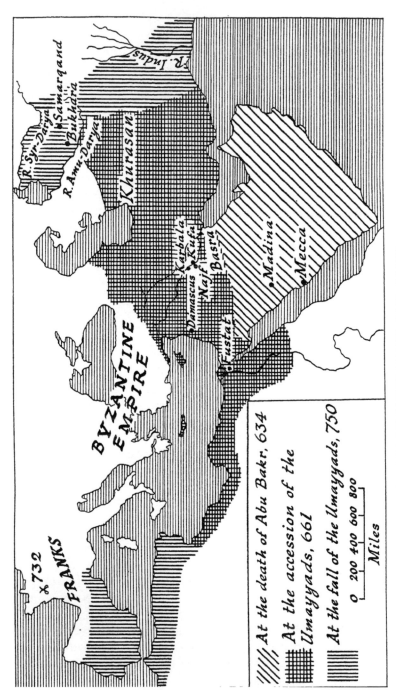

FRANKS
×732

BYZANTINE
EMPIRE

Khurasan

R. Indus

R. Syr-Darya
Samarqand
Bukhara
R. Amu-Darya

Karbala
Kufa
Najaf Basra
Damascus
Fustat
Madina
Mecca

At the death of Abu Bakr, 634

At the accession of the
Umayyads, 661

At the fall of the Umayyads, 750

0   200 400 600 800
Miles

3.   THE EXPANSION OF THE ARAB EMPIRE

and the constant necessity for such supplementation gave rise in succeeding decades to the production, first orally and later in writing, of many scores of thousands of Traditions of the Prophet's conduct, each enshrining some legal or ritual principle. Many of these Traditions were fictitious, but the fiction was an innocent device whereby religious sanction could be obtained for some necessary piece of legislation, generally borrowed at this early stage from the customary law of Madina.[1]

It was also necessary, however, for the new Arab rulers to regulate the legal position of the millions of their non-Muslim subjects, who represented the overwhelming majority of the population of the Empire.[2] In this 'Umar followed the example of Mohammed, who had left undisturbed the Christian and Jewish communities of the northern Hijaz whom he brought under his sway, on condition of the payment of an annual tribute. 'Umar extended this usage to all the Christian and Jewish inhabitants of the Empire and to the Zoroastrians of Persia; and these subjects thus became known as the Ahl adh-Dhimma or 'people of the covenant'. Far from there being any idea of compulsorily converting them to Islam, their role was to provide revenues for the Arab ruling-race by the payment of taxation, which apparently was at first lighter than that of the Byzantine Empire; and since Muslims were exempt from such taxation, the conversion of non-Muslims was actually discouraged, as it would have lessened the number of taxpayers. Since moreover the Muslim law (the Shari'a) was not applicable to the non-Muslim majority, they were left under the jurisdiction of the civil code which had obtained before the Conquest, such jurisdiction being now placed in the hands of their own religious dignitaries. This was the origin of the system of self-administering religious communities or *millets* which was to prevail throughout Islam until the collapse of the Ottoman Empire, and still survives for the purposes of civil law in that majority of Middle Eastern countries which have not yet undergone a thorough secularization.[3]

[1] For the compilation of fictitious documents by the early Christian Church with similarly innocent motives, cf. C. Delisle Burns, *The First Europe* (London, 1947), 354f.
[2] It is hardly necessary in these days to remark that the traditional Christian account, that the Muslim conquerors gave the conquered Christians and Jews the choice only of conversion to Islam or death by the sword, is totally erroneous.
[3] The institution had indeed already been foreshadowed in the dealings of the Hellenistic monarchies and the Roman Empire with the Oriental temple-communities under the authority of local priesthoods. In Alexandria under the

In spite of these statesmanlike foundations laid for the Empire by 'Umar, it was not destined to enjoy a long period of peaceful consolidation. After the murder of 'Umar by a discontented slave after a reign of ten years, the caliphate passed by election among the Muslims to the elderly and ineffectual 'Uthman, a member of the aristocratic House of Umayya, a section of the Quraish tribe of Mecca which had been one of the last to accept conversion to Islam. Under 'Uthman his Umayyad kinsmen acquired most of the leading positions in the Empire, and aroused the active jealousy of the earlier converts, the Muhajirun and the Ansar. 'Uthman was murdered in 655, and the caliphate passed by election to Ali, who as cousin and son-in-law of the Prophet was his male next-of-kin, but had been passed over in the previous three elections. Nor did he now show that the doubts of the Muslims concerning his fitness to govern had been misplaced. 'Ali had almost every virtue except those of the ruler: energy, decision, and foresight. He was a gallant warrior, a wise counsellor, a true friend, and a generous foe . . . but he had no talent for the stern realities of statecraft, and was outmatched by unscrupulous rivals who knew that "war is a game of deceit" '.[1] When his attempt to remove the Umayyad governors appointed by 'Uthman was resisted by a show of force by Mu'-awiya, the able Umayyad governor of Syria, Ali weakly agreed to submit the matter to arbitration. This brought upon him in Iraq, a strategic centre of the Empire to which he had removed his seat of government from too-remote Madina, the revolt of a group of Arab conservatives, who insisted that he had no right to submit the caliphate to arbitration, as it had been conferred upon him by the God-guided judgement of the whole body of the Faithful. One of this group, the Khawarij or Seceders,[2] murdered Ali in 661, after the arbitrators had awarded the caliphate to Mu'awiya, no doubt on the grounds of his greater fitness to govern.

Mu'awiya ruled for some twenty years, and for seventy years more the caliphate remained hereditary in the House of Umayya, thus bringing to an end the original elective caliphate and replacing it by a hereditary monarchy of the traditional oriental kind. Syria,

Ptolemies the Greek civil law applied only to the Greek community and to Hellenized Egyptians; the large Jewish community and the non-Hellenized Egyptians remained subject to their traditional civil law administered by their own priesthoods.

[1] Nicholson, op. cit., 191.
[2] In the singular, Kharij. The movement survives to this day as the Ibadi sect of Oman and Zanzibar, and some scattered communities in North Africa.

the seat of Mu'awiya's power before his elevation to the caliphate, now became the centre of gravity of the Empire, and Damascus its capital.

Under the Umayyads the military extension of the Arab Empire continued, until by 732, the centenary of the Prophet's death, it had reached its geographical limits, Transoxiana and Northern India in the east, Spain in the west. The Muslims had indeed invaded France, but in the centenary year itself were decisively checked half-way to the English Channel, at a battle fought between Tours and Poitiers, by the Frank Charles Martel. Though the Muslims had conquered Crete, they had twice failed to take Constantinople, which remained the capital of a substantial Byzantine Empire comprising the Balkans and Asia Minor.[1] In the south the Sahara remained a barrier, and it was some centuries before Islam effectively penetrated up the Nile beyond Aswan.

The Umayyads maintained the broad lines of internal administration laid down by 'Umar, those of an Arab military aristocracy. The Arab military governors of the provinces throughout the vast Empire enjoyed a freedom from central control amounting almost to independence. Civil administration remained in the same non-Arab and mainly non-Muslim hands as before. For a whole century, from the Arab conquest in 636 down to 743, the financial administration of the city of Damascus itself remained in the hands of a Syrian Christian family, one of whose members has been canonized by the Church as St. John of Damascus.

Already at this stage however, the great social defect of the Arab character, its unreadiness to subordinate its overmastering self-will and self-interest, whether of individual, of family, or of tribe, to the good of a larger group, was manifesting itself in incidents that boded ill for the future of the Arab Empire. 'The Arabs are incapable of founding an empire', wrote the fourteenth-century Muslim historian Ibn Khaldun, 'unless they are imbued with religious enthusiasm by a prophet or a saint'; and the social cohesive force of Mohammed's teaching was already largely spent on the generation which personally knew him. The most im-

---

[1] Their recognition of the de facto independence of the Byzantine Empire conflicted with their theoretical duty to bring about the conversion of the whole world to Islam. The orthodox explanation was that a respite had been granted to the Byzantine Empire because Heraclius, unlike the Persian King who had torn to pieces the Prophet's fictitious letter bidding him adopt Islam, had preserved his letter in musk! (D. S. Margoliouth, *The Early Development of Mohammedanism*, 103.)

portant dissident group, the Shi'at 'Ali (party of Ali), upheld the rights of the dead Ali and maintained that the caliphate should pass hereditarily to his sons Hasan and Husain. The elder son Hasan was a colourless figure who did not press his claim; but Husain raised his banner in Iraq and was killed by the Umayyad troops at Karbala in 680. Round his tomb, and that of Ali in the neighbouring city of Najf, there rapidly grew an emotional Shi'i martyrology among the large numbers of poor Arabs who had not benefited materially from the spoils of conquest and the Persian converts to Islam who were denied equality of status by the race-proud Arabs. They evolved the doctrine that Ali and his descendants had inherited with the caliphate, not merely Mohammed's temporal authority over all Islam, but also his spiritual inspiration. Some Shi'is indeed went so far as to maintain that Ali was greater than Mohammed; that while the mission of the latter was merely to transmit to mankind the text of the Qur'an, its inner spiritual significance was contained in Ali; while the Muslim profession of faith declared Mohammed the apostle of God, the Shi'is proclaimed Ali the *saint* of God. His death and that of Husain were conceived as a martyrdom for the salvation of mankind, a notion probably inspired by the Christian doctrine of the Atonement. The spiritual inspiration of Ali and his sons was held to be passed on to their descendants, the Saiyids descended from Husain and the Sharifs descended from Hasan, who are to this day objects of Shi'i veneration. In particular, both temporal and spiritual power was believed to pass from Husain to his legal heir in each generation, to whom as the infallible Imam (leader) the implicit obedience of the Shi'a was due in all matters, religious or secular. Had any of the descendants of Ali possessed something of the political talent of the best Umayyads, he would certainly have been able to supplant them, such was the superstitious reverence of the Shi'is for their imams;[1] but in fact the Umayyads, whose power rested on the mass of moderate people, Muslim and non-Muslim alike, who wanted above all things law and order, were able with some difficulty to maintain their ascendancy.

In addition to the rising of the Shi'a the early Umayyads had to contend with a revolt of Madina, the city of the Prophet, which resented the passing of authority from it to Damascus; there were feuds between great Arab tribal groups drawn originally from

[1] Snouck Hurgronje, *Mohammedanism*, 91.

Northern and Southern Arabia respectively; and the Khawarij overran Iraq, Southern Persia, and the greater part of Arabia. As a contemporary poet sang:

> 'They are split in sects: each province hath its own Commander of the Faithful, each its throne. . . .'

Thus the Arab nation was torn asunder by the old tribal pretensions which Mohammed sought to abolish. That they ultimately proved fatal to the Umayyads is no matter for surprise; the sorely-pressed dynasty was already tottering, its enemies were at its gates. But by good fortune it produced in this crisis an exceptionally able and vigorous ruler, 'Abd ul-Malik (685–705), who not only saved his house from destruction, but re-established its supremacy and gave the Muslim civilization an opportunity to enrich itself culturally. His iron-handed governor of Iraq ruthlessly put down the rebellion in the eastern provinces, and for twenty years provided peace and security by his despotic rule. In order to knit together the far-flung empire and curb the separatist tendencies of the provinces Abd ul-Malik borrowed from earlier empires the institution of an official postal system by means of relays of horses; he substituted for the Byzantine and Persian coins, which had hitherto been in general use, new gold and silver pieces on which he caused sentences from the Qur'an to be engraved; and he made Arabic, instead of Greek or Persian, the official language of financial administration.[1]

This reform does not mean that the non-Arab personnel of the administration, largely Christian by religion in the Levantine provinces, were replaced. But by this time the social barrier which 'Umar had attempted to impose between the Arab garrisons and the non-Arab and non-Muslim majority of the population was beginning to break down. The Arab cantonments had soon grown into towns and cities; Arabs had acquired land; and, as formerly between Alexander's Greeks and Orientals, social contact and intermarriage (for Muslims were permitted to take non-Muslim wives) were doing their levelling work. Moreover, non-Muslims

---

[1] Nicholson, op. cit., 199 ff. It is of interest that, because these coins bore quotations from the Qur'an, the eighth-century founder of one of the four schools of Muslim jurisprudence objected to their being given in payment to non-Muslims. (D. S. Margoliouth, *The Early Development of Mohammedanism*, 119.)

were being attracted to Islam by reason of the social prestige and freedom from taxation that it conferred, to such an extent that under the later Umayyads of the early eighth century new legislation compelled Muslims acquiring land, and non-Arab converts to Islam, to continue to pay the appropriate tax.

Nevertheless, the majority of the inhabitants of Syria and Lower Egypt were still Christian in the ninth century, and Baghdad itself is stated to have had as late as A.D. 900 a Christian population of 40–50,000. Except for the brief reigns of two bigoted Umayyad caliphs the still influential Christian Church was tolerated. The adoption of the Arabic language and of Islam seems to have been most rapid in Iraq, where the Semitic mass of the population had been comparatively little affected by Greek influences. In Syria and Palestine the process was slower, and Aramaic remained the principal language there till the ninth century. In Persia with its strong national culture Arabization was very superficial, and the Arabic language was adopted only temporarily and by a small proportion of the population for official purposes. Islam had made considerable headway in Persia by 750, and a reliable class of Muslim Persian officials had come into being; but Persia did not become completely Muslim till the tenth or eleventh century. In conservative Egypt the official adoption of the Arabic language under Abd ul-Malik affected only the smallest fraction of the population; but the language of their Arab rulers was gradually adopted, and by the tenth century a Coptic ecclesiastic had to write in Arabic to be understood by his coreligionaries. 'The chief factor in the spread of Arab culture in Egypt, which gave it so much greater effect than the preceding Hellenism, was the gradual settlement of the country districts by Arab nomads. . . . Sections, or even whole tribes, gradually succumbed to the advantages of settled life, and thus a strong strain of Arab blood was constantly being added to that of the Copts. It was apparently a considerable migration, which even sent offshoots as far as the Sudan. . . . The ancient civilization of the Nile Valley assimilated these nomad Arabs, and only their Arabic language remained. The Arabs became Nilotized, but also the Copts were Arabicized, and it is inexplicable that the essentially conservative Copts should have adopted another language without a great deal of mixing.'[1]

The Umayyad caliphs were descendants and representatives of

[1] C. H. Becker, *Encyclopaedia of Islam*, art. Egypt.

C

the pagan aristocracy of Arabia who, fully exposed in their new Syrian environment to the influences of the old blend of Greek and Oriental civilization, were ready to assimilate it and adapt it to both their secular and religious purposes. The almost total deficiency of Arab culture in the sciences and liberal and useful arts, and the supremacy in these matters of the Christians, Jews, and Persians, were freely acknowledged. The conquered peoples were regularly employed in commerce and industry, banking, the arts, as architects, engineers, and irrigation-specialists, as schoolmasters and secretaries, even as court-physicians and political advisers. The caliphs at Baghdad in the ninth and tenth centuries had some Christian wazirs (viziers), and most of the court-physicians in the early centuries of Muslim rule were Nestorians. The employment of Christian advisers in Egypt as late as the fourteenth century was a cause of annoyance to fanatical Muslims.[1] The only function absolutely reserved to Muslims was service in the army and navy. Not only were the Umayyad caliphs' country-palaces decorated in a mixture of Graeco-Syrian and Mesopotamian-Persian styles which completely disregarded the orthodox Muslim ban on the human figure,[2] but also Graeco-Syrian influences strongly affected the development of the mosque, whose architecture was still rudimentary at the beginning of the Umayyad period. Though the Dome of the Rock at Jerusalem (often miscalled the Mosque of Omar), which was founded in 691 by Abd ul-Malik, was a shrine built for Muslim worship, it must nevertheless be regarded as a product of Christian art. Its plan, a circle within an octagon, existed in the Church of the Ascension then standing on the Mount of Olives, and elsewhere in Palestine and Syria. The geometric setting-out of the plan and elevation of the Dome of the Rock appears to be derived from Syrian-Christian architectural practice. Before its exterior was re-covered with Persian tiles in the sixteenth century it was covered with marble and mosaic, and its external appearance must then have been as Byzantine as its internal appearance still largely is.[3] The Great Mosque at Damascus, founded in 708, was likewise the work of architects and builders supplied from the Byzantine Empire.

---

[1] A. S. Tritton, *The Caliphs and their Non-Muslim Subjects*. J. H. Kraemer, *Encyclopaedia of Islam*, art. Egypt, 7.
[2] e.g. the recently-discovered palace at Khirbat Mafjar near Jericho: *Quarterly of the Dept. of Antiquities of Palestine*, XII (1945), 17 ff.
[3] E. T. Richmond, *Moslem Architecture* (623–1516), ch. II.

The increased penetration of the Muslim culture by Christian and Persian civilization even affected Muslim law and theology. The greater complexity of the civilization of which the Muslims now found themselves a part made necessary new elaborations of their legal code, mainly by the assimilation of the Roman Law existing in the conquered provinces of the Levant. By the end of the Umayyad period a new critical approach to the mass of Traditions had begun to appear, and the science of Muslim jurisprudence was beginning to take shape. Contact with the older and more subtle Christian religion, which had retained some of the questioning Greek spirit, was causing some Muslims to look more deeply into the foundations of their own faith, where they found numerous ambiguities and inconsistencies amid the obscure and uncoordinated phraseology of the Qur'an. This new spirit of inquiry in Islam was stimulated, as it had been among the Christians, by the disputes of rival sects: in this case the Shi'a and the Sunnis, as the mass of moderate believers called themselves, claiming to be following the custom (Sunna) of the Prophet. In particular, some were brought to question the Prophet's doctrine of the eternal and uncreated Qur'an, which seemed to them to place a second eternal existence in conflict with the essential unity (*tawhid*) of God. Secondly, they were exercised by the alternative of free-will or predestination, which the Qur'an characteristically left ambiguous. Thus a sect, known to Muslim historians as the Mu'tazila or secession, which came into being towards the end of the Umayyad period, adopted a rationalist attitude towards both of these questions, and was to exert an important influence on the history of the following century.

In spite of the readiness with which they had assimilated what survived of Greek civilization, the Umayyad period is marked by a certain economic decline when compared with the later Roman Empire. Mediterranean commerce, already shaken in the West by the Germanic invasions, was even more seriously affected by the partition of the Mediterranean coastlands between two conflicting civilizations, the Christian on the northern shores and the Muslim on the south. Moreover the Muslims in the West had conquered Spain and were energetically raiding into Italy and Provence, while in the East they were making every attempt, though vainly, to conquer the remainder of the Byzantine Empire. Though in spite of frequent Muslim raids the trading cities of Southern Italy maintained some commerce with the Southern Mediterranean and the Levant, the effect of the Muslim conquests was gradually to check the flow of Oriental goods to Christian Western Europe.[1]

The fertility of Egypt was maintained on about the same level as before the Muslim conquest by a policy of non-interference with the Coptic administration and irrigation-specialists. Historians no longer hold, as formerly, that the Muslim conquest abruptly ended the prosperity of Syria and Palestine; instead they ascribe the beginnings of their economic decline to the shifting of the centre of gravity from the Levant to Iraq and Persia which followed the transfer of the capital from Damascus to Baghdad with the accession of the Abbasid dynasty in the middle of the eighth century.

The Umayyads never succeeded in securing the loyalty of the whole of even the Arab inhabitants of their vast Empire; and their non-Arab subjects became increasingly estranged by the oppressive rule of their deputies. The Arabs 'lived as soldiers at the expense of the native population whom they inevitably regarded as an inferior race. If the latter thought to win respect by embracing the religion of their conquerors, they found themselves sadly mistaken. The new converts were attached as clients (mawali) to an Arab tribe: they could not become Muslims on any other footing. Far from obtaining the equal rights which they coveted, and which, according to the principles of Islam, they should have enjoyed, the Mawali were treated by their aristocratic patrons with contempt, and had to submit to every kind of social degradation.... And these Clients, be it remembered, were not ignorant serfs, but men whose culture was acknowledged by the Arabs themselves—men who formed the backbone of the influential learned class and ardently prosecuted those studies, divinity and jurisprudence, which were then held in highest esteem. Here was a situation full of danger. Against Shi'is and Khawarij the Umayyads might claim with some show of reason to represent the cause of law and order, if not of Islam; against the bitter cry of the oppressed Mawali they had no argument save the sword. . . .'

Active propaganda against the Umayyads was made, not only by the Shi'is, but also by a branch of the Prophet's family descended from his uncle Abbas. These Abbasids 'had genius enough to see that the best soil for their efforts was distant Khurasan, the extensive north-eastern provinces of the old Persian Empire.

[1] H. Pirenne, *Mahomet et Charlemagne,* 148 ff.

These countries were inhabited by a brave and high-spirited people who in consequence of their intolerable sufferings under the Umayyad tyranny, the devastation of their homes and the almost servile condition to which they had been reduced, were eager to join in any desperate enterprise that gave them hope of relief.'[1] While the Abbasids succeeded in persuading the Shi'is into allying themselves with them, the Umayyad rulers had become soft and negligent in the civilized luxury of sophisticated Syria. Quarrels broke out within the royal house over the succession to the caliphate, which changed hands no fewer than four times in the Muslim year 743/4. In these circumstances the warnings of the loyal governor of Khurasan were disregarded. In 747 the Abbasids openly raised the standard of revolt. By 750 they had supplanted and virtually exterminated the Umayyads, and the victor transferred the seat of the new dynasty to Iraq, where in 762 a new capital was founded at Baghdad.

*   *   *

This shifting of the political centre of gravity brought with it a decline in the Arab influence which had formerly been predominant, and an increase in that of the Persians who had done so much to place the Abbasids in power; for the first fifty years of their rule, for example, the Abbasid caliphs drew their prime ministers (wazirs) from the Persian Barmaki family, the 'Barmecides' of the Arabian Nights. With this relative decline of Arab supremacy, the many races of the Empire became fused into a common Muslim culture, the non-religious aspects of which were shared by the many Christians and Jews who had not embraced Islam. In the Empire as a whole, the relative decline in the importance of Syria was far more than compensated by the economic advance of its eastern provinces. The Abbasids, completing the work of the Sassanian Persians, restored to Lower Iraq a rudimentary but sound system of irrigation and land-drainage which checked the formation of stagnant water and the salination of the land. Baghdad, the new capital, rapidly became a rival of Constantinople in its material prosperity. A second centre of agricultural development and urban civilization was promoted in Transoxiana, with its great cities of Bukhara and Samarqand, and in Khurasan. This

[1] Nicholson, op. cit., 248 ff.

agricultural progress was of special benefit to the landowning class, but wider circles of the population must also have profited from it. Sea-borne trade through the Persian Gulf, already of great antiquity owing to the eminence of Mesopotamia as one of the earliest centres of urban civilization and commerce, underwent a great revival, with Basra assuming great importance as the port of Baghdad. By about 850 Muslim ships had reached China to trade for silk, and there was a considerable Muslim colony at Canton; some Muslim traders pushed further north, and probably reached Japan and Korea. Trade with East Africa was less important, but was carried as far south as Madagascar. There was even some re- vival of trade between the Levant ports and those of Christian Europe, especially Venice and the ports of southern Italy, with Jews playing an important part as middle-men, since they enjoyed a comparative toleration from both sides which neither Christian nor Muslim was yet prepared to extend to each other. More im- portant than the Mediterranean trade at this period, however, was that with the Swedish masters of Russia and the Baltic, evidence for which is furnished by the enormous numbers of Muslim coins found in that region: they were struck in the mints of Tashkent and Samarqand and extend over a period from A.D. 700 to 1500. Mus- lim indirect influence even reached the British Isles: a gold coin struck by King Offa of Mercia in the eighth century closely imi- tates an Arabic dinar, even to the Arabic inscription; and a gilt- bronze cross found in an Irish bog bears the inscription *b'ismi'llah* (in the name of God) in Arabic characters.[1]

This material prosperity has become legendary through the popularity of the Arabian Nights, with their stories of Baghdad under the Abbasid caliph Harun ar-Rashid (786–809), the con- temporary of Charlemagne with whom he was on friendly rela- tions. Of the immense cultural superiority of the Muslim East to Western Europe at this time there can be absolutely no question. With its material wealth there went also an increasing interest in matters of the intellect. The rising Muslim civilization felt the growing need of certain branches of practical knowledge which could be supplied by the higher civilizations on which it had im- pinged: medicine; mathematics for land-survey, architecture, and navigation; geography for the promotion of commerce; and

[1] J. H. Kramers, in *The Legacy of Islam*, 94 ff. Christopher Dawson, op. cit. 243 f.

4. MUSLIM DOMINION IN THE TENTH CENTURY

astronomy, to determine the direction of Mecca and the dates of the beginning and end of Ramadhan, the month of the sacred fast, and also for astrology. Already the Umayyads had employed architects and craftsmen trained in the Byzantine-Syrian or the Persian tradition. They had also attracted to their court physicians and other scholars from Jundishapur in south-west Persia, which had had since Sassanian times an important medical school and academy where Greek, Syrian, Persian, and Indian scientific knowledge was pooled; but the Umayyads had done little consciously to promote and encourage learning. The second Abbasid caliph al-Mansur (754–75), the founder of Baghdad, on the other hand, had astronomers, engineers, and other learned men at his court, and the plans of his new city were prepared by a Persian astronomer and a Jew. From this time began the translation of scientific works into Arabic from Greek, Syriac, Persian, and Sanskrit, the work being done in the main not by Arabs, but by Syrian Christians and Persians. This work was put on an organized basis by the caliph al-Ma'mun, who founded at Baghdad in 830, in the interests of the rationalist Mu'tazila sect which he favoured, a Bait al-Hikma or 'house of learning', which was a combination of academy, library, translation-bureau, and observatory. By means of such translation-enterprises the Arabic-speaking world soon became possessed of the outstanding works of Greek science and philosophy at a time when Western Europe was almost entirely ignorant of the Greek learning. Translation from the Greek was sometimes direct, but more frequently through the Syriac versions which had been made some centuries before by the Syrian Christians; the Nestorians in particular had been assiduous in translating the Greek philosophers in order to use them as ammunition in theological controversy with their orthodox opponents. In addition, Persian and Indian mathematical and astronomical works were translated into Arabic; and early in the ninth century the simple Indian system of numerals with its arrangement in columns by powers of ten and the all-important use of the zero (our so-called 'Arabic' numerals) was introduced into the Middle East, which had previously known only the clumsy Semitic, Greek, and Roman numerals.[1]

[1] It was not until the twelfth century that Christian arithmeticians in Europe began to adopt the 'Arabic' system. (Carra de Vaux, in The Legacy of Islam, 384 ff.)

Following this work of translation it was not long before original research, observation, and speculation began to be practised within the Muslim Empire. But before this the *political* unity of that Empire had been shattered for ever. Ibn Khaldun, looking back over Muslim history from the end of the fourteenth century, came to the conclusion that kingdoms are born, attain maturity, and die within a period which rarely exceeds three generations, or 120 years.[1] The Umayyad Empire had been precariously maintained by the awe with which his Sunni subjects regarded the caliph as temporal successor of the Prophet. But dynastic struggles were bound to diminish that awe: in the West the success of one of the few Umayyad survivors of the collapse of their dynasty in making himself independent ruler of Spain in 756 was followed in the next half-century by the breaking-away from the Abbasids of North-West Africa under two separate dynasties. In the heart of the empire, moreover, the Abbasid caliphs, realizing from the fall of the Umayyads that the fickle and inconstant Arab individualism intolerant of discipline provided a most unstable military basis for their authority, had begun to recruit from the north-eastern confines of the Empire mercenaries from among the Turks, a people less gifted intellectually than the Arabs and Persians, but with those more solid and stable qualities of obedience and endurance that have made them such excellent soldiers through the centuries. Already in 808 we find Turks serving in Egypt; but they soon realized the military and moral weakness of their Arab masters, and were not content to remain subordinates. The Turkish bodyguard with which the caliph al-Mu'tasim had provided himself clashed so frequently and violently with the populace of Baghdad that the caliph was obliged in 836 to quit the city and found a new capital at Samarra, three days journey up-river, where he and his successors rapidly came under the political domination of the commanders of their own mercenaries. In 868 the Turkish soldier Ahmed ibn Tulun made himself the independent ruler of Egypt, Palestine, and Syria, and introduced a short period of sound government in place of the reckless exhaustion of the economic resources of Egypt which she had suffered under the tax-farming governors of the Abbasids, and which had provoked a great rising of the oppressed Copts in 831.[2] In 874 Transoxiana and the

---

[1] Nicholson, op. cit., 440.
[2] C. H. Becker in *Encyclopaedia of Islam*, art. Egypt.

greater part of Persia, which had already been in revolt against the Abbasids, became finally independent under the Persian Samanid dynasty. In Iraq itself, which was practically all that now remained under the direct rule of Samarra, the authority of the caliph was challenged by the ferocious revolt in Lower Iraq of the Zanj or negro slaves (870–83). And worse was to follow. Though the Shi'is had helped the first Abbasid to overthrow the Umayyads, the new dynasty proved itself no less oppressive of the Shi'a than its predecessor had been, no doubt because the sect with its tendency to fanatical extravagances was regarded as potentially subversive of all ordered government. Driven underground by oppression, the Shi'is remained numerous especially in Lower Iraq, and both there and in the cities of Persia they perhaps found especial support from the artisan class, as an expression of class-consciousness against the ruling aristocracy, whether composed of Arabs, Persians, or Turks.[1]

In this atmosphere of suppressed ferment it was natural that schisms over doctrine should occur within the Shi'a. In particular there was a difference of opinion which of the two sons of the sixth Imam, who died in 760, should succeed him. The minority who supported the claim of the elder son Isma'il held that the succession of imams ended with him. They thus regarded Isma'il as the Hidden or Expected Imam, who according to Shi'i doctrine was shortly to return among men as the Mahdi (the divinely-guided) to restore true Islam, conquer the whole world, and introduce a short millenium before the end of all things. In the ninth century a Persian, Abdullah ibn Maymun, began to organize a secret esoteric cult of Isma'il in nine degrees in which all religious belief was progressively allegorized away until only an atheistic philosophy was left.[2] This cult was extensively propagated by enthusiastic missionaries and made many converts among the unhappy and discontented who always constitute the majority of mankind. At the end of the century an Isma'ili sect, called the Qaramita or Carmathians, organized itself as an independent political state on the Arabian coast of the Persian Gulf and in the Yemen. Declaring total war on all non-Isma'ilis its armies menaced Baghdad, interfered with the pilgrim-traffic, and in 930 actually sacked Mecca and carried off

---

[1] H. A. R. Gibb, in Toynbee, *A Study of History*, I, 400 ff.
[2] The most recent study of this intricate subject is Bernard Lewis's *The Origin of Isma'ilism.*

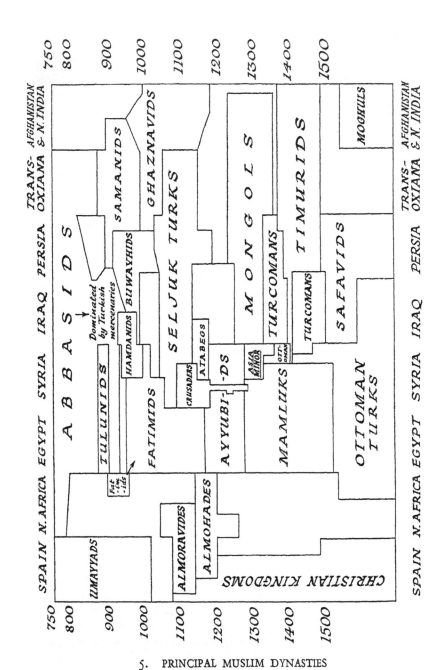

5. PRINCIPAL MUSLIM DYNASTIES

(after S. Lane-Poole, *The Mohammedan Dynasties*)

the Black Stone. Meanwhile the grandson of Abdullah ibn May-mun, in danger in Syria, escaped to Tunisia, where he won sup-port, was proclaimed Imam in 909, and succeeded in overthrowing the reigning dynasty. Claiming descent from Husain, the son of Ali and the Prophet's daughter Fatima, he thus became the founder of the Fatimid dynasty. This dynasty was the first to throw off even the nominal authority of the Abbasids by pro-claiming an independent caliphate, and extended its conquests along the North African coast until in 969 it captured Cairo and made the city its capital. Western Arabia, Palestine, and Syria were also brought under Fatimid rule. Meanwhile the hapless Ab-basid caliphs had in 945 passed under the domination of the Buwayhids, rough mountaineers from North Persia, who were moderate Shi'is. Thus the Shi'a had become politically the domi-nant sect in the greater part of the Muslim world, though it never converted the majority of Muslims. Egypt had taken the place of Iraq as the centre of gravity, and the famous University of Al Azhar[1] was founded at Cairo in 972 for the propagation of Isma'ili doctrine. The fatal Arab tendency to political separatism and restiveness under authority had had free rein: for the next thousand years down to our own day the Arabic-speaking world was to remain divided, and for the most part under foreign domination.

But when a civilization begins to break down, the deterioration is not uniform over the whole range of its activities; and just as in a diseased human body, the deterioration may actually be masked for a time by an increased stimulation of certain functions.[2] For the Muslim civilization the first effect of its political disruption on its rising science and scholarship was temporarily favourable. Scholars required the patronage of a benevolent ruler in order to be able to pursue their studies. Now, instead of scholarship being confined to the caliph's court at Baghdad and dependent on the will of one sovereign who might or might not be interested in furthering such pursuits, it was fostered in the courts of a dozen dynasties from Samarqand to Spain. Among the most notable of these centres of learning were Baghdad, Cairo, Bukhara and Samarqand; Shiraz, Isfahan, and Nishapur; Aleppo and Damascus; and Cordoba. Like their medieval European successors, students

[1] Pronounced, Áz-har.
[2] cf. Lewis Mumford, *The Condition of Man*, 153.

made long and laborious journeys to sit at the feet of some famous master. For example, al-Ghazzali, born at Tus in north-east Persia, studied at Nishapur, Baghdad, and Damascus, a total journey of some 1,400 miles.

Though Arabic was the principal language of scholars, with Persian steadily increasing in importance, only a small minority of the scientists and scholars of the Muslim world were Arabs by race. An analysis of the origins of the leading scholars and scientists of the Muslim East indicates that over the whole chronological range of Muslim culture from its rise to its decline Persia and Transoxiana furnished consistently some 40 per cent. of the distinguished names. Christians were predominant in the initial period of the translators, but fell away later, and Jews in the East were relatively unimportant in contrast to their great contribution to the culture of Muslim Spain.[1]

The assessment of the contribution of the Muslim world to science and scholarship has tended to run to two extremes. On the one hand, some protagonists of Greek civilization have been willing to see little originality in the Muslim achievement, and to concede them only the credit for preserving and handing on what survived of Greek learning to Western Europe in the later Middle Ages. On the other hand, modern Arab writers, and also some European historians of science, reacting too far against the excessive exaltation of Greek civilization by students of the classics, have claimed too much for the medieval Muslim scientists, exaggerating their original achievement out of all proportion to what they had received from the Greeks or from their oriental forerunners. The true assessment lies between these two extremes, and has been well embodied in a vivid word-picture: 'Islamic medicine and science reflected the light of the Hellenic sun, when its day had fled; and shone like a moon, illuminating the darkest night of the

[1] This is based on data given by A. Mieli, op. cit., for three successive periods: (I) the period of translators and first beginnings, eighth-ninth centuries; (II) the 'Golden Age', tenth-eleventh centuries; (III) the age of decline, twelfth-thirteenth centuries:

	I	II	III
Christians	12	8	5
Jews	0	3	4
Persians (including Transoxiana)	10	23	18
Iraqis	2	9	3
Syrians	3	7	9
Egyptians	1	4	5
Arabians	0	0	0

In Spain one-quarter of seventy-three names cited by Mieli are those of Jews.

European Middle Ages; some bright stars lent their own light; but moon and stars alike faded at the dawn of a new day—the Renaissance.'[1]   The Muslim contribution to mathematics and astronomy is exemplified by the number of Arabic loan-words in the terminology of these sciences: algebra, azimuth, zenith; and the names of many stars, such as Algol, Aldebaran, Betelgeuze.   In medicine considerable progress was made, thanks to the numerous hospitals founded in the principal cities by benevolent rulers: there were said to be six thousand medical students in eleventh-century Baghdad.   Though Muslim law forbade dissection of the human body, the course of diseases was carefully and systematically observed and recorded.   The knowledge of chemistry and other natural sciences was advanced, and Muslim cartography and descriptive geography greatly influenced medieval European map-making in the Mediterranean.   When all has been justly claimed for the originality of Muslim science, however, the fact remains that it was essentially the pupil and continuation of Greek science, Though it made some important original contributions to learning, its great service lay in the systematization and preservation of older learning at a time when Western Europe was ignorant of it and incapable of preserving it.   The Muslim scholars lacked in general the scientific imagination and originality of thought of the Greeks: they found difficulty in passing from the accumulation of practical data to a theoretical conclusion, and in the unifying of detail into a harmonious system.[2]

Muslim thought at its best has had its gaze turned upwards toward the One God; and, entirely absorbed by contemplation of Him, has not looked about itself at Man.   Muslim society has always tended towards aristocracy; and Muslim science and learning, as compared with that of the Greeks, has suffered in the absence of a substantial middle-class, which has given it less vitality to survive great political upheavals.   When all the necessary discounting of the 'democratic' character of the ancient Greek city-state has been done, the fact remains that Greek culture was genuinely the property of a considerable urban middle-class, which grew in importance till it reached its peak in the second century A.D. Islam, on the other hand, 'has known periods of intellectual life only under the protection of isolated princes here and there. It has

[1] Max Meyerhof, in The Legacy of Islam, 354.
[2] cf. Edward Atiyah's criticism, in An Arab Tells His Story, 186

had Augustan ages; it has never had great popular yearnings after wider knowledge. Its intellectual leaders have lived and studied and lectured at courts; they have not gone down and taught the masses of the people.'[1] The masses have remained in much the same economic and social conditions and at much the same intellectual level as their ancestors four thousand years ago.

Little Muslim science and scholarship found its way to medieval Europe via the Byzantine Empire, whose cultural contacts with the Muslim world were tenuous, though Arabic medical works were being translated into Byzantine Greek in the eleventh century.[2] The Crusaders, settled during the twelfth and thirteenth centuries in a strip of the Levant lands whose depth from the coast rarely exceeded fifty miles, were for the most part rough, unpolished adventurers, whose contacts with the native population were mainly with the peasantry, not with its scholars. Consequently, though there was an appreciable cultural interchange between the 'Franks' and the people of the Levant, it was mainly of a material kind. In any case, by the time of the First Crusade (1099) the intellectual ossification of the Muslim East was already beginning, and consequently the Crusades played no greater part than the Byzantine Empire in the transmission of Muslim learning to the West.[3]

Of considerably greater importance in this connexion was Sicily, which had been conquered by the Muslims of North Africa in the course of the ninth century, and enjoyed a period of stable and orderly Muslim government from c. 950 until Sicily was reconquered for Christendom towards the end of the eleventh century by the Normans, 'a dynasty of gifted pirates' which had entered the service of the Byzantine Greeks and then wrested Southern Italy from them. At the time of the Muslim conquest Sicily had long been rich with the past civilization of Greece and Rome. Though Eastern cultural currents had streamed in during the period of Muslim domination, the Arab rulers had been too involved in warfare to develop the finer arts of peace. But under the tolerant rule of the Normans the varied culture-strains were able to intermingle and flower. H. A. L. Fisher draws an attractive miniature pen-picture of the civilization of Sicily under Roger II (1130-54), whom his critics called the 'half-heathen king': 'His kingdom was

---

[1] D. B. Macdonald, op. cit., 153 f.
[2] R. Walzer, in *Bulletin of the John Rylands Library*, 1945, 171.
[3] Hitti, op. cit., 662.

half-oriental, half-western, providing a shelter for Greek, Latin, Moor, and Jew, and better organized . . . than any other European government of that age.   Among the orange-groves of Palermo Roger, the descendant of the Vikings, sat upon his throne, robed in the dalmatic of the apostolic legate and the imperial costume of Byzantium, his ministers part Greek, part English, his army composed as to half of Moors, his fleet officered by Greeks, himself a Latin Christian but, in that balmy climate of the south, ruling in half-Byzantine, half-oriental state . . . a true representative of his lovely island, shared then as ever between east and west.'[1] Roger's grandson Frederick II (1215–50), Holy Roman Emperor and King of Sicily, still kept a semi-oriental court, and incurred the excommunication of the fierce Pope Innocent III by his reluctance to undertake the Crusade; for he was in friendly political and commercial relations with Muslim rulers, and eventually won back Jerusalem temporarily for Christendom, not by the way of the sword but by a treaty-compromise with the tolerant Sultan of Egypt.   In 1224 Frederick founded the University of Naples,[2] and encouraged the translation into Latin of Arabic science and philosophy. Here at Naples studied St. Thomas Aquinas (1226–74), who made a profound study of the Arabic commentators on the Greek philosophers, but had the originality to go beyond them to the original Greek texts, which were now at last becoming available to the Western world.

But the country of outstanding importance for the transmission of Muslim learning to the West was Spain, whose level of civilization at the time of the Muslim conquest had been almost as high as that of Sicily. In particular, her cities contained many thousands of literate and energetic Jews, endowed with that spirit of restless inquiry which characterizes their race.   During the ninth century Muslim Spain became one of the wealthiest and most thickly-populated lands of Europe, sending abundant industrial and agricultural exports both to Christian Europe and to the Muslim East. Cordoba, the capital, was the most cultivated city in Europe, the rival of Constantinople, Baghdad and Cairo. With its population of half-a-million, its three hundred public baths, its seventy libraries, and its miles of paved streets lit at night, it was centuries in

---

[1] *History of Europe*, one-vol. ed., 190 f.
[2] For Muslim influence on the Medical School of Salerno in the eleventh century or even before, see Mieli, op. cit., 219 f.

advance of the barbarous condition of contemporary Paris or London, and was the cultural metropolis for the Christian rulers of the petty states of Northern Spain. Nevertheless, the intellectual tone in Muslim Spain was still one of rigid orthodoxy and strict conservatism. There was scant sympathy with the rationalist innovations of some of the Abbasid caliphs, and little evidence yet of intellectual originality. Both Muslims and Jews wishing to complete their education went to the Eastern Mediterranean and on to Iraq. In the first half of the ninth century, however, the Umayyad Abd ur-Rahman II sent a scholar to Iraq to obtain copies of translations of Greek and Persian scientific works, and surrounded himself with a group of astronomers.[1] A century later the University of Cordoba was founded by Abd ur-Rahman III, who proclaimed himself Caliph independently of the Abbasids. His successor invited professors to Cordoba from the East, established twenty-nine free schools in the city, and employed agents to buy learned manuscripts in the eastern cities. At the same time the centre of Jewish scholarship began to be transferred from Iraq to Spain. Early in the eleventh century the Umayyad dynasty collapsed, and for eighty years Spain was torn by civil wars, with Muslim military commanders playing the same role as they had done in the East when the Abbasid dynasty fell into decline. But just as in the East, the partitioning of the caliphate among provincial rulers led to the diffusion of the culture of the metropolis over a number of provincial capitals, such as Seville, Toledo, and Granada. And as the Christian kingdoms of Northern Spain seized the opportunity to invade the disunited Muslim state, so they began increasingly to absorb Muslim cultural influences.

The Muslims, finding themselves hard-pressed by the aggressive Christians in the north, appealed for help to the Berbers of North-West Africa, who had been united for the last fifty years in a militant Muslim brotherhood, al-Murabitun (whence their Spanish name of Almoravides). At the end of the eleventh century these defeated the Christians under their legendary leader the Cid, but remained in Spain as the ruling Muslim dynasty, only to succumb to its luxuries. Meanwhile another Puritan movement, al-Muwahhidun (Almohades in Spanish) had arisen among the Berbers. These overthrew the Almoravides in the middle of the twelfth century and replaced them as rulers of an empire extending from

---

[1] E. Levi-Provençal, *La Civilisation arabe en Espagne* (Cairo, 1938), 65.

D

Central Spain to the borders of Egypt. Both Berber dynasties were rigidly orthodox in matters of Muslim thought, and according to a fairly reliable tradition even had the writings of the great Ghazzali, the 'restorer of the faith', publicly burned in the market-place of Cordoba. While, however, they imposed the severest orthodoxy on the mass of the people, they did not interfere with the speculations of the Muslim philosophers, provided that these did not reach the multitude and disturb their faith. Thus twelfth-century Spain, ruled by religious conservatives, was yet the home of two outstanding Arabic philosophers, Ibn Bajja (Avempace) and Ibn Rushd (Averroes), the latter of whom asserted that the Qur'an, being but an imperfect presentation of truths which might be learnt more completely and correctly from Aristotle, was a dis-cipline fit only for the masses whose intelligence neither desired nor was capable of philosophical reasoning. But while the Moorish rulers tolerated such heresy, so long as it did not reach the people, they vigorously persecuted the many thousands of Christians and Jews in their Spanish province, and periodically expelled to the Christian North all who refused conversion to Islam. The twelfth century thus marked the beginning of the decline of scholarship in Muslim Spain. The refugees took north with them their advanced culture, especially to the kingdom of Toledo, which had been cap-tured by the Christians in 1085. Here Archbishop Raymond set up early in the twelfth century a college for the translation of Arabic philosophy and science, which flourished for 150 years and attracted scholars from all parts of Europe, including Britain.[1] The following century, the thirteenth, was the great period of translation from Arabic into Latin. It was encouraged notably by Alfonso the Wise of Castile, who was interested in philosophy and astronomy, and had two Jews translate an Arabic record of planet-ary movements which was still authoritative enough to be con-sulted by Galileo and Kepler in the seventeenth century. It was through such translations that in the following centuries the cream of Arabic scholarship, the legacy of their Greek and oriental fore-runners and the original Muslim contribution, was passed on to the rising universities of the West.

*   *   *

[1] An attractive and imaginative picture of the procedure followed by these scholars, and the linguistic and interpretative difficulties they encountered, is given by Chas. and Dorothy Singer, in The Legacy of Israel, 204 ff.

Already by the second half of the tenth century the acute and manifest disunity of the Muslim East had encouraged the Byzantine Empire, which 250 years before had been threatened at its very heart by the Arab armies, to take the offensive against its enemies, raid the Levant coasts, recover Cilicia, Cyprus and Antioch, and push its frontiers into North Syria and east to the Euphrates. In Hitti's words, 'in the first half of the eleventh century . . . political and military confusion prevailed everywhere. Islam seemed crushed to the ground.'[1]

Nor was this confusion confined only to externals. It penetrated to the very core of the Muslim faith. The caliph al-Ma'mun, who had founded the enlightened Bait al-Hikma in his enthusiasm for the rationalist views of the Mu'tazila, had encountered the opposition of the rigorous theologians of Baghdad. Regarding this opposition with considerable justification as obscurantist and pernicious, the Caliph proceeded to impose on theologians and lawyers the rationalist doctrine, that the Qur'an was created and not eternal, by the illiberal mechanism of an inquisition.[2] The death of al-Ma'mun's successor was followed by an officially-supported orthodox reaction, upholding the Qur'an and the Sunna as the only valid sources of knowledge, and again enforced by inquisitorial methods. The more extreme theologians, led by Ibn Hanbal, rejected all the findings of exact science and philosophical speculation, as leading to heresy, unbelief, and atheism. But speculation could not be completely suppressed, and Islam could not exist in a self-created vacuum. To justify its first principles to those Muslims of an enquiring mind, and they were not a few, it had to resort to those very methods of logical argument, derived from the Greek philosophers, which the extreme reactionaries deplored. A compromise was attempted early in the tenth century by al-Ash'ari, using logical argument in the demonstration of theological truth. But while this satisfied a large central block of Muslim thought, it offended on the one hand the philosophers, who were tending increasingly to reject the Qur'an and Sunna where they conflicted with the more subtle and plausible speculations of Aristotle and later Greek philosophy; and on the other hand it outraged the followers of Ibn Hanbal, who rejected any process of thought or argument, including al-Ash'ari's logical defence of Muslim revelation,

[1] op. cit., 473.
[2] *Encyclopaedia of Islam*, art. Mihna.

which was not expressly authorized by the scriptures. Meanwhile a third strain of Muslim religious thought, the mystical strain of Sufism, which had developed in the eighth and ninth centuries, had gained many adherents.[1] The mystics were impelled by the insistent desire to find a more intimate and personal approach to, and union with God than was provided by Sunni formalism and detachment, which placed Man at an almost infinite distance from his Creator and provided the Prophet as merely an interpreter of God's word, but not as a mediator between God and Man. Though the Sufis sought justification for their ritual practices in some few and exceptional passages of the Qur'an, their main inspiration was in fact drawn from other religions, in particular from Christian mysticism, the Zoroastrians of Persia, and the mystery-religions of the pre-Christian Middle East. So great is man's natural desire, amid the trials of this unsympathetic world, for consolation in grief and hope in adversity from some more-than-human source, that many thousands of Muslims were attracted as disciples of the mystics, who originally practised their devotions individually and without any sort of mutual association. Following only their individual inspirations, some of them were led into doctrinal extravagances, imagining themselves filled with the divine spirit, even declaring 'I am the Truth' and so claiming to be the Godhead, and disparaging orthodox Islam as a 'religion of the limbs' immeasurably inferior to their own 'religion of the heart'.

Thus by the eleventh century Muslim theology was undergoing a real internal crisis, from which it has never completely recovered. 'While the (mystic) saints, with their innumerable followers and worshippers, menaced the Islam of history and tradition, the ortho-dox party, divided against itself, either clinging fanatically to the letter of the Qur'an or disputing over legal and ritual minutiae or analysing theological dogmas in the dry light of the intellect, was fast losing touch with the inward spirit and life which makes religion a reality. Many earnest Muslims must have asked themselves how long such a state of things could last. Was there no means of preserving what was vital to the Faith without rending the com-munity asunder?'[2]

[1] Sufi was originally a nickname, derived from *suf*. wool: the wearer of an ascetic woollen garment, like that of the Christian monks.
[2] R. A. Nicholson, in *The Legacy of Islam*, 220 f.

In this desperate political, religious, and moral crisis, the salvaging of what could be saved of Muslim civilization was to come through human instruments as unpredictable as the salvaging of what could be saved of the Graeco-Roman civilization at the end of the third century A.D. through the rough Illyrian soldiers Diocletian and Constantine. Like that earlier first-aid process, the permanent loss of lifeblood from the wounded body-politic was considerable, and the lesion was repaired only with coarser, and less sensitive and flexible tissue.

The rise in the tenth century of the Fatimid and the lesser Shi'i dynasties, Arab and Persian, had for the time deprived the Turks of the political ascendancy they had been gaining in the Muslim world; but it did not make them any the less indispensable as garrison-troops and bodyguards. The Arab and Persian dynasts—Fatimid, Buwayhid, Samanid—continued to employ Turks in considerable numbers. Early in the eleventh century the Turkish tribe which later became known as the Seljuks pressed down from north of the Oxus into north-east Persia, becoming converted to Sunni Islam as they did so. |To these unlettered, unimaginative soldiery the pedestrian matter-of-factness of orthodox Sunni Islam was more attractive and suitable than the spiritual exaltation or over-elaborated subtleties of the Shi'i sects or the Sufis. By 1055 the Seljuk Turks had entered Baghdad at the invitation of the effete Abbasid caliph to rescue the caliphate from its Shi'i masters who were intriguing with the rival and schismatic Fatimid caliphate. To the Sunni majority of the Muslim world, whom a century of Shi'i political supremacy and systematic religious propaganda had failed to convert, the Turks were the more acceptable masters. In 1071 the Seljuks inflicted a crushing defeat on the Byzantine army, which delivered into their hands the greater part of Asia Minor, never conquered by the Arabs, as a region for Turkish settlement; from this time onwards Asia Minor has continuously been predominantly Turkish in speech and Muslim in faith. The Seljuks\ now ruled a vast empire extending from the Aegean to India. While its first Sultans remained culturally uncouth, they were fortunate in having as their wazir a gifted and intellectual Persian who bore the title Nizam al-Mulk. This statesman founded at Baghdad in 1066 the first real university of the Muslim world, named after him the Nizamiya, a centre for propagating the Sunni orthodoxy of al-Ash'ari as a counterblast to the Shi'i heresies taught at Al Azhar in Fatimid Cairo, and for training administrators for the Seljuk Empire.[1]

One of the lecturers at the Baghdad Nizamiya at the end of the century was a thirty-four-year-old Persian, al-Ghazzali, who had made a comprehensive study of theology, philosophy, and the sciences, and became a great success as a teacher and interpreter of Muslim law. But, as he tells us in his Confessions, he went through an intellectual and spiritual crisis of scepticism, finding that orthodoxy lacked an adequate logical basis, and that on the other hand philosophy failed to answer the ultimate problems raised in man's quest for understanding, and led only to heresy and unbelief. Accordingly he gave up his lectureship at the age of thirty-eight, and spent the next two years of his life in strict ascetic retreat. After his re-emergence he lived for fourteen years more, mainly in retirement devoted to study and writing, but with short periods of public teaching at Baghdad, Damascus, and Nishapur. His teaching rejected the subtleties of both the professional theologians and the philosophers, and sought to lead men back to living contact with the Qur'an and the Traditions, while admitting the use of logical thinking as an intellectual discipline. His great contribution was to demonstrate the validity and importance of the personal mystical experience which, he taught, enabled the human soul to renew the contact with the changeless world of divine Reality from which it had become separated by its entry into the mortal body: in this way a direct communion with God, bringing enlightenment and revelation, was possible. But he insisted that mystical practice must conform with both the letter and the spirit of the Prophet's teaching, and condemned such extreme forms of mystical belief as pantheism and the individual's identification of himself with God. Thus, while on the one hand al-Ghazzali referred Islam back from theological and philosophical subtleties to its first principles, on the other hand he reconciled the mystical appeal to the spiritual emotions with those same austere first principles, and so gave mysticism a legitimate place in the system of Muslim belief. Called the 'Restorer of the Faith', it has been said that 'Islam has never outgrown him, has never fully understood him.'[2] For nearly eight centuries he found no worthy suc-

---

[1] Nizam al-Mulk also founded in Iraq and Persia five other colleges which bore his name, and was the patron of 'Umar al-Khayyam.
[2] Macdonald, op. cit.

cessor, with the result that, while the transfusion of warm and living blood which he administered to the Muslim religion averted a fatal outcome of its crisis, he could not arrest the creeping paralysis, the choking of the spirit by the letter, which in the following centuries spread progressively over its members. The only vitality that survived was in the mystics, and as the centuries passed they diverged ever further from orthodoxy into extravagance or vulgar chicanery. Meanwhile, original scientific and scholarly speculation tended to be abandoned for less original and intellectually-exacting pursuits, such as the compilation of encyclopaedias and universal histories; and even the Nizamiya was devoted to the amassing of conventional learning rather than the promotion of research.

The Seljuk Turkish unification of the greater part of the Middle East lasted less than forty years. Immediately after 1092 their empire broke up into independent Seljuk principalities, leaving Syria and Palestine a crazy quilt of Turkish and Arab petty states. Christian Europe, which saw in the pilgrimage to the Holy Land a means of absolution from the most grievous sins, and had enjoyed access to the Holy Places with only the minimum of molestation from the Fatimids and their predecessors, had found that a generation of warfare between the Seljuks and the Fatimids had made travel more hazardous for the pilgrims. After the Seljuk conquest of Asia Minor the Byzantine Emperor had appealed to the Pope for a Christian alliance against Islam. The energetic Nordic peoples who dominated Western Europe were seeking new outlets for their warlike instincts, and now that the expulsion of the Muslims from Spain was making progress, they were attracted further afield. The feudal laws of succession produced a numerous class of landless younger sons who, with other adventurers, were eager to carve out for themselves estates in new lands. The Italian and other rising commercial cities of the Mediterranean were anxious to develop a larger trade in the luxury products of the Levant and further Asia. All these martial and material impulses were canalized, directed, and consecrated by the powerful influence of the Church into the First Crusade, which took the Levant by storm in 1099.

The importance of the Crusades in the cultural history of Western Europe can hardly be overestimated for their effect in throwing open the windows of men's minds to the influences of the Middle East, whose level of civilization was still far higher than that of the West; but their influence on the history of the Middle East itself is much more restricted. The cultural contribution which the Crusader settlers in the Levant could make was comparatively slight, except in the field of military architecture and tactics; and their presence in the Levant for two centuries was detrimental to it, in that their final expulsion was accompanied by the destruction of such important cities as Antioch, Tripoli, and Akka. The psychological impact of their invasion on the Muslim world was much smaller than might be supposed. While the Christian minorities in the Levant welcomed the Franks and gave them valuable help, the petty Muslim princes of Syria, impressed by their warlike prowess, preferred to pay them tribute rather than to resist. Appeals for help to the feeble Abbasid caliph in Baghdad were ignored. The centre of Seljuk authority was now in Isfahan, six weeks' journey from the Levant coast in those days; and the Seljuk sultan paid no heed to such distant alarms. The Crusaders were unable to consolidate their position more deeply than some fifty miles inland from the coast, and never occupied such strategic Muslim cities as Aleppo or Damascus. They were not, therefore, regarded for some time as a dangerous enemy to Islam, and no general jihad was declared against them. Instead they became a factor in the internecine intrigues and petty wars of the Muslim principalities, the parties to which had no aversion from making alliances with the Crusaders against their own coreligionaries. Hence for the first thirty years the Crusaders had matters much their own way, and succeeded by their expansion across the Jordan in cutting the communications between Fatimid Egypt and Muslim Syria. Then, however, they found themselves threatened by the Turkish atabeg (prince) of Mosul, whose ambitions for territorial aggrandizement found the exposed Crusader County of Edessa in 1144 an easier victim than his Muslim neighbours. As the Fatimid dynasty was now fast degenerating, the contest between the Crusaders and the Atabegs resolved itself from 1154 onwards, when the Atabegs had occupied Damascus, into a struggle for the possession of Egypt. This was won by the Atabegs, whose Kurdish commander became the master of the Nile Valley in 1169. Two years later his nephew, the famous Saladin (Salah ud-Din al Ayyubi), deposed the last feeble Fatimid and reigned as Sultan in his stead. Asserting his independence of the Atabegs, he made himself by 1183 ruler of a kingdom comprising Egypt and inland Syria,

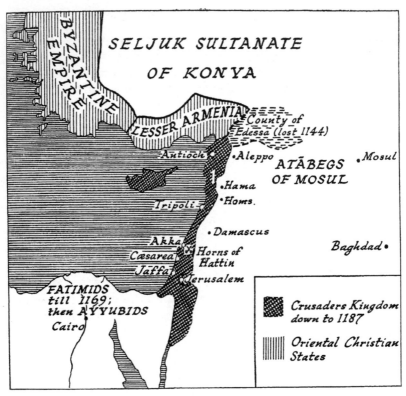

6. THE CRUSADER 'BEACH HEAD'.

completely enveloping the Crusader kingdom except for its outpost on the Red Sea at Aqaba. The Crusader freebooter Raynald
de Chatillon provoked Saladin to a jihad by an abortive attempt to
seize Mecca and Madina by way of the Red Sea. At the Horns of
Hattin above Tiberias Saladin outgeneralled and shattered the
Crusader army in 1187; Jerusalem fell, and two years later all that
was left of the Frankish kingdom were the ports of Antioch,
Tripoli, and Tyre.

The Third Crusade, in which Richard Coeur-de-Lion of England played a prominent part, failed to do more than recover
Cyprus and a strip of the Levant coast with Akka as its principal
port; and for fifty years (1192–1244) the situation was a stalemate
with, on the whole, peace between the Franks and their Muslim
neighbours. Characteristic of the new age, in which both the
fierce Crusading spirit and that of the jihad were out-of-date, was
the peaceable accommodation between the Holy Roman Emperor
Frederick II and Saladin's successor on the throne of Egypt, by
which in 1229 the Frankish kingdom recovered the Holy Places of
Jerusalem, Bethlehem and Nazareth and a strip of territory connecting them with the port of Akka. In these pacific conditions the
most important contribution of the Crusades was able to take root:
namely, the great development of the Eastern trade by the Italian
and other commercial cities, notably Venice, Genoa, and Pisa.
Already in the early years of the Crusader kingdom they had obtained from the Frankish feudal rulers important concessions for
their traders as the price of their participation in the material
fitting-out of the Crusades: exemption from taxation and customs-
dues, and legal autonomy in their special quarters in the Levant
ports under the jurisdiction of their own consuls. Their friendly
relations with Egypt at the beginning of the thirteenth century enabled them to extend their commerce to that country, by treaties
with the Ayyubid sultans dating from 1208, and so to lay the
foundations of the prosperous Levant trade of Mediterranean
Europe.

After Saladin's victories the Muslims no longer had any fear of
the Crusader power, but treated them as a convenient minor piece
on the Middle Eastern chessboard. Early in the thirteenth century,
however, the Muslims had to face a far more deadly menace in the
invasion of their eastern lands by the heathen and desperately cruel
Mongols, who, under their leader Jingiz Khan, came out of the

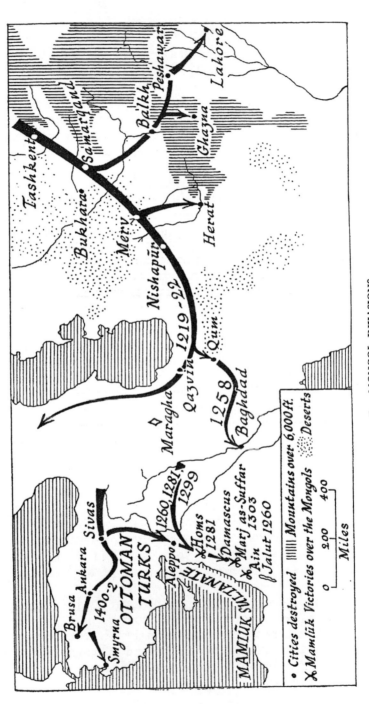

Tashkent

Samarqand

Bukhara

Balkh

Peshawar

Lahore

Ghazna

Herat

Merv

Nishapūr

1219-22

Qazvin

Qum

Maragha

1258

Baghdad

Sivas

Ankara

Brusa

1400-2

Smyrna

OTTOMAN TURKS

Aleppo

1260,1281,
1299

Homs
1281

Damascus

Marj as-Suffar
1303

Ain
Jalut 1260

MAMLŪK SM

MAMLŪK STATE

• Cities destroyed ||| Mountains over 6,000 ft.

✗ Mamlūk Victories over the Mongols ∷∷ Deserts

0   200   400

Miles

7. MONGOL INVASIONS

steppes of Eastern Asia that still bear their name. Between 1219 and 1224 they overran Transoxiana and North Persia, and utterly destroyed the highly-civilized cities of those lands and massacred their inhabitants, before passing on across South Russia to establish an empire which extended from the Vistula to the Pacific. Such is the mental tortuousness of political strategists, especially those dominated by an ideology, that the directors of Christian policy actually conceived the idea of an alliance with these savages against the civilized and treaty-keeping Muslims of the Levant. In 1245, following the loss of Jerusalem, largely as a result of Crusader intrigue against Egypt, Pope Innocent IV sent John de Piano Carpini on a political mission to Mongolia, and three years later St. Louis of France was also negotiating with the Mongols and sent the friar William of Rubruquis to their homeland. These missions brought no political success to the Crusader cause; but in 1253 another and more grievous blow fell on the Muslim world in a Mongol invasion under Hulagu, the grandson of Jingiz. He overran South Persia and in 1258 captured Baghdad, massacring its inhabitants. He laid open Iraq to uncouth Turcoman[1] and Mongol herdsmen from the north-east, who by their neglect allowed the elaborate irrigation-system on which the country's fertility depended to fall gradually into decay. Hulagu finally put an end to the Abbasid caliphate in Baghdad, that pitiful relic of former Arab greatness. The triumphant Mongols pressed on to invade Syria and destroyed Aleppo, but were decisively defeated in North Palestine by the armies of Egypt in 1260. In Egypt, meanwhile, an important dynastic revolution had taken place: the last feeble sultan of Saladin's line had been deposed by the Turkish commander-in-chief of his slave armies, himself originally a slave (mamluk); and for the next 250 years a 'dynasty' of these Mamluk commanders—usually Turkish by birth, sometimes Mongol or Circassian—was to rule Egypt, Palestine and Syria. The succession to the throne was sometimes hereditary, but more often the prize of the strongest, and intrigue and assassination were the rule. The millions of native Egyptians and Syrians, Muslim and Christian alike, had even less part in the government of their countries under this turbulent foreign soldateska than they had known in previous

[1] Medieval Arab and Persian historians apply this term to all the Turks of Western Asia, including the Seljuks and even sometimes the Ottoman Turks (*Encyclopaedia of Islam*, art. Turcoman).

centuries; but the day-to-day administration of Egypt, inherited from its Byzantine and Fatimid governors and in all probability the most efficient instrument of government which existed in the Middle Ages,[1] remained in the same patient Coptic and Jewish hands as before, sometimes to the unruly indignation of the Muslim city mobs, who vented their anger in pogroms.

Some of the Frankish towns and strong-points of the Levant had assisted the Mongol invasion; and now the Mamluk Sultan Baybars took a merciless revenge. Between 1265 and 1268 he wrested from them Jaffa, Caesarea, Nazareth, and the great city of Antioch. From 1272 to 1282 there was a precarious truce, during which his successor Qalawun inflicted another heavy defeat on the Mongols in Syria. In 1289 the Crusaders lost Tripoli, and two years later Akka, their last stronghold, fell and the seat of the Frankish kingdom was withdrawn to Cyprus. A third Mongol invasion of Syria c. 1300 was again checked by the Mamluk armies.

By thus turning back from the Levant the threat of Mongol invasion, with its insensate lust for destruction of all that was finest and most civilized, the early Mamluk sultans have deserved well of history. Like the Ayyubids they were given overmuch to self-indulgence in military and palace architecture and the pleasures of the flesh. Nevertheless, consciously imitating Saladin and his forerunner the Atabeg Nur ud-Din of Aleppo, the earlier Mamluks did spare an appreciable fraction of their revenues for the development of irrigation-canals, aqueducts and harbours, and for building hospitals, libraries, and schools. The primary purpose of these schools, however, was not so much to promote science and general learning as to propagate Sunni orthodoxy and combat the Shi'a, which was evidently still formidable.[2] The great Jewish physician and philosopher Moses Maimonides had found a welcome at Saladin's court when Moorish intolerance had driven him from his native Spain; and for a century Jewish and other doctors continued his medical tradition in Egypt. By 1300, however, original scientific research was almost at an end in the Muslim East. In Egypt ancient superstition and magic, deeply rooted in the masses of the people as it still is, was reasserting itself; and scientific and scholarly activity was running to seed in unoriginal imitativeness

[1] H. A. R. Gibb, *Ibn Battuta: Travels in Asia and Africa*, 20.
[2] Saladin had grimly closed the Fatimid network of Shi'i schools, the Diyar al-'Ilm, and dispersed their libraries. It was now that al-Azhar became a *Sunni* mosque.

and facile compilation. A high level of esoteric scholarship had been maintained in the higher grades of the Isma'ili sect, which was re-propagated c. 1090 in North Persia and North Syria; but both these centres were practically exterminated in the late thirteenth century by the Mongols and the Mamluks respectively.[1] Strangely enough, a temporarily fertile ground for at least some branches of science and scholarship was provided in North Persia and Transoxiana by the courts of the Mongols themselves. Inspired by his unlettered interest in astrology as a means of foretelling the future, Hulagu, the destroyer of Baghdad, founded an astronomical observatory and library at his capital of Maragha near Tabriz. About 1300 one of his descendants, who had been converted to Islam, endowed an observatory, library, and schools at Tabriz. A century later the Turco-Mongol conqueror Timur Leng (Tamberlane) deported to his capital at Samarqand scholars, architects and craftsmen from the cities he had destroyed, such as Aleppo and Damascus; and his successor was patron of a flourishing astronomical observatory at Samarqand in the first half of the fifteenth century.

Instead of the resurgence of uncouth Turk and Mongol ending abruptly the growing commercial penetration of the Middle East from Europe, as might be supposed, it actually fostered it. Although the Mamluks severely punished the native Christians of the Levant for their complicity, real or suspected, with the Mongol invaders,[2] the Christian pilgrim-traffic to the Holy Places was too profitable a source of Mamluk revenue to be stopped; and this material consideration applied still more to the trade in the silks, spices, and other products of the further East, for which the peoples of Europe, now growing in sophistication, had acquired an insatiable appetite. Consequently, the Mamluks encouraged and took a heavy toll of this trade through Alexandria and the Levant

---

[1] On Alamut, the Persian centre, see Freya Stark, *The Valley of the Assassins*. The Isma'ilis continued a ruthless underground struggle against the Sunni rulers of the Muslim world, and gained the sinister title of 'Assassins' (originally Hashshashin) by allegedly furnishing with 'Dutch courage' in the form of hashish members chosen from their lower grades whom they used to murder their political opponents. One of their first and most distinguished victims was the enlightened Seljuk wazir Nizam ul-Mulk.

A minority of the Isma'ilis survived the destruction of their centres, and to-day some 200,000, who have long abandoned the aggressive tendencies of their forerunners, venerate as their Imam the Agha Khan, who claims descent from Ali in the forty-seventh generation, through the medieval Grand Masters of Alamut.

[2] V. Minorsky, *Royal Central Asian Journal*, XXVII (1940), 436.

ports, while the Mongols permitted Marco Polo and his kinsmen to make their famous journeys to Mongol-dominated China in the late thirteenth century. In the following century we find merchants of Venice, Genoa, and other European cities trading with the Mongol capital at Tabriz via the Black Sea; and though the re-assertion of exclusive Chinese independence under the Ming dynasty once more closed China to Europeans, Timur Leng and his successors in the fifteenth century continued to encourage European trade with their dominions in West-central Asia. Trade with the Mamluk kingdom in the Levant became a virtual monopoly of Venice, who had finally disposed of her rival Genoa in a ruthless commercial war. Both Venice and the Mamluks extracted an exorbitant profit from the trade; but in the fifteenth century Mamluk predatoriness became too much even for the Venetians, and when the exacting Sultan Bars-bay raised his excise-duty on pepper to 160 per cent. they successfully brought pressure on him by threatening to withdraw their merchants from Alexandria.

Meanwhile, the political stability of the Middle East countries had continued to deteriorate, until only an enforced re-unification, however roughly and arbitrarily imposed and with whatever further loss of cultural vitality, could save the whole from ruin. The raids of Timur Leng c. 1400 had ruined Aleppo, Damascus, and other Syrian cities; had erected 120 towers of skulls of the inhabitants of Baghdad alone; and had completed the work begun by Hulagu in converting Iraq from a land of irrigated agriculture to a land given over in the main to the nomadic herds of the Turcoman and the Bedouin. Mamluk rule likewise deteriorated sharply after c. 1340. In the next 128 years there were no fewer than twenty-nine Mamluk sultans, ruling for an average of only four and a half years apiece. In Egypt, Palestine and Syria alike the cultivator was oppressed by the irresponsible Mamluk feudal land-lords, whose incomes depended on the amount of land-tax they could extort from their peasantry. Bedouin and Turcoman raiders pillaged the settled lands, and the former actually sacked Jerusalem in 1480. The cities of Syria and Palestine were largely ruined by the continual revolts of local governors, and the public benefactions of better days, such as schools and hospitals, were extensively converted by the trustees to their personal profit. A contemporary Muslim historian estimated that the population of the Mamluk empire was reduced to one-third of its figure at the beginning of their rule;[1] and though his figures cannot be statistically verified, the hundreds of archaeological sites, which are abundantly covered with medieval Arab pottery but are now abandoned, bear material testimony to the extent of the depopulation. An important factor contributing to this depopulation in the later fourteenth century was the Black Death and the famine which accompanied it in two appalling visitations in successive generations. 'In a young and vigorous society the effects of such a disaster soon disappear; but where the social order is already reeling, many decades are required before equilibrium can be regained. This respite was not granted to the Islamic world.'[2]

For already the political forces which were to fill the anarchic vacuum of the Mamluk empire and of equally disorganized Iraq and Persia were taking shape. The Seljuk unity of Asia Minor had been shattered by the Mongol invasions of the mid-thirteenth century, but without basically altering the Turkish character of the dominant section of the population. About 1300 a small Turkish principality founded by one Othman around Brusa in the north-west of the peninsula was beginning to expand at the expense of its Turkish neighbours and the moribund Byzantine Empire to the north. In 1353 Othman's descendants invaded Europe and in 1361 established their European capital at Adrianople (Edirne), blocking the route from Constantinople to the Balkan hinterland and so isolating the capital of Orthodox Christianity from its potential Orthodox allies, the Slavs. A powerful coalition led by the Serbs was shattered by the Ottoman Turks in the battle of the Kossovo Plain in 1389. By 1400 they had extended their northern frontier to the Danube and incorporated the greater part of Asia Minor; Constantinople itself was on the point of falling; but at this moment the irresistible thunderbolt of Timur Leng struck them. Crushingly defeated at Ankara in 1402, the Ottomans lost Asia Minor, but their kingdom survived in the Balkans. From 1420 onwards they began to acquire from Western Europe the use of firearms; in 1453 they gave the coup-de-grace to the Byzantine Empire by taking Constantinople; and by 1468 they had completed the reconquest of Asia Minor, and so became neighbours and rivals of the Mamluk empire on the borders of North Syria. For a generation they were kept in check by Qait Bey (1468–95), a

[1] Hitti, op. cit., 696.
[2] H. A. R. Gibb, *Ibn Battuta: Travels in Asia and Africa*, 24 f.

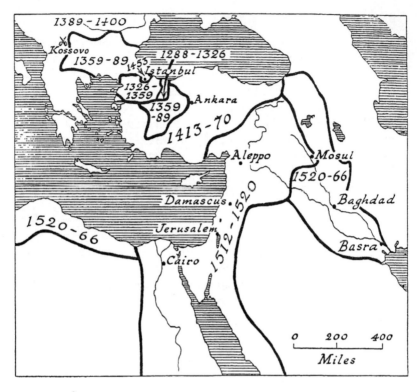

8. THE EXPANSION OF THE OTTOMAN EMPIRE

Mamluk sultan at last worthy of his first predecessors. Instead they successfully assaulted Persia.[1] In 1514 the Turkish troops armed with muskets and supported by 300 cannon were too much for the Persian cavalry without firearms. It was now the turn of the Mamluks, who were suspected of complicity with the Persian shah. They also had no guns as yet, and their cavalry were routed near Aleppo in 1516. They hastened to acquire some few pieces of ordnance to meet the advancing Ottoman army, but the outcome of a second battle outside Cairo next year was the same. The Mamluk sultanate was no more. The pitiful Abbasid puppet-caliph, last of a line which had been set up in Cairo by the first of the great Mamluks in 1260 following the Mongol sacking of Baghdad, and under whose nominal authority the Mamluks had continued to rule, was carried off from Cairo to Constantinople. By this token the centre of gravity once more passed from Egypt to the city on the Bosporus; and Cairo sank to the level of a provincial capital.

APPENDIX: THE PRINCIPAL DOCTRINES OF ISLAM.

The essential core of Muslim belief is the Oneness of God. The Muslim Creed begins with the words *la ilah ill'Allah*, 'There is no god but God'. From this follow his various attributes of omnipotence, omniscience, omnipresence, etc.

The Creeds ends, *wa-Mohammed rasul Allah*, 'and Mohammed is the apostle of God'. No divinity is thereby claimed for the Prophet. He is wholly human, the last and greatest of an ascending series of prophets, borrowed from the Jewish Old Testament. The series comprises the Patriarchs culminating in Moses, and the kings David and Solomon, but not the prophets of the periods immediately before and after the Exile. Higher than all, and next in rank to Mohammed himself comes Jesus, 'from the breath (spirit) of God' as the Qur'an describes him. He and His Mother are honoured by Muslims; but Jesus again is regarded as wholly human, and the Christian doctrines of His Incarnation, Crucifixion, and Resurrection are held to be misguided.

The doctrine of the Trinity is especially obnoxious to Muslims, who consider it to conflict with the essential Unity of God; yet

---

[1] A new dynasty, the Safavid, winning the support of the populace of the Persian cities by its adoption of moderate Shi'i doctrines as the religion of dynasty and state, had newly unified Persia c. 1500 after centuries of disunion and anarchy. Their dynasty lasted until 1722.

Muslim orthodoxy itself through its belief in the eternal, uncreated Qur'an, the archetype of that dictated to Mohammed by the Archangel Gabriel, elevated the Qur'an to a status co-existent and co-eternal with God, and caused the important seventh-century sect of the Mu'tazila to protest that the Unity of God was thereby infringed.

Muslims believe in a Resurrection of the body preceding the Last Judgement, with physical rewards in Heaven and punishments in Hell. These Last Things will be preceded by the coming of the Mahdi, the divinely-guided, having the same names as the Prophet himself. This concept of the Mahdi has been left obscurely in the background of orthodox Sunni Islam, but among the poor and underprivileged sections of the Sunni community self-styled Mahdis have appeared from time to time to deliver them from oppression and institute a reign of righteousness; and in the Shi'a the Mahdi has much greater importance, since he is there none other than the Hidden Imam returning to his people.

In its dogmatic essentials Islam is thus closely akin to Judaism, with some superficial borrowings from Christianity, the whole given a distinctively Arabian orientation after its rejection by the Jews of Madina. Its importance in world-civilization lies not so much in its undistinguished dogmatic as in the cohesive force of the system of legal and social regulations for the direction of the Muslim community, begun by the Prophet himself and incorporated in the Qur'an, and continued under the Caliphs in the form of the Traditions. It was these regulations, superimposed on the simple dogmatic foundation, that originally brought together the individualist Arab tribes as a conquering force, that imposed a social unity upon the national and cultural diversity of the Muslim world in its greatest days, and that maintains a sense of unity even to-day after centuries of decay and neglect. The present machine-age may have undermined the belief of many 'educated' Muslims in the dogmas of their religion; but though they have become free-thinkers or even atheists, they remain notwithstanding within the social community of Islam.

CHAPTER III

The Ottoman and Persian Empires and the Growth of European Enterprise (1517–1770)

LIKE THE Byzantine Empire, the Ottoman Turks had to divide their effective power between the Middle East and their even more important interests in the Balkans. Both empires were essentially Levantine; but they wasted their resources in continual wars against a powerful rival in Persia, from which they were estranged by deep religious differences. Just as the inconclusive Byzantine-Persian wars weakened both states and exposed them to the Arab invasion and conquest, so the inconclusive Ottoman-Persian wars of the sixteenth-eighteenth centuries weakened both and exposed them to European commercial penetration, leading eventually to their helpless manipulation by European Powers in the nineteenth century. In both the Byzantine and the Ottoman periods the possession of Iraq was disputed with Persia, and in both periods likewise the sovereign in Constantinople, being also the master of Egypt, was led by force of geographical propinquity to seek to control the opposite Arabian coast of the Red Sea; but with little permanent effect, so that in both periods the greater part of the Arabian peninsula remained practically independent of the Great Power ruling in the Levant, and was only lightly touched by its civilization.

The Ottoman principles of provincial administration were not unlike the Byzantine, though in a cruder form. The Empire was essentially military in its organization, and its object was frankly the power and well-being of the state, personified by the sovereign, with little thought for the well-being of its subjects. It distributed large tracts of land in feudal fiefs to its military commanders, though without disturbing the existing tenant-cultivators. The function of the provinces was to provide the central government with revenue in the form of material wealth and manpower for the armies, and the function of the provincial governor to collect this revenue, with only secondary thought for the social or economic good of the provincials. Provided that these demands were met, there was little deliberate interference with the racial or religious status of the population, except such as might arise locally from the presence of garrisons and officials of the ruling race and creed. The Christians in the Ottoman Empire continued to fare much as they had fared under preceding Muslim rulers, and their lot was distinctly better than that of the Jews in medieval and twentieth-century Central and Eastern Europe. The Turks showed greater toleration to the Christians in the Asiatic provinces, where they were a small and submissive minority, than in the Balkans, where they constituted a rebellious majority constantly intriguing with the neighbouring enemy Powers, Austria and Russia.[1] Catholic missions were admitted, not only to the Levant, but to Baghdad and Basra as early as the seventeenth century, though they were always exposed to the caprice of changing local authority. In the depopulated Palestine of the eighteenth century the pilgrim-dues were the most important item of revenue. The yearly pilgrimage of some 4,000 persons c. 1750 had risen to 10–12,000 when the French traveller Volney visited Palestine in 1784, and the tax collected for their visit to the Jordan alone amounted to three times the tax-assessment of the town of Gaza, then the most populous town in Palestine.[2]

The Turks were a racial minority in their great empire, and made no attempt at the general colonization of the conquered provinces. The empire was conceived on no narrow Turkish-national basis, but was a comprehensive empire like the Abbasid or the Roman. Whatever a man's race or birthplace, he was eligible for government-service and could attain the highest office, provided that he conformed to the general cultural pattern of the empire: the religion and social customs of Sunni Islam; a military background of training and experience; and the Turkish language, which under the Ottomans (while absorbing a multitude of forms of expression and loan-words from Arabic and Persian) had yet triumphantly asserted itself as the language of the ruling-class against those two languages of an older and higher civilization. While the bulk of

---

[1] The Armenian atrocities of the last fifty years had their origin in the rise of an insistent Armenian nationalism encouraged by Turkey's traditional enemy, Russia. Cf. the contemporary comments of D. G. Hogarth, *A Wandering Scholar in the Levant* (1896), 146 ff.
[2] De Haas, op. cit., 357 f., with references.

senior officials were Turks, Syrian and Palestinian townsmen gained by their innate keenness of intellect an appreciable number of senior posts; the sturdy and vigorous Kurds found openings in the military and administrative career; but Iraqis were mainly confined to the lower grades; and before 1850 the native Egyptian was treated, like the fellahin everywhere in the empire, as a beast of burden. The Turks left considerable local authority to non-Turkish ruling-groups, especially in the less accessible districts: examples are the Kurds in their mountain-valleys; the Shi'i Arab tribal chiefs of Lower Iraq; the Druze[1] amirs who then dominated the Lebanese mountains. Even the defeated Mamluks remained more numerous than the Turkish officials and soldiery in Egypt. They were indispensable for the administration of that country; their amirs remained governors of the sanjaqs (sub-provinces); and they continued through the centuries to maintain their numbers by importing fresh slaves, especially from the Caucasus. By 1600 no distinction could be made between the Mamluks and the Ottoman Turks in Egypt. Both were called 'Turks' to differentiate them from the native Egyptians; Turkish blood and speech had preponderated among the Mamluks from the beginning. To sum up, it has been well said that at its best Turkish rule was marked by 'a skilful, vigorous opportunism, well informed of conditions, well executed within limits, gaining limited and immediate ends, rather cunning than wise. It lacked ideals, save the vaguest that Islam and humanity could prompt; it lacked knowledge and theory; it abounded in follies, abuses, injustices; yet it met each immediate problem with a suitable expedient, and gained the applause of the moment without thought for the larger morrow.'[2]

The absence of a constructive long-term policy of administration was greatly aggravated by the shortness of tenure of the pashas, or provincial governors. They were often changed annually; in 280

---

[1] The Druze sect, numbering to-day some 150,000 persons in the Jebel Druze (Southern Syria), Lebanon and North Palestine, originated in the eccentric Fatimid caliph al-Hakim, the fanatical destroyer of the Church of the Holy Sepulchre in Jerusalem, who in 1017 declared himself the incarnation of God on earth, and shortly afterwards mysteriously disappeared. His followers declared that he was not dead, but merely in hiding till his return as Mahdi. Persecuted by his successors on the Fatimid throne, they found a refuge in Syria under the leadership of one Darazi, after whom the Druze are named. Practising their cult in secret to avoid persecution through the centuries, they have always been considered by Muslims of all sects to be so extreme in heresy as to constitute a distinct religion.

[2] Longrigg, op. cit., 169.

years of direct Ottoman rule Egypt had 100 pashas, while Damascus had 133 in the first 180 years of Ottoman dominion. High office was purchased by bribery, and retained only by the prompt forwarding of tribute to Istanbul and repeated bakhshish to powerful courtiers. The pasha compensated himself out of the provincial revenues, and by farming out the collection of taxes to the highest bidder. Such impermanent and irresponsible administration could not be better than indifferent. The far-seeing Sultan Sulaiman III (surnamed by Turks the Lawgiver, and by contemporary Europeans the Magnificent, 1520–66) carried out useful public works, such as the improvement of the water-supply of Jerusalem and Mecca, and work on canals and flood-prevention in stricken Iraq. There were pashas who founded new mosques under the impulse of piety or the prickings of overburdened consciences; but on the whole the Ottoman administration built very few roads, or hospitals, or schools; as late as 1838 a traveller could not find a single bookshop in either Damascus or Aleppo. The Turks paid little attention to the improvement or maintenance of agriculture and irrigation, or to the settlement and control of the Bedouin, who had greatly encroached on the settled lands in the Time of Troubles of the preceding centuries. Many villages were abandoned and towns dwindled in size, except such ports as were temporarily favoured with European trade. Great Alexandria, by-passed by the opening of the Cape Route and left with only a meagre trade in the products of Egypt, the Sudan, and Southern Arabia, shrank from a populous city to a town of 10,000 people or less. The peasant sowed only sufficient land to produce a crop he could harvest quickly and hide away from the tax-collector. In Syria cultivators abandoned their fields and sought a living in the towns or took refuge in the less accessible mountain-valleys. In Egypt irrigation was allowed to decay, and the orderly distribution of water lapsed. 'Village fought village for the right to a water-channel; farmers came in the night, cut the dykes, and emptied their neighbours' water on to their own land. Deprived of water, beaten and oppressed by their overlords, many of the fellahin deserted their land and turned to a life of brigandage and crime on the waste lands between the villages.'[1] By the eighteenth century Egypt, once the granary of the Roman Empire with seven to ten million inhabitants, had become barely self-supporting in food,

[1] Crouchley, op. cit., 14.

even though her estimated population had fallen to two and a half millions. Famine was frequent, and so was pestilence, by which half-a-million died in Egypt in 1619, and 230 villages were desolated in 1643. In the mid-seventeenth century the country between Aleppo and that part of the Euphrates nearest to the city was fertile and efficiently irrigated, but a century later the land had become a desert;[1] and at the end of the eighteenth century it is stated that only one-eighth of the villages formerly on the tax-register of the Aleppo pashaliq were still inhabited. The population of Syria and Palestine combined was then estimated at only one and a half millions, with that of Palestine shrunken to perhaps under 200,000.

Already by 1600 the authority of the provincial governors was weakening as the brief noontide of the Ottoman Empire passed. Sometimes the provinces relapsed into anarchy; but sometimes the power of the pashas was superseded by that of local rulers who afforded greater internal stability, the possibility of sounder economic life, and freer commercial enterprise to European merchants, than did the transient and rapacious Turkish administrators. The Druze amirs of the Lebanon became virtually independent of the Porte, and the relative security of life under their rule attracted a considerable immigration from other parts of Syria. Outstanding among them was Fakhr ud-Din, who carved out a kingdom for himself in Lebanon and North Palestine between 1585 and 1635. He made his own diplomatic agreements with European Powers; encouraged the production and export of silk and cotton through his ports of Sidon and Beirut in exchange for European goods; and introduced Christian missions and European engineers. From 1600 to 1669 the pashaliq of Basra enjoyed firm government and prosperity under the local family of Afrasyab. Later it was the turn of the Baghdad pashaliq to find stability and tolerant rule under Hasan Pasha and his son Ahmed Pasha, 1704–47. After the death of the latter, effective control remained till 1832 in the hands of a corps of Georgian Mamluks, the majority Christian by birth, which the two pashas had built up. The Georgian Sulaiman Pasha the Great united the three pashaliqs of Baghdad, Basra, and Mosul from 1780 to 1802, paying only formal recognition to the Ottoman Sultan in the form of 'constant reports, rarer presents, and yet less frequent tribute.'[2] Until about 1750 Egypt was less fortunate. The

[1] C. P. Grant, *The Syrian Desert*, 161, n. 1.
[2] Longrigg, op. cit., 199.

Ottoman pashas had long ceased to exercise any real authority, and the unhappy country was torn by the struggles for supremacy of the Mamluk beys. Their tyranny and oppression of the weak went uncontrolled. 'In no province did Muslim fervour burn so bright against the infidel; nowhere was the power of the Sultan more relaxed; and the Franks who dwelt there were subjected to a régime of extortion and ill-treatment at the hands of the beys, which in its insolence and regularity far exceeded that experienced elsewhere in the Levant. . . . The natives seem to have had an innate antipathy to all Europeans, and lost no opportunity of molesting or reviling them with ferocity and fanaticism.'[1] The situation was temporarily improved by Ali Bey, who tried to reform the financial system and the administration of justice and suppress the brigandage of the Bedouin. In 1770 he declared his complete independence of the Sultan, and allied himself with adh-Dhahir, the governor of Galilee, who had expelled the Turkish officials from his province, revived the derelict port of Akka for the export of cotton and silk, and was in the habit of distributing free seed to the fellahin and remitting their taxes in bad years. Before the two rebels could achieve much in their respective provinces, however, they met their deaths in 1773 at the hands of jealous rivals.

*   *   *

In antiquity the Mediterranean had been the main focus of European civilization and commerce; and though the importance of that sea as a channel of cultural contacts had been diminished when the Muslims overran and conquered its southern shores, the Crusades had done much to restore its former commerce. Even after the expulsion of the Franks from the Levant, the Mediterranean trading-cities, especially Venice and Genoa, had continued to enjoy a lively commerce with the Muslim East. In the meantime, however, the small Atlantic kingdom of Portugal had succeeded in the fourteenth century in freeing itself from the Muslims, and under the inspiration of Prince Henry the Navigator (1394–1460) her seamen began to explore the Atlantic coast of Africa southwards. Henry's general motive was evidently to carry on the Crusades by an attempt to outflank the Dar ul-Islam both strategically and commercially; to divert the trade in the gold and other

[1] Wood, op, cit., 124, 234.

products of West Africa from Muslim hands; to make contact south of the Sahara with the Negus of Ethiopia ('Prester John') and jointly assail the Muslims from the south; and he may also have planned in his later life to win control for Portugal of the Indian trade, which was now the main source of wealth of the Muslim world.[1] The progress of Portuguese exploration was naturally slow at first, and by the time of Henry's death had gone no further south than Sierra Leone; but in the following generation their seamen pushed onwards, until in 1488 Bartholomew Diaz at last rounded the Cape of Good Hope. Ten years later Vasco da Gama went on to reach the Muslim coastal towns of East Africa, where he secured an Indian pilot who conducted him on to Southern India. The King of Portugal now adopted the grandiose title of 'Lord of the Conquest, Navigation, and Commerce of Ethiopia, Arabia, Persia, and India', and in spite of Muslim resistance further trading expeditions were sent to their station at Calicut, bringing home cargoes of spices.

The Mamluks of Egypt and the Republic of Venice were equally alarmed at this by-passing of their extremely profitable joint monopoly of the Indian trade with Europe. The Mamluk Sultan threatened to destroy the Christian Holy Places if the Portuguese did not abandon their Indian voyages, and the Prior of St. Catherine's Monastery on Sinai actually journeyed to Rome and tried to persuade the Pope to forbid them. The Venetians, who had instigated the so-called Fourth Crusade against Constantinople in order to destroy a trade-rival and had looked with complacency on the fall of the same city to the Ottoman Turks, even went so far as to supply timber to the Mamluks to build warships in an attempt to sweep the Portuguese from the Indian Ocean. But the Portuguese ocean-going ships and mariners were more than a match for the Muslim vessels and sailors, accustomed in the main to the more sheltered seas of the Levant and the Middle East. They occupied the strategically-placed islands of Socotra and Hormuz in an attempt to blockade the Muslim fleets within the Red Sea and the Persian Gulf respectively, and repelled a Mamluk naval attack on their Indian ports. Lisbon rapidly took the place of Venice as the European clearing-house for Indian goods, and the Cape Route began to supersede the old sea and land-routes to the Mediterranean. Admiral de Albuquerque is even said to have formed a

[1] Prestage, op. cit., 29 ff., 165 ff.

plan to divert the Upper Nile into the Red Sea and so deprive Egypt of her vital water-supply.

In the Persian Gulf the Portuguese had occupied by 1515 the strategic and trading posts of Muscat, Hormuz, and Bahrain; but they were never able to seize permanent bases in the Red Sea, since the opposition of the Mamluk and subsequently the Ottoman navies held them in check. Though they enjoyed for the moment a monopoly of the Cape Route, they had by no means diverted all the traffic from the Overland Route. Throughout the sixteenth century Arab traders were still bringing the silks, spices, dyes and drugs of the East and the coffee of the Yemen up the Red Sea and across the desert to Cairo and Alexandria, and trade also continued to follow the route from the Persian Gulf via the Syrian steppe to the Levant ports. Caravans of four to six hundred camels were common, and Aleppo became the leading trading-centre of Syria; there are several references to the city in Shakespeare. In 1521 Venice obtained from the Sultan a commercial concession of the form which was to become common, granting her traders freedom from customs-duties or other taxation beyond a stated limit, and judicial extraterritoriality under the authority of their own consuls. These were the so-called Capitulations (i.e. the 'chapters' of the concession) modelled on precedents of the Crusader and Mamluk periods.[1] Commercial pre-eminence in the Mediterranean was now, however, passing from Venice to France, to whom capitulations were granted in 1536. By the time Elizabethan England entered upon the Levantine commercial scene, founding in 1581 the Levant Company of Merchants to trade her good woollen cloth and tin for eastern products, the French were already well established; and though they could not prevent the English from opening a consulate in Aleppo, they did successfully obstruct the opening of an English consulate at Alexandria. In any case, the stout English woollens found little sale in torrid Egypt.

Already before the accession of Queen Elizabeth the English had begun to chafe at the Portuguese monopoly of the Far Eastern trade. The population was increasing. The manufacture of woollen cloth was outstripping the demands of the home market; but not yet feeling strong enough to challenge the Portuguese by attempt-

---

[1] They were destined to survive down to the twentieth century and make difficulties for diplomats and administrators in the altered conditions of the Middle East.

ing the Cape Route, the English tried to by-pass it by seeking a North-East Passage round northern Europe to the Far East, and in 1553 founded the Muscovy Company for this purpose. 'The advocates of the scheme asserted with confidence that in Cathay with its cool climate, its teeming and (it was believed) wealthy population, a lucrative market for English woollens would certainly be found; while, once the dangers of the northern ice had been passed, it would be a comparatively easy matter to proceed from Cathay to the Moluccas, and there lade for the return voyage the spices so much in demand in the European markets.'[1] The climatic difficulties of the North-East Passage frustrated these hopes; but Antony Jenkinson, commander of the Company's fleet, travelled from Moscow down the Volga and crossed the Caspian to establish trade-relations with the Persian capital at Qazvin in 1561. This roundabout route was, however, abandoned twenty years later owing to the founding of the Levant Company and to the anarchy which was already threatening Persia.

In 1583 four English travellers set out on an exploratory journey from Aleppo to Malacca via Baghdad and the Persian Gulf. In 1591, the year in which the sole survivor of this expedition arrived in England, three English ships were sent via the Cape to the Far East on a voyage of reconnaissance, the Portuguese power being now in decline. Meanwhile the Dutch had in 1581 wrested their independence from Spain, and were now ready to embark on the commercial enterprises which the dense population of their small country, totalling about half that of contemporary England, forced upon them. By 1599 the Dutch had sent successful expeditions to the East Indies; and in that year the English East India Co. was founded, largely by merchants of the Levant Co., 'to set forth a voyage to the East Indies and the other isles and countries thereabouts.' In its infancy the Company undertook a voyage only once every two or three years, each being separately financed by subscriptions and levies from its members. The Dutch companies, on the other hand, were federated in 1602 into the 'United East India Company', practically a department of state with a permanently subscribed capital of the then immense sum of over half-a-million pounds.[2] Soon it was 'covering the Indian Ocean with its fleets, threatening to displace the loose Portuguese monopoly in favour

---

[1] Foster, op. cit., 5 f.
[2] J. A. Williamson, *Short History of British Expansion*, I, 219.

of one far more complete and aggressive, and making the effort of the English company seem puny.'[1] The English company was indeed for the first fifty years of its existence chaotically financed and administered, and it was obstructed rather than helped by the early Stuart governments.[2]

Meanwhile the English brothers Sir Antony and Sir Robert Sherley had in 1598 received a warm welcome from the illustrious and enterprising Shah Abbas the Great of Persia (1587–1629), who was seeking the most favourable market for Persia's raw silk, her main commodity for export and largely a royal monopoly. The Persian Gulf was still dominated from Hormuz by the Portuguese, who 'were everywhere hated by the native populations on account of the savage cruelty which they had constantly used to mask their deficiency in real force';[3] the route to the Levant coast was controlled by the Shah's enemy, the Ottoman Sultan, for his own profit; and the Caspian route was impossibly roundabout. The Shah accordingly sent first Antony and then Robert as his ambassador to the capitals of Europe to seek alliance against the Ottoman Empire and trade-relations. The East India Co., which had already opened a factory (trading-station) at Surat north of Bombay in 1612, accepted the Shah's proposals, and sent ships in 1616 to the Persian Gulf to trade with his capital at Isfahan. The Portuguese at Hormuz made a determined attempt to intercept the Company's merchant-ships, in return for which a joint Anglo-Persian expedition in 1622 expelled them from Hormuz and the Persians drove them out of Bahrain also. Their decline was accelerated by their loss of Muscat in 1650 and the closing of their factory at Basra.

The East India Co. now had factories at the Shah's new port of Bandar Abbas, with branches at Isfahan and Shiraz; at Mokha for the Yemen coffee-trade; and soon afterwards at Basra for trade by river-boat with Baghdad. However, the reorganization of the Company in 1661 was followed by a change of policy and the abandoning of all these factories. Experience had shown that it was not profitable for the Company to operate the local coastal trade, which was the natural business of the highly efficient Asiatic shipping. The Company accordingly concentrated its staffs at a few

---

[1] Foster, op. cit., 183.
[2] J. A. Williamson, *The Ocean in English History*, 104 ff.
[3] Williamson, *Short History*, I. 223.

central factories, but without losing the local trade, since its regular liners making the Cape passage continued to be fed by the 'country ships' not under its command.[1]

The successful development of the Cape Route had largely diverted the trade in East Indian products from the Overland Route. The transport costs of the long desert crossing and the profits exacted by the several middlemen through whose hands the goods passed raised the cost of pepper from $2\frac{1}{2}d$. per lb. in India to 2s. at Aleppo, and that of cloves from 9d. per lb. to 4s. The spices which reached Western Europe via the Cape cost only one-third of what they cost via Aleppo, and thus it was actually profitable for the Levant Co. in 1614 to re-export Indian goods from England to the Levant, since they could still undersell the same commodities brought there by the Overland Route. By the second half of the seventeenth century the Levant Co., three-quarters of whose imports into England had consisted of Persian silk, was feeling severely the competition of the East India Co., which was importing Persian raw silk and Indian manufactured silks and calicos via the Cape Route. But the Privy Council had the foresight to support the East India Co.; and the silk trade through Aleppo continued to decline to one-half of its former figure.

The strain of the wars of the later seventeenth century, first against England and then against Louis XIV of France, was too much for the vitality of the Dutch state, and her commercial activities in the Indian Ocean and the Persian Gulf began to flag. Meanwhile France, under Louis XIV's far-seeing minister Colbert, had begun to plan the creation of a maritime commercial empire. He opened factories in India, sent an embassy to Persia in 1664 and obtained trading-rights at Bandar Abbas and Isfahan. French competition in the Levant also was stimulated by Colbert, and during the eighteenth century her commercial interests in these lands were always greater than the English. In Egypt France secured a virtual monopoly, with fifty merchants in Cairo in 1702 and other establishments at Alexandria and Rosetta, compared with only two English merchants at Cairo and Alexandria. The policy of the Levant Co., which was content to secure a high rate of profit on a comparatively small volume of sales, was partly responsible for the

---

[1] Williamson, *The Ocean in English History*, 101 ff., and especially 109 ff., correcting the older hypothesis that the withdrawal of the East India Co. from local trading was primarily due to successful Dutch competition.

sharp decline in English trade in favour of France. While the English cloth had the highest reputation, the French was lighter and better suited to the climate, It was, moreover, 10 per cent. cheaper; and when English clothiers did produce a thinner and cheaper cloth its quality was so inferior that the Levant merchants would not touch it. It was said that the Turks of Istanbul 'could neither be clothed, at the price and in the manner they wished, nor have coffee to drink' without buying from the French.[1] French trade with the Levant increased with extraordinary rapidity, and on the eve of the French Revolution was three times as great as the volume of English trade to those countries. Between 1778 and 1791 the English Levant Co. was compelled to close down its four factories in Syria, leaving the French in full possession of the trade. Politically also France was acknowledged by the Sultan as protector of all the Catholics within his Empire.

In Persia and Iraq however, the commercial situation in the eighteenth century was far different. The French East India Co. was ill-organized and ill-supported from Paris; and consequently the decline of the Dutch left the English to enjoy the bulk of the Persian Gulf trade through the prosperous factories which it re-opened at Bandar Abbas and Basra. As a result of the internal anarchy in Persia which followed on the Afghan invasion of 1722, however, most of the European factories in that country had eventually to be closed, and in 1761 the main seat of British trade was shifted to Basra, where the East India Co.'s resident was raised to the rank of consul. In 1766 the Company lent the Pasha of Baghdad six ships to deal with unruly tribesmen in Lower Iraq, and in 1780 it helped Sulaiman Pasha the Great to secure his succession to the pashaliq and so won his friendship. Britain's commercial position in the Gulf was now pre-eminent, and she was acquiring through it a growing political influence also. In 1798 the Company's Resident at Bushire, which had become the principal station on the Persian coast after the closing of Bandar Abbas, was asked to arbitrate in a dispute between the Pasha of Baghdad and the Sultan of Oman.

Like the Chinese, the rulers and inhabitants of the Ottoman Empire continued, long after their civilization and power had passed its peak, to regard the European strangers in their midst as

[1] They had made a trade treaty with the Governor of Mokha in 1709, and in 1738 temporarily occupied the port in a dispute over debts to French traders.

immeasurably their inferiors. Till about 1830 a foreign ambassador was kept waiting on a bench in the courtyard of the Serai to await the Grand Vezir's pleasure, and was finally introduced to the Sultan as 'the naked and hungry barbarian who has ventured to rub his brow upon the Sublime Porte'. The Grand Vezir informed the English Ambassador c. 1680: 'You and all other ambassadors are sent here by your respective princes to answer for the lives and estates of all Muslims all over the world that are endangered or suffer by their respective subjects, and you are a hostage here to answer for all damage done by Englishmen all over the world.' As late as 1798, when the Ottoman Empire went to war with a European state its ambassador was flung into the Prison of the Seven Towers, 'a pile of noisome dungeons'. If this was the prevailing tone of diplomatic courtesies, it is not surprising that European merchants in the Levant were obliged to wear Oriental dress to minimize the risk of insult by the populace. The merchants were beginning to revert to European dress c. 1700 in Istanbul and Smyrna, and about 1750 in Aleppo; but in the more distant parts of the Levant, and especially in Egypt, they were still obliged to wear full Turkish dress till nearly 1800. It is entertaining to speculate whether the English merchants in Aleppo continued to wear the enormous Turkish turbans and voluminous pantaloons for the games of cricket which they played on the 'Green Platte' outside the city.

CHAPTER IV

Britain and Her Rivals in the Middle East,

1770–1914

'Power-politics is the only kind of politics there is.'
(James Burnham, *The Struggle for the World*).

IN THE EARLY eighteenth century European political influence in the Middle East and India was still slight. The Ottoman, Persian and Mogul Empires were still relatively strong; and though Western Europe was now well in advance of the stagnating East in technical skill and in the quality of its manufactures, its traders still lived in these lands as clients, dependent on the good-will of the Oriental rulers and officials. Their insecurity led them to make common cause among themselves, and even the outbreak of a general war in Europe did not greatly affect their mutual relations. In 1696, for example, the English chaplain at Aleppo and his companions travelling to Jerusalem met with hospitable treatment from French merchants on their journey and at their destination, even though their countries were at war; and during the same war British and Dutch merchants in the Persian Gulf made an agreement with the French merchants for their mutual protection against the nuisance of piracy.

However, with conditions in the Oriental empires becoming more anarchic, local Oriental rulers increasingly courted the assistance of the European traders with their gold, their garrisons and naval units, and it was not long before the Europeans began to enter into the complexities of Oriental political intrigue and turn it to their own advantage. In this way the strategic rivalries of the European Powers at home were at length reproduced in the East. Since the Mogul Empire was the most advanced in decay, it was there that the English and French trading companies first came into conflict. As late as the outbreak in Europe of the War of Jenkins' Ear in 1739, indeed, the French company was still

F

anxious that it and the English company should continue to observe a strict neutrality. Hostilities however broke out between them in 1745, and there followed sixteen years of fierce Anglo-French struggle with each company using Indian rulers as allies. By 1761 the French hopes of empire had been shattered and the English East India Co. was on the way to becoming the supreme authority over large parts of India.

The next country to become the scene of these Anglo-French rivalries was Egypt. On the initiative of Ali Bey, for a few years the independent ruler of Egypt, and of Warren Hastings, the vigorous and unconventional governor of Bengal, the East India Co. sent more than one expedition in the 1770's from India to Suez,[1] whence the freight was transported under Egyptian guarantee to the Mediterranean for shipment to England. By opening up this route, which foreshadowed the speeding-up of communications in the following century, Calcutta was brought within two months of London, as compared with five months by the Cape Route. Although a variety of jealous influences interrupted this traffic after a few years, it had been enough to alarm the French for the future of their virtual monopoly of the Egyptian trade; and English and French interests competed for the favour of the Mamluk rulers of Egypt, with control of the Red Sea–Mediterranean route as the prize, until the attention of both countries was diverted by the French Revolution and the European war which grew out of it.

By 1797 Napoleon, commanding the French armies at the age of twenty-eight, had knocked Austria out of the coalition of counter-revolutionary Powers, leaving France free to turn on her next most formidable enemy, Britain. Since a direct invasion across the Channel was considered too difficult, the French government decided on an expedition to conquer Egypt. This project, which had been mooted by French political thinkers at various times since the beginning of the century, had been considered impolitic as long as Egypt was an integral part of the Ottoman Empire, with which France had continually been on good terms in opposition to their common enemy Austria. But now that the Ottoman authority over Egypt had ceased to be more than nominal and that Britain had shown signs of establishing commercial interests there, the

---

[1] The Ottoman government, jealous for its customs-revenues, did not allow European trading-ships to sail north of Jidda.

French case for annexation was strengthened, especially now that her victories in Italy and her alliance with Spain had caused the British fleet to withdraw from the Mediterranean to the shelter of Gibraltar. The instructions which the French government gave Napoleon for the Egyptian expedition included the expulsion of British interests from the Red Sea in favour of France and the cutting of a canal through the Isthmus of Suez. If the expedition were successful, there were reasonable hopes of ousting the British from India, since their hold on that country was still far from complete, and French military adventurers and mercenary troops exerted a powerful influence on several important Indian princes.

Napoleon's force landed near Alexandria in July 1798, and proclaimed its ostensible purpose of overthrowing the Mamluks and restoring the authority of the Ottoman Sultan. But though the French met with little resistance from the decadent Mamluk army, their hopes of consolidating their position were shattered by Nelson's destruction of the French fleet at the battle of Abuqir on 1 August. Napoleon was now cut off by superior British sea-power from supplies, from reinforcements, and even from news from France; and he could do little more than mark time in Egypt. In January 1799 Britain, Russia, and the Ottoman Empire reached an agreement to expel him. Learning that an Ottoman army was being assembled in Syria for the invasion of Egypt, he advanced through Palestine to meet it, but was checked before the fortress of Akka, which was held by its Bosnian tyrant Ahmed al-Jazzar ('the Butcher') supported by a British naval squadron. After two months Napoleon was forced to raise the siege and retire with his plague-stricken army to Egypt. Meanwhile the situation in Europe had deteriorated for the French, and Napoleon himself slipped away ignominiously to France in August 1799. The French army stayed on ineffectually, and was eventually withdrawn by agreement with Britain in 1801. Its only direct achievement was the great 'Description of Egypt' compiled by the staff of scholars which had accompanied it. Nevertheless, it had the enormously important indirect effect of 'bringing to the attention of a few men in Egypt a keen sense of the advantage of an orderly government, and a warm appreciation of the advance that science and learning had made in Europe', with results that were to galvanize into new life the torpid economic and social system of Egypt and the Levant.

The romantic interest of the Egyptian expedition has over-shadowed other, and not less significant, proceedings in other parts of the Middle East. Until about 1770 Britain had been content to be represented in the Middle East by trader-consuls 'humbly asking for nothing but capitulations and to be left alone'. From 1770 on-wards, in their dealings with an Ali Bey or a Sulaiman Pasha of Iraq, her representatives were attaining the status of equals in power and authority. But, just as it had been the bid to create a French empire in India which turned the East India Co. from trade to the tasks of empire, so it was Napoleon's threat to that growing empire in India which first constrained Britain to increase her political influence in the Middle East; and in both instances, once committed, she followed the course thus imposed on her with greater tenacity than the more opportunist French, and so achieved success and empire almost in spite of herself.

In the Southern Red Sea Britain immediately countered Napoleon's thrust towards India by occupying Perim, in the nar-rowest part of the Straits of Bab al Mandab. But soon, when living conditions on this torrid rock had proved intolerable, the occupy-ing force was moved to Aden, by agreement with its ruler, the Sultan of Lahaj. A treaty was made with him in 1802, and six years later Lord Valentia commented prophetically, 'Aden is the Gibraltar of the East'. In 1799 Napoleon had made overtures from Egypt to the Sultan of Oman, who by his possession of harbours on either side of the Straits of Hormuz (he held Bandar Abbas at this time) could control the entrance to the Persian Gulf. The Sul-tan was however persuaded to conclude with the East India Co. a treaty excluding from his territories French and Dutch subjects (Holland was now under French domination) for the duration of the war; and in 1800 the Company established a permanent Resident at Muscat.

Both at Basra and Baghdad French consuls had been established earlier than those of the East India Co.; but since they were ill-paid, ill-provided, often ill-chosen, and no great volume of French trade passed through their hands, they failed to impress the ruling Pashas. In 1798 the French consuls were arrested, their papers confiscated, and their premises occupied. It is not clear whether this was done entirely on the initiative of Sulaiman Pasha on ac-count of the Ottoman declaration of war on France following the invasion of Egypt, or whether perhaps it may have been suggested to him by the East India Co.'s Resident, now permanently established in Baghdad and on friendly terms with him. The French consuls were eventually released, but the Pasha rejected with little ceremony their claim to formal precedence over the British representatives. In 1802 the Resident at Baghdad was promoted to the rank of Consul with a guard of Sepoys, and Britain's position in Iraq grew in prestige and prosperity to the jealous indignation of the French.

For nearly ten years, from 1800 to 1809, the French were engaged in tortuous intrigues with Fath Ali Shah of Persia, with a view to an overland invasion of India in which they hoped to have the Russians as allies; and after the crushing French victories in Europe in 1805–6 a French military mission was sent to Persia following a treaty between the two countries. But this entente was broken when Napoleon went on in 1807 to make the Treaty of Tilsit with Russia, who had been steadily encroaching on Persian territory in Transcaucasia for the past eighty years and against whom the Persians looked for French assistance. In these new circumstances the British authorities in India had little difficulty in reasserting their own influence with the Shah and squeezing out the French military mission.

Meanwhile in 1806 Britain had regarded an ephemeral alliance between the Sultan of Turkey and Napoleon as likely once more to open Egypt to the French. A small British force accordingly occupied Alexandria, but twice failed to take Rosetta and suffered considerable losses. The Albanian Mohammed Ali, who had made himself Pasha of Egypt in 1805, now offered, provided that the British force was withdrawn, to oppose any European force that might attempt either to occupy Egypt or pass through it en route for India. He had rightly concluded that the French army was a much more remote instrument of power than the British navy, which in the later years of the war practically drove the French merchant fleet from the Levant. There was a flourishing British trade with Egypt in grain for the Mediterranean naval squadrons and for the army in the Iberian Peninsula.[1]

In 1810 the British capture of Mauritius, which had been the base for French privateers in the Indian Ocean, was a severe blow to

---

[1] Nevertheless, Mohammed Ali was already so intent on consolidating his position as master of Egypt that in 1810 he offered the French an alliance if they would recognize him as independent; but in view of the French desire to remain on good terms with the Ottoman Empire, they rejected his proposal.

what remained of French prestige in the Persian Gulf area. In the following years France's increasing difficulties in the Russian and Peninsular campaigns gave her no opportunity for further adventures in the Middle East; and the fall of Napoleon left Britain as the dominant and unquestioned authority in that region.

★   ★   ★

Mohammed Ali combined ambition with perspicacity to a greater degree than any other Oriental ruler of the nineteenth century. Conscious of the declining powers of the Ottoman Empire, he was anxious to confirm himself and his heirs in hereditary possession of Egypt. He was content to recognize the nominal suzerainty of the Sultan provided that he enjoyed autonomy in practical matters. But the impact of the Napoleonic wars had taught him that, if he was to attain and maintain such a position, he must have an army and navy equipped and trained on Western lines; and to Western Europe he consequently turned for armaments and technical experts. He would have preferred to obtain these from Britain, for whose dominant position as a sea-power he always had the greatest respect, and of whose friendship he was always genuinely desirous. He told the Swiss traveller Burckhardt in 1815, 'The great fish swallow the small . . . England must someday take Egypt as her share of the spoil of the Turkish Empire.' But the main imperial principle of British governments was already the maintenance of the British position in India, and to this the preservation of the status quo in the Middle East, i.e. the support of the Ottoman Empire which had assisted in checking Napoleon's ambitions in this direction, was a corollary. As Palmerston put it in 1833, with reference to the pan-Arab policy of Mohammed Ali's son Ibrahim Pasha in Syria. 'Turkey is as good an occupier of the road to India as an active Arabian sovereign would be.' When therefore his overtures to Britain were declined, Mohammed Ali turned for material help and guidance to France, who, in spite of the fall of Napoleon, survived through Talleyrand's diplomacy as a leading European Power. French officers, doctors, and savants accompanied Mohammed Ali's armies in the successful campaigns which subdued the wild Wahhabis of Central Arabia (1811–18).[1]

[1] The religious teacher Mohammed ibn Abdul Wahhab, a follower of the school of the ninth-century Ibn Hanbal in his desire to return to the simplicity of the Qur'an and the Sunna and cleanse Islam of all later excrescences, had

A French colonel, who became a Muslim and is commemorated as Sulaiman Pasha by one of Cairo's principal streets, was engaged to reorganize and train the Egyptian army on French lines. Another Frenchman planned and organized the naval dockyard, and others came as doctors, engineers, surveyors, and as managers of the numerous factories founded by Mohammed Ali in his attempt to modernize and develop the whole productive economy of Egypt. Anxious to build up a cadre of young Egyptians with a modern technical training, it was natural that he should send them to France, whose educational system had been entirely modernized since the Revolution and now provided the finest scientific and technical instruction in the world. In contrast, all that contemporary England could offer was the unreformed medieval structure of Oxford and Cambridge, the few great collegiate schools, and the country grammar schools, all greatly mouldered by the neglect of two centuries—a crumbling monumental ruin not unlike the Great Pyramid, and of about as much utility to the ambitious Pasha. It was therefore to Paris that his young men were sent to study.

French educational influence was predominant in the fifty elementary and secondary schools which were opened in Egypt from 1836 onwards, and French scientific and technical works were translated into Arabic as text-books. A French military mission and ten naval officers were lent to Mohammed Ali in 1824 to accompany the forces with which he undertook to suppress the revolt of the Greeks against the Ottoman Sultan; and when the Great Powers had finally agreed on a joint intervention to end the Revolt, lest it should provoke a general European war, the French naval officers were withdrawn only two days before Ibrahim Pasha's fleet was destroyed by a joint Anglo-French fleet at Navarino. The French continued to intrigue with Mohammed Ali for their own ends and, having set their minds on annexing Algeria but not wishing to disturb the concert of Europe by a direct attack on what was still nominally Ottoman territory, they suggested to the Pasha in 1829 that he should conquer and annex the whole of North Africa with French help. But the British government

won the ear of the Najdi noble Mohammed ibn Sa'ud about the middle of the eighteenth century. The Wahhabi tribesmen, influenced by this puritan creed, extended the domain of the Sa'udi rulers, and at the beginning of the nineteenth century occupied and 'purified' Mecca and Madina and sacked the Shi'i shrine of Husain at Karbala. These acts brought down upon them the vengeance of the Ottoman Empire, with Mohammed Ali as its instrument.

warned him off such a scheme, and he then turned in 1831 to the conquest of Syria and Palestine, which he had been previously promised by the Sultan for his part in opposing the Greek Revolt; moreover, he wished to use the forests of the Lebanon to rebuild the fleet he had lost at Navarino. By 1833 Ibrahim Pasha had conquered Syria and his army, for which the feeble Ottoman army was absolutely no match, was less than 150 miles from Istanbul. 'We rejoice,' commented the French Foreign Office, 'that we have facilitated the birth and development of a Power worthy of our collaboration and as interested as we are in the prosperity of the Mediterranean. We shall always be ready to give to the Pasha in the future the same evidence of our friendship and goodwill as he has received in the past from the French government.'

The Ottoman Sultan appealed to Britain for support; but Britain, preoccupied with a delicate situation in Western Europe, could spare no naval detachments for the Eastern Mediterranean at this moment. In his helplessness the Sultan was compelled to accept an offer of aid from Russia, who had emerged a Great Power from the Napoleonic Wars.[1] She had encouraged the Greek Revolt, in the hope of eventually dominating that country through the medium of the Orthodox Church; and now a Russian force was promptly sent to the Asiatic side of the Bosporus to 'protect' the Sultan. Alarmed at the prospect of Russian domination of the Ottoman Empire, Britain and France were at length impelled to concerted action. Mohammed Ali was pressed to recall his army from Anatolia; the Sultan ceded him Palestine, Syria, and Cilicia, which were henceforth administered by Ibrahim Pasha; and the Russian force was withdrawn from Turkey. The crisis of the First Syrian War was over; but it had had the effect of stimulating in the mind of Palmerston, who was to dominate British foreign policy for the next thirty years and whose constant concern was the possibility of a Franco-Russian combination against Britain, a lasting, deep, and possibly exaggerated mistrust of Mohammed Ali as a pawn in the hands of these Powers.

[1] Her bid to replace the Ottoman Empire as the dominant power in the Black Sea had begun with Peter the Great's invasion of the Ukraine a hundred years before, and had advanced her frontiers by 1815 to the Lower Danube. In 1813 she had forced Persia to acknowledge the cession to her of Transcaucasia including the Baku region, the value of whose oil-deposits was not then understood; and when Persia attempted to set aside this treaty by an ill-advised act of aggression, Russia forced on her in 1828 the Treaty of Turkmanchai, which made serious inroads on Persian sovereignty to the economic advantage of Russia.

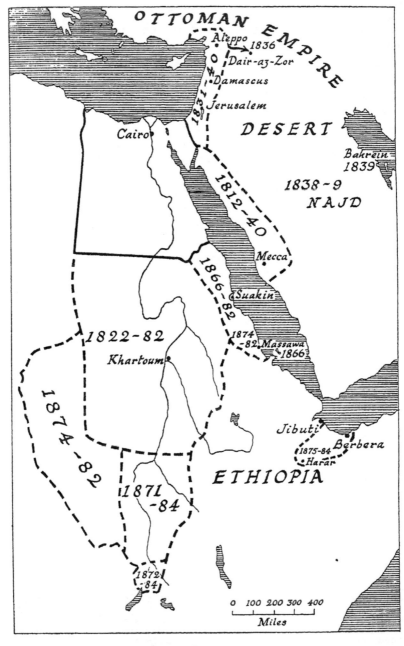

9. THE EGYPTIAN 'EMPIRE' IN THE NINETEENTH CENTURY

Encouraged by their success, Mohammed Ali and Ibrahim pressed on with their ambitious schemes for uniting the whole of the Arab lands under their rule. While the Pasha encouraged the British in developing once more the Mediterranean-Red Sea route to India, this time using the first paddle-steamers which reduced the voyage from London to Bombay from four months to six weeks, Ibrahim was less favourably disposed to a British experiment in 1835-6 at steamship-navigation on the Euphrates, as being liable to limit his expansion south-eastwards from Syria. The Foreign Office suspected that this obstruction was not unconnected with Russian intrigues, and the French Consul at Basra had also attempted the physical sabotage of the Euphrates expedition.[1] When in the following years the Pasha's ambitions brought him into political and military contact with the Arab sheikhdoms of the Persian Gulf and with Southern Arabia respectively, regions in which the East India Co. had been steadily consolidating its commercial and strategic position since the Napoleonic Wars, Palmerston's response was swift. He warned the Pasha off any encroachment on the Turkish pashaliq of Baghdad and declared that 'H.M. Government could not view with indifference any advance by Mohammed Ali towards Baghdad and the Gulf.' In 1839 Britain acquired the ancient and decayed port of Aden in the teeth of a drive by Mohammed Ali into the Yemen, and suggested that he should withdraw his troops, with the menace that any attempt on Aden would be regarded as an attack on a British possession.[2]

In the same year the Ottoman Sultan, whose army had been trained by the rising young Prussian officer Von Moltke, invaded Syria with the intention of avenging the humiliation of the First Syrian War and crushing his rebellious subject; but Ibrahim's French-trained forces decisively defeated them, and the Ottoman fleet deserted to Alexandria. The Ottoman Empire lay at the mercy of Mohammed Ali, who continued to enjoy French support. But by this time Palmerston, who was simultaneously engaged in the First Afghan War in an attempt to check Russian intrigues in that country, had become convinced that Mohammed Ali was acting in the interests of Russia; and he decided that the only way to

[1] Longrigg, op. cit., 293.
[2] H. L. Hoskins, 'The Background of the British Position in Arabia,' in Middle East Journal, I (Washington, 1947), 137 ff.

prevent the collapse of the Ottoman Empire was to oust Ibrahim from Syria. He accordingly succeeded in July 1840 in bringing about an agreement between Britain, Russia, Austria, and Prussia, by which Mohammed Ali was presented with an ultimatum to evacuate Syria, with the threat of losing all his possessions if he procrastinated unduly. This threat to their protégé caused great indignation in Paris and the French government threatened war; but Palmerston knew that it was unprepared for such extremes and kept up the pressure of the Powers on Mohammed Ali. While the French government vacillated and eventually fell, British and Ottoman forces blockaded and occupied Beirut and Akka, and forced Ibrahim to evacuate Syria and Palestine. His father had to give back the Ottoman fleet, but was confirmed in the hereditary pashaliq of Egypt. The Second Syrian War was over. As the French historian Driault ruefully comments, 'All the advantages had fallen to Britain. She had pushed back Mohammed Ali and France in the south, Russia in the north, and kept open for the future the overland route to India via Iraq. She had made safe the development of her influence along this route. She was pre-eminent in the lands of the Levant.'

In the previous twenty years, while numbers of French officials were being introduced into Mohammed Ali's service, Britain was less obviously, and certainly less consciously, establishing her commercial predominance in Egypt. The key to this was the Egyptian production of high-grade cotton, which had been fostered by Mohammed Ali and was first introduced to the spinners of Lancashire in 1821. The export of cotton from Egypt actually increased 200 times in the next three years and became from now on her principal export. It was absorbed in the main by Britain, whose factory-made cottons now displaced the more expensive hand-woven French fabrics. Soon after 1830 British trade with Egypt was greater than that of any other country. By 1849, the year of Mohammed Ali's death, she provided 41 per cent. of Egypt's imports and took 49 per cent. of her exports.

But since the defence of her position in India remained a cardinal feature of her overseas policy, she was not anxious to see communications through the Middle East modernized or made more speedy to give an opportunity to any jealous and aggressive Power to assail her. She had refused in 1834 to give any financial guarantees for a proposed railway to connect Alexandria, Cairo, and

Suez; and when the French government showed itself ready to sponsor the cutting of the Isthmus of Suez, Palmerston commented that however great the commercial advantages might be, this 'second Bosporus' might be a source of grave political embarrassment to Britain. In the declining years of the aged Mohammed Ali the project was not pressed, and nothing could be done under his reactionary and anti-European successor Abbas I.[1] But the murder of Abbas brought to the throne in 1854 the fat, indolent, and easygoing Sa'id, who had as a boy been friendly with Ferdinand de Lesseps, the young son of the French Political Agent. On his friend's accession de Lesseps, who had subsequently been French Consul at Alexandria for seven years, sent him a letter of congratulation and was invited to revisit Egypt. These were the go-getting days of Napoleon III: within ten days of his arrival de Lesseps had presented the Pasha with a detailed scheme for the cutting of a Suez Canal which Sa'id accepted; and a fortnight later the Pasha signed the concession for the 'Compagnie Universelle', subject to the approval of his Ottoman suzerain. It was alleged that he had not even read the agreement, and it had certainly not been examined by his judicial and financial advisers. But de Lesseps was his friend, and he was promised 15 per cent. of the profits. What more was needed?

De Lesseps took the opportunity of the Franco-Ottoman friendship during the Crimean War to go to Istanbul to obtain the Sultan's approval for the concession. He found himself however vigorously opposed by the British Ambassador, who represented to the Ottoman government that such a concession would eventually lead to a French protectorate over Egypt. That British opposition to the scheme was not without justification is shown by the fact that the anti-British section of the French press had been exulting that 'in piercing the Isthmus of Suez, we are piercing the weak point in the British armour'. While British commercial interests, such as the East India Co. and the P. & O. Steamship Co., favoured the scheme, Palmerston strongly opposed it as 'profitable to France, but hostile to British interests'. In 1858 the British government warned the Turks that if the Sultan gave his consent he could no longer count on Britain to maintain the integrity of his Empire. When work on the alignment of the Canal began in 1859, Sa'id replied blandly to British protests that under the

[1] Ibrahim had died before his father.

Capitulations he had no control over what French subjects did in Egypt. The French won the support of Russia and Austria for the scheme. Britain, thus isolated in her opposition, was reduced to creating prejudice against it by attacking the use of forced Egyptian labour, though she had urged its use on the British-built Cairo-Suez railway a few years before. Nevertheless the work went on; Palmerston, its arch-opponent, died in 1865 and the British opposition died with him. The Sultan finally approved the undertaking in 1866, and the Canal was opened to the shipping of the world by the Empress Eugenie in 1869.

Britain's statesmen had not however been content merely with obstructing the Canal project. They had also taken active steps to strengthen her defences along the short sea-route to India in case the Canal became an accomplished fact. In 1863 the harbours and docks of Malta were extended, and its fortifications strengthened. In 1854 Britain had acquired from the Sultan of Oman for use as a cable-station the Kuria Muria Islands, which the French also had made several attempts to acquire. In 1857 Britain re-occupied Perim. In 1862 she reached a mutual agreement with France to respect the independence of Oman, which was in fact already under strong influence from the Government of India. By 1870 British influence was being extended from Aden along the southern coast of Arabia to the ports of Mukalla and Shihr, whose trade with East Africa passed largely through Aden and whose ruling sultan usually resided in India. Britain thus established here a protectorate in fact, if not yet in name; and in 1876 she took Socotra under her formal protection.

★   ★   ★

During the nine years of his occupation of Syria (1831–40), Ibrahim Pasha had encouraged European and American missionaries to settle there. In particular the French Jesuits were eager to resume their work, which had stagnated since the temporary suppression of their order by the Pope in 1773; and by 1840 they had re-established a powerful influence over the Maronites[1] of the Lebanon, which was exercised not only in ecclesiastical matters

---

[1] This Christian sect, which forms the majority of the inhabitants of the Mountain Lebanon, entered into communion with the Church of Rome at the time of the Crusades, but is distinguished by its retention of Syriac as its liturgical language.

but also for the furtherance of French policy in the Levant. During the intrigues of the Second Syrian War Britain, on the other hand, had made use of the friendship of some of the Druze chiefs of Southern Lebanon. Ibrahim Pasha's government, and the steady increase of population in the mountain-valleys of the Lebanon, had had the effect of unsettling the peasantry and making them less tolerant of their subservience to their landlords. Social relationships were complicated by the fact that, while in North Lebanon landlords and peasantry were both mainly Maronite, in the South there were both Maronite and Druze peasantry in the service of Druze lords. The proclamation in 1839 of the equality before the law of all religions within the Ottoman Empire had encouraged the Christian communities; and the Maronite priesthood, which was drawn largely from the peasantry and was anxious to extend its influence over the people, stimulated the social unrest. It finally came to a head in 1857, when the peasants of North Lebanon, incited by their clergy, rose against their Maronite lords and divided up the large estates, while those in South Lebanon were forbidden by their priests to pay rents to their Druze landlords. This show of Maronite truculence had the effect of uniting the Druze peasantry with the Druze lords, since they saw that the Maronites already outnumbered them in fighting-men and were increasing at a faster rate. The antagonism of the two unruly communities was fanned by the Turkish Pasha in Beirut, who hoped to see them weaken one another; while the rival intrigues of French and British agents, the one taking seriously France's rôle as protector of the Maronites, the other giving some encouragement to the Druze, added to the tension. In 1860 the Druze made a general attack on the Maronites, in which some 14,000 of the latter were massacred.[1] In Damascus the Druze, helped by Kurdish and Syrian Muslims, attacked the Christian population and killed some 5,000. The news of the Damascus massacres caused horror in Western Europe, coming as it did soon after the attacks on Christians in Jidda in 1858 as a second example of anti-Christian fanaticism in the Ottoman Empire. In France it was welcomed as providing an opportunity for a military adventure in the Lebanon, for which immediate

[1] It is stated that the smaller Protestant communities, evangelized in the main by the American missionaries, were left for the most part in peace, except where they sided with the Maronites to resist the Druze (J. Richter, *History of Protestant Missions in the Near East*, 199). See in general the objective summing-up by Pierre Rondot, *Les Institutions Politiques du Liban* (Paris, 1947), 44 ff.

preparations were made. The other Powers gave their consent to the French expedition. When it landed at Beirut there was little for it to do, as the Turks had already practically completed the task of restoring order. The French wished to keep the force there indefinitely as a guarantee against a recurrence of the disorders, but the British government insisted that, calm having been restored, the French should withdraw after nine months. This they reluctantly did: 'the undertaking had failed to realize the hopes of the Protecting Power'.[1] In place of the protectorate envisaged in Paris, an international commission created in 1864 the autonomous sanjaq of the Lebanon, no longer subject to the Pasha of Beirut, but to a Christian governor appointed by the Ottoman Government. Under this satisfactory compromise, which kept the peace in the Lebanon down to the First World War, French educational missions were free to continue their cultural work, and it was claimed that in 1914 more than half of the school-going children in Syria and Palestine attended French schools.[2]

Immediately after the Damascus massacres Napoleon III had summoned to Paris from Syria the Jesuit priest William Gifford Palgrave, who had been an Indian Army officer before he took Holy Orders. He presented himself to the Emperor as a likely envoy to Arab societies, on account of his facility in Semitic languages (his grandfather was a Jew), and was sent on a mission to the Amir of the Shammar in Northern Arabia, 'the one effective power in the lands east of the Red Sea'. The nature of his mission has never been disclosed, but it was regarded by the British government sufficiently seriously for the Resident at Bushire to counter it by a visit in 1864 to the rival North Arabian Power, the Sa'udi Amir.

At the same time France also took an active interest in the efforts of the Ottoman government to reform and modernize itself. 'The Turks were the only bond capable of preventing all the races of the Empire—Slav, Greek, Arab—from disintegrating into Russian, Austrian, or British dust. It was necessary to change Muslim habits, to destroy the age-old fanaticism which was an obstacle to the fusion of races, and to create a modern secular state. It was necessary to transform even the education of both conquerors and subjects, and inculcate in both the unknown spirit of

---

[1] Lammens, op. cit., II, 186 f.
[2] id., II, 201.

tolerance—a noble task, worthy of the great renown of France.' In 1863 the Ottoman Bank was founded with the controlling interest in French hands, British interests being secondary; it had the monopoly of the banknote-issue and branches in every important town in the Empire. In 1867 the French government invited the Sultan to visit Paris, and recommended to him a system of secular public education and the undertaking of great public works and communications. As a contribution to the first, there was opened in 1868 under the joint direction of the Turkish Ministry of Foreign Affairs and the French Ambassador the Lycée of Galata-Serai, a great secondary school open to Ottoman subjects of every race and creed, where more than six hundred boys were taught by Europeans in the French language—'a symbol of the action of France, exerting herself to teach the peoples of the Orient in her own language the elements of Western civilization'. In the same year a company consisting mainly of French capitalists received a concession for railways to connect Istanbul and Salonica with the existing railways on the Middle Danube.[1]

But all these schemes for establishing a French cultural and financial dominion in the Middle East were 'brutally interrupted' by the disaster of the Franco-German War of 1870. France emerged from the War permanently weakened, and her imperial energies were now focused in the main on her expanding colonies in N.W. Africa. Not that she has ever renounced her aspirations in the Middle East; but after 1870 her relation to Britain in this region was that of an envious, and sometimes spiteful, loser in a race, rather than that of a serious rival. She could for twenty years obstruct the efforts of Lord Cromer to restore the financial stability and promote the economic progress of Egypt;[2] in the 'nineties she could intrigue against Britain at Muscat, or seek to forestall her in establishing a position on the Upper Nile,[3] but whereas from 1815 to 1870 British imperial interests in the Middle East had been thought to be challenged by France and Russia to a roughly equal degree, from 1870 to 1900 there is no doubt that the Russian challenge, real or imagined, easily assumed the first place.

*   *   *

Palmerston's fears of a Franco-Russian coalition against Britain

[1] Driault, op. cit., 187 ff.
[2] Lord Milner, *England in Egypt*, ch. XIII.
[3] Temperley and Penson, *Foundations of British Foreign Policy*, 501 ff.

had been allayed by the development of a dispute between those two Powers over the respective claims of the Catholic and the Orthodox Churches to the Holy Places in Palestine. In the first half of the nineteenth century the Russians had established numerous claims which the Ottoman Empire had accorded in previous centuries to the Catholic Church and its French protector, but which had been allowed to lapse during the Revolution and the Napoleonic Wars. Napoleon III, however, wishing to win for his régime the support of French Catholics, revived in 1852 all the Latin claims to the Holy Places which had been conferred by the Capitulations of 1740, and demanded that any subsequent concession to the Orthodox Church which conflicted with them should be set aside. The Russian government responded with counter-claims, and went so far as to demand the right to protect all Orthodox Christians of whatever nationality throughout the Ottoman Empire. Such a claim was deemed by the Powers to disturb the European Balance of Power by encroaching on the authority of the Sultan over his millions of Orthodox subjects in the Balkans. Negotiations produced agreement on the question of the Holy Places, but on the larger issue Russia remained obdurate. She allowed herself to be diplomatically outmanoeuvred by the British Ambassador in Turkey, and had to fight the Crimean War against an alliance of Britain, France, and the Ottoman Empire. The Treaty of Paris which ended the war in 1856 forbade the Russians to launch warships on the Black Sea, and thus removed one potential danger from Britain's Mediterranean route to the East.

While the other Powers were preoccupied with the Franco-German War, however, Russia resumed her freedom of action in the Black Sea. She had for forty years been progressively bringing under her direct rule what is now Russian Turkestan, for her important trade-route across Siberia, the forerunner of the Trans-Siberian Railway, had been continually harassed by the lawless Turcomans to the south. Her southward expansion seemed to have been completed with the ratification of the Anglo-Russian Convention of 1873, in which the Amu-Darya was recognized as the definitive Russian frontier, and the Russian government acknowledged that Afghanistan was 'completely outside the sphere within which Russia might be compelled to exercise her influence'. Within four years Russia was engaged in a war against the Ottoman Empire which would certainly have left her pre-

G

dominant in the Balkans, had it not been for the intervention of
the other European Powers. Simultaneously, British opinion was
alarmed 'almost to the point of panic'[1] by the Amir of Afghanistan's leanings towards the dynamic Russians rather than the
seemingly irresolute British. While Britain embarked upon the
Second Afghan War to reassert her authority in this vital quarter,
her apprehensions extended also to the Persian Gulf, and Lord
Salisbury, the Foreign Secretary, proclaimed that 'The people of
this country will never allow Russian influence to be supreme in
the valleys of the Euphrates and Tigris'. Britain had for sixty years
been steadily establishing her authority over the Arab sheikhdoms
of the Persian Gulf: first using her good offices to put down piracy
and the slave-trade; then arranging for the submission of disputes
between the sheikhs to the British Resident at Bushire, who thus
became virtually ruler of the Gulf; and finally in 1869 persuading
the sheikhs of the Trucial Coast to undertake not to make any
territorial concessions or enter into agreements with any government other than Britain. Following the Russian scare of 1878,
this 'exclusive agreement' was extended to the sheikhs of Bahrain
and Qatar when treaties with them were renewed in 1880, with the
additional proviso that they should not accept any diplomatic or
consular representatives, except with the approval of Britain. In
1885, after a further Russian annexation to the very borders of
Afghanistan, war between the two Great Powers was narrowly
averted, and British apprehensions once more inflamed. Curzon,
at thirty years of age a budding British authority on the Middle
East, could in 1889 express the moderate view that Russian movements in the direction of India were designed, not for conquest,
but to draw British attention from her real objectives in the Balkans;[2] but three years later, having been appointed Under-
Secretary for India, he wrote: 'I should regard the concession by
any Power of a port upon the Persian Gulf to Russia (that dear
dream of so many a patriot from the Neva or the Volga) as a
deliberate insult to Britain, as a wanton rupture of the status quo,

---

[1] K. W. B. Middleton observes that 'As a maritime Power, with comparatively weak land-forces, Britain has always been particularly nervous about the
frontier of her Indian possessions, by far the most valuable and important part
of her subject empire. She has therefore tended to magnify out of proportion to
reality any development which could conceivably constitute a threat to Indian
security.' (*Britain and Russia* (1947), 11).
[2] cf. W. E. Wheeler, in *Journal of the Royal Central Asian Society*, XXI (1934),
596 f.

and as an international provocation to war; and I should impeach the British minister who was guilty of acquiescing in such a surrender as a traitor to his country.' At the same time he applauded Britain's imposing on the Sultan of Oman the customary prohibition from ceding or leasing any concessions, and commented, 'We subsidize its ruler; we dictate its policy; we should tolerate no rival influence'. While the two Powers were locked in tense rivalry for obtaining preponderance in Persia through loans and commercial concessions, several countries were canvassing plans for a railway connecting the Levant with the Persian Gulf. The Russian Consul at Baghdad was scheming to obtain a Russian port and naval base on the Gulf; and it was learnt in 1898 that an Austro-Russian syndicate had applied to the Ottoman government for a concession for a railway from Syrian Tripoli to Kuwait, the finest natural harbour on the Persian Gulf. Britain had recently declined a request for protection from Sheikh Mubarak of Kuwait, who had come to the throne by murdering his pro-Turkish brother; but in these new circumstances Lord Curzon, now Viceroy of India, sent the Resident in the Persian Gulf to negotiate a secret agreement with the Sheikh, in which he too undertook to grant no leases or concessions without Britain's agreement. Curzon now summed up British policy in this region in a series of Olympian rhetorical questions. 'Are we prepared to surrender control of the Persian Gulf and divide that of the Indian Ocean? Are we prepared to make the construction of the Euphrates Valley Railroad or some kindred scheme an impossibility for England and an ultimate certainty for Russia? Is Baghdad to become a new Russian capital in the south? Lastly, are we content to see a naval station within a few day's sail of Karachi, and to contemplate a naval squadron battering Bombay?'

At this stage no one could have foreseen that within seven years of the beginning of the new century these longstanding and bitter conflicts of interest between Britain on the one hand, and Russia and France on the other, were destined to be temporarily liquidated in the powerful flux of a still more formidable challenge to all three Powers from the recently-born German Empire.

★   ★   ★

Until 1870 German interests in the Middle East had been confined to missionary activities in Syria and Palestine and to a small volume of trade, and her political influence had been negligible. But the War of 1870 naturally increased her prestige greatly with the Turks, ever respectful of military power and success. The influence of France in the Ottoman Empire was correspondingly reduced. The steps Britain had recently taken to render her influence in the Persian Gulf exclusive were resented by the Turks as an encroachment on their nebulous territorial sovereignty over the coasts of Arabia, which they were at this time attempting to make more real; and Britain's occupation of Cyprus in 1878 and Egypt in 1882 prejudiced her further in the eyes of the Turks. Consequently, when in 1872 the Ottoman government was seeking an adviser for the construction of the Balkan railway-system, it was a German engineer whom they called in; and in 1883 the German Ambassador had little difficulty in persuading Sultan Abdul Hamid II to invite the Kaiser to send a German military mission to Turkey.

By 1886 the Balkan railways were approaching completion, and the forward-looking Sultan was already contemplating their extension to his Asiatic provinces in order to strengthen his administrative control and assist their economic development. After overtures to British and American financiers had met with no response, a German syndicate undertook in 1888 the extension of the railway to Ankara, under the name of the Anatolian Railway Co. The new company was not exclusively German: more than a quarter of its first loan was subscribed in Britain, and the British chairman of the Ottoman Public Debt Administration became one of its directors. In 1889 Kaiser Wilhelm II, who had succeeded his father in the previous year at the age of twenty-nine, visited Istanbul, and the Deutsche Levant Linie was formed for steamship services between the North Sea and the Levant. This was followed by a German-Turkish trade agreement in 1890, and from this time onwards German consuls in the Ottoman Empire were assiduous in the help they gave to German commercial interests. The Kaiser's visit to Istanbul and this forward commercial policy were not favoured by the veteran Bismarck, who was primarily concerned in keeping France weak and isolated, and in avoiding any other foreign disagreements: he thus disliked the idea of commercial expansion in Asia Minor as likely to arouse the hostility of Russia, whom he had continually sought to draw into friendly association with Germany and Austria. But in 1890 the young Kaiser dismissed the old Chancellor and became himself the pilot of foreign

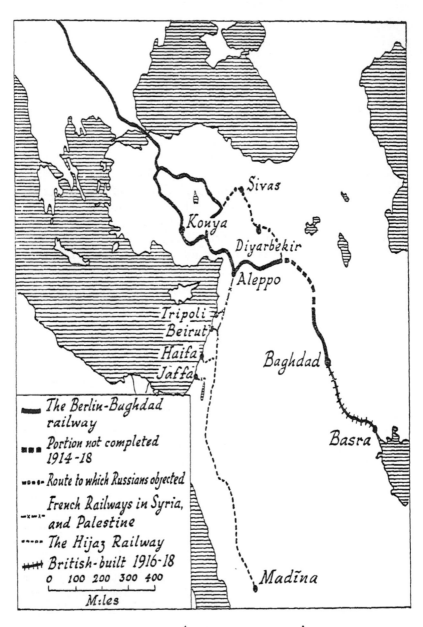

The Berlin-Bughdad railway

Portion not completed 1914-18

Route to which Russians objected

French Railways in Syria, and Palestine

The Hijaz Railway

British-built 1916-18

0   100 200 300 400

Miles

IO. THE 'DRANG NACH OSTEN'

policy. Bismarck's intentness on not disturbing the status quo was indeed becoming obsolete: Germany's rapidly increasing population, in a country where the possibility of expanding food-production had evident limits, impelled her to a policy of industrial expansion with a quest for foreign markets; and her naval inferiority suggested that the direction of such commercial expansion should be continental, rather than oceanic.

By 1893 the railway to Ankara had been completed, and the preliminary survey of the further route to Baghdad begun. The first proposal, for a route via Sivas and Diyarbekir, was opposed by Russia on the grounds that it would lie too near her Caucasian frontier and might be used strategically against her; and eventually in 1898 the Anatolian Railway Co. applied for a concession for the route Konya-Aleppo-Mosul-Baghdad. Although there were certain competing interests, German commercial influence was now preponderant in Turkey beyond any doubt, and she was supplying a large proportion of Turkey's armament needs. Consequently the German company obtained the concession, buying out French opposition by an agreement which gave French railway and banking interests an equal share in the undertaking.

At this stage the British attitude to the German project was still favourable. The threat to Britain's position in the Middle East still came overwhelmingly from Russia and France. In 1892 the British Ambassador in Berlin had urged the Germans to develop a commercial interest in the Persian Gulf as a counterpoise to Russia in that region, and in 1898 the British reaction to the German railway-concession was favourable. Lord Salisbury was reported to have said, 'We welcome these concessions, for in this way Germany comes into line with our interests in the Persian Gulf'. *The Times* commented that if the development of the Turkish railways was not to be in British hands, the Germans were to be preferred to any other. The *Morning Post* remarked that the concession gave Germany a reason for resisting aggression in Asia Minor from the North. Imperialists of the standing of Cecil Rhodes and Joseph Chamberlain also gave the scheme their blessing. The Under-Secretary for Foreign Affairs alone sounded a warning note by stating that the government had every intention of maintaining the status quo in the Persian Gulf.

In 1900 the German technical mission which was planning the route the railway was to follow visited Kuwait and made a tempting offer to the Sheikh for a concession for a terminus and port. When he resisted their offer in accordance with his secret agreement with the Government of India a year before, the Germans induced the Ottoman Government, which the Sheikh nominally regarded as his suzerain, to send an expedition to assert its authority over him; but the presence of a British gunboat at the head of the Gulf caused them to desist. In other parts of the Gulf German traders were beginning to find the British 'exclusive agreements' an obstacle to their enterprises.

In 1903 the Anatolian Railway Co. had carried its plans for the Baghdad Railway to the stage at which it required to raise additional capital for their execution, and invited British capitalists to participate on equal terms with the existing German and French interests. The Balfour government favoured the acceptance of the offer, but the Cabinet was not unanimous, remembering perhaps Curzon's dictum of 1892 that 'Baghdad must be included in the sphere of indisputable British supremacy'. The proposal was hotly attacked by the imperialist and big-business section of the press, which was concerned by the progress made by German commercial competition in capturing overseas markets from Britain, and resented the German support for the Boers in the South African War; moreover, German publicists had been tactless and provocative in discussing the opportunities which a war in the Middle East involving Britain would present for German expansion. Consequently the government declined the German offer, and the Foreign Secretary, Lord Lansdowne, redefined Britain's policy in the Persian Gulf: her aim was to promote and protect British trade without excluding the legitimate trade of other powers; the establishment of a naval base or fortified port in the Gulf by any other power would be a very grave menace, 'and we should certainly resist it with all the means at our disposal. I say that in no minatory spirit because, as far as I am aware, there are no proposals on foot for the establishment of a foreign naval base in the Gulf.'

The following year, 1904, saw the culmination in the Entente Cordiale of the negotiations into which the British and French governments had been impelled by their growing fear of the expansionist policy of their 'vigorous and talented competitor' Germany. In this emergency all the outstanding points at issue between Britain and France were settled. In particular, France at last acknowledged Britain's de facto position in Egypt, though she insisted to the end on her stating a time-limit for her occupation, and only yielded on Britain's undertaking not to alter the legal status quo.[1] In 1907 the Entente Cordiale was extended to include Russia, whose prestige and sense of security had been abased by her defeat in the Japanese War of 1904–5, and who was consequently more ready to compromise with her long-standing British rival. An Anglo-Russian Agreement was reached 'to obviate any cause of misunderstanding in Persian affairs' and to delimit the Russian and British spheres-of-interest in North and South Persia respectively, leaving a no-man's-land between them. The Russian government acknowledged that Afghanistan lay within the British sphere of influence, while Britain undertook not to encourage the Amir to take any action threatening Russia. The Russian government 'explicitly stated that it did not deny Britain's special interest' in the Persian Gulf. The Agreement has subsequently been severely criticized by political moralists as a cynical partitioning of Persia, 'absolute respect for whose independence and integrity' was declared to be the fundamental principle of the two Powers; but the fact is that Persia had ceased to be a Great Power since the time of Shah Abbas the Great, three hundred years before; she had become a minor piece in the game of Great-Power chess at the time of Napoleon; and had ceased to be effectively independent since Russia imposed on her the Treaty of Turkmanchai in 1828. In her weakness Persian politicians had been reduced to playing off Britain and Russia against one another. The Agreement did at least have the effect of temporarily reducing the tension of Anglo-Russian rivalry in Persia; and it consolidated Britain's position in South Persia, where British concessionaires at last struck oil at Masjid-i-Sulaiman in 1908, actually after the directors in London, disappointed by several years' efforts without results, had cabled orders for the work to be abandoned. In 1909 the Anglo-Iranian Oil Co. was formed with a capital of £2,000,000, the Shell Co. being the principal participant.

The 'Committee of Union and Progress' which made the Young Turk Revolution of 1908 aimed at substituting a liberal and constitutional government for the autocracy of Abdul Hamid, and so looked initially for support to liberal and constitutional Britain and France rather than to autocratic Germany. However, the enthusiasm for liberalism and modernization was short-lived,

---

[1] *Round Table*, December 1936, 111.

and was soon followed by a nationalist reaction of which the Armenian massacres of 1909 were a feature. While the British and French press denounced these atrocities, the Germans were silent. In the next year, after the Turks had applied to France and Britain for a loan without success, they eventually obtained it from Germany on conditions which, unlike those proposed by France, were 'consistent with the dignity of Turkey'.

Meanwhile, in 1907 the new Liberal government in Britain had announced that its objection to a railway to the Persian Gulf would be removed if the construction and operation of the section south of Baghdad were left to British capitalists. Negotiations were protracted over a period of six years, and eventually resulted in an agreement between Britain, Germany, and Turkey in 1913-14. Britain finally consented to the construction of the Baghdad Railway on terms which may be summarized as follows:

(1) Basra was to be the terminus. The existing status of Kuwait was confirmed. No harbour or railway-station was to be built on the Persian Gulf, and Germany was not to support the effort of any other Power to this end.

(2) Britain was to have two directors on the board of the Baghdad Railway Co.

(3) An Ottoman River Navigation Co. with exclusive rights on the rivers of Iraq, and an Ottoman Ports Co. to build and administer ports and termini at Baghdad and Basra, were to be formed on British initiative, generous shares being allotted to the Turkish government and the Baghdad Railway Co.

(4) The Germans recognized the exclusive right of the Anglo-Iranian Oil Co. to prospect for and extract oil in South Persia and the vilayet of Basra. The oil-exploitation of the vilayets of Baghdad and Mosul was to be entrusted exclusively to a Turkish Petroleum Co., in which British interests were to hold three-quarters, and German interests one-quarter, of the shares.

It seemed, therefore, as if a compromise over this tangled question had at last been reached, and Britain's jealously-guarded control over the Persian Gulf preserved in its essentials. But it has been rightly said that Germany's interest in the Railway, like Britain's interest in the Persian Gulf, was now as much imperial as economic. The 'Drang nach Osten' had become a principal aspiration of German imperialists, while on the other hand their Social-Democrats warned against the Railway as the 'first great triumph of

German capitalist-imperialism' and likely to embitter relations with Britain. A Turkish liberal Minister of Finance had said, 'When you entered the board-room of the Baghdad Railway Co., you breathed the atmosphere of the Minister's office in the Wilhelmstrasse'. Germany had made great efforts to gain influence in Persia also, exploiting the extreme Persian dislike of the Anglo-Russian Agreement of 1907. Her Ministers 'fished assiduously in the troubled waters of Tehran'; there was a steady increase in German imports; and a new college at Tehran received a handsome subsidy from the German government and was staffed with German teachers. The energetic and resourceful German Consul at Bushire, Wassmuss, recruited a strong pro-German faction among the tribesmen of Fars province. The officers of the Persian gendarmerie, and the Swedish officers who had been training them, became in effect German agents. So successful was this German penetration of the British and neutral zones of Persia that, following the outbreak of the First World War, by the end of 1915 German influence was predominant there, except for the Gulf ports. The Allied colonies had to be withdrawn, and seven branches of the British-controlled Imperial Bank of Persia fell into enemy hands. The German Meissner Pasha had undertaken for Abdul Hamid the building of the Hijaz Railway which, besides its ostensible purpose of taking Muslim pilgrims to the Holy Cities, had the strategic advantage of affording the rapid movement of Turkish troops to Western Arabia without passing through the Suez Canal. In Egypt the Germans were at some pains to establish friendly relations with the growing Nationalist party.[1]

Britain likewise had not been slow to strengthen her position in the Middle East. Already in January 1912 a special committee set up by the Government of India had proposed the occupation of Basra in the event of war. In 1913 the Admiralty, having decided to convert the Navy to the use of oil-fuel, bought a controlling interest in the Anglo-Iranian Oil Co., which had by now sunk two hundred wells and completed the pipeline from its fields to the Abadan refinery. The Sheikh of Muhammara, Arab by race but a Persian subject, who ruled the Abadan district, was assured of British support in maintaining his local authority against the Sultan and the Shah alike. In anticipation that oil might be found in Bahrain, its Sheikh had been induced in 1911 to undertake to

[1] Sir Ronald Storrs, *Orientations*, definitive ed. (1943), 120 ff.

grant no concessions without the agreement of the Government of India.

Meanwhile in Europe the naval and military armament-race had gone on inexorably gathering momentum, like a huge fly-wheel which those who had set it in motion were apparently powerless to stop. Turkey was drawn irretrievably into the German orbit by her nationalist leaders. After all, the privileged positions of Britain and France in Lower Iraq and Syria respectively were encroachments on full Turkish sovereignty; Russia, ever anxious to expand at the expense of Turkey, was constantly encouraging the Balkan, Armenian, and Kurdish nationalists; whereas Germany was the one Power whose interest it was to favour a stronger Turkey. In October 1913, two months after the French General Joffre had gone to Petersburg to re-organize the Russian army, the German General Liman von Sanders was chosen to re-organize the Turkish army, and introduced hundreds of German staff and regimental officers. When the Triple Entente Powers protested, the Turks pointed out that their navy was trained by British officers, their gendarmerie by French, and that the military connexion with Germany went back thirty years. In March 1914 plans were concerted between Germany and Turkey for the co-ordination of their railway-systems in the event of war; and following the murder of the Austrian Archduke Ferdinand, which precipitated the First World War, Turkey was formally admitted as a member of the Triple Alliance.

CHAPTER V

Modernization and the Growth of Nationalism
(1800–1917)

A T THE BEGINNING of the nineteenth century Muslim civilization in the Middle East, once far in advance of anything that the Europe of the 'Dark Ages' could show, was but a ruin, picturesque when viewed superficially by the romantic traveller, but displaying all the marks of squalor and decay when approached more closely. Such innovations as had been effected by missionaries in the Levant, under the Amir Fakhr ud-Din in the early seventeenth century for example, were limited in their geographical scope and did not penetrate deeply into the lives of the people; the Muslim majority was practically untouched by them. Agriculture, the mainstay of the economy of the region, languished under a régime which taxed unmercifully and could not provide security against administrative extortion or the raids of the Bedouin. In the cities little public building had been done for three hundred years, and the imposing remains of the Mamluks or earlier dynasties were crumbling unheeded and unrepaired amid the encroaching congestion of ramshackle dwellings. Outside the decaying city-walls vast mounds of rubble and garbage accumulated for centuries, the haunt of lawless beggars and scavenging dogs, extended like veritable ranges of hills towering fifty feet or more above the natural ground-level, or invaded waste plots within the city itself. Water-supply, sanitation, the care of the sick, depended on such benefactions as had survived the slow ruin of the centuries or were left for the individual to arrange for himself. Periodic famine and epidemic were regarded as a normal visitation of the wrath of Allah, not as inconveniences which might be prevented by human action. Government was rapacious, arbitrary, venal, slipshod; the life of the subject depended on the whim of the ruler, and might be lightly taken for the slightest fault.[1] Higher

[1] e.g. Lord Zetland, *Lord Cromer*, 161 f.; Clara Boyle, *A Servant of Empire*, 45 ff.

education was confined to the study of the theology and jurisprudence of Islam; elementary education, to the learning of the
Qur'an by heart; and only the exceptional individual could read a
book or write more than his own name. The establishment of
Islam had inhibited the development of political ideas. Travel was
slow and beyond the means of the majority: Damascus was three
weeks' journey by caravan from either Baghdad or Cairo; such
rare travel-books as existed were accessible only to a few; and the
average man's experience and imagination were therefore confined to his immediate environment. Consequently the idea of
nationality was unknown; all were subjects of the Padishah, but no
one thought of himself as belonging to a Syrian or an Iraqi, still less
an Arab nation. Instead men were distinguished by their *millet*, or
by the town of their origin: as Sunni Muslim, Orthodox, Jew,
Druze, Armenian, or Shi'i; as Baghdadi, Halabi (Aleppine),
Shami (Damascene), or Misri (Cairene).

The dominating purpose of Mohammed Ali was to secure his
personal position in Egypt, by making the country a formidable
military and naval power, and to this end he consistently devoted
one-half of the revenues of the state. The well-being of the people,
to whom he was foreign, did not interest him in the slightest; but
to provide the necessary finances for his military schemes, he had to
raise the agricultural productivity of Egypt from the miserable
state to which nearly five hundred years of misrule had reduced it,
and to create industries which did not yet exist. By 1814 he had
bought out or expropriated almost all the landowners of the
Mamluk period, vesting the ownership in his own government,
i.e. in himself, but leaving the use and cultivation of the lands in the
hands of the existing tenants. From about 1820 he began the construction of numerous canals in the Delta for the purpose of cultivating that district by perennial irrigation in place of the artificial
basins into which the annual Nile flood was admitted to fertilize
the ground for the main winter crop. By superseding the age-old
basin-irrigation by this new system, incomplete and imperfect
though it was in its beginnings, two or three crops could be grown
from a plot in one year, producing profitable yields of cotton,
indigo, flax, or rice as well as the basic winter grain-crop. Thus it
is estimated that between 1824 and 1840 the area under cultivation
was increased by about a quarter, in spite of the heavy demand on
man-power for military and industrial conscription. Agricultural

policy was closely centralized, as it had been under the Greek rulers of Egypt after the conquest of Alexander the Great. Mohammed Ali directed what crops should be grown, giving preference to those which were exportable at a good profit, especially cotton. Seeds were lent to the cultivators, and funds advanced to cover the cost of cultivation. A large staff of inspectors was employed to ensure that the Pasha's orders were faithfully carried out. Most classes of crops were declared government monopolies, compulsorily purchased by the government at a fixed price which was sometimes a half or less of their market-value. The goods were then either consumed for state needs, as supplies for the army or raw materials for the state factories, or they were sold abroad at a handsome profit. In 1836 it was estimated that 95 per cent. of Egypt's exports, and 40 per cent. of her imports, were for the government's account. In 1816 the existing manufactures had similarly been declared government monopolies. The government, at a considerable profit to itself, supplied the artisans with the raw materials it had purchased from the fellahin, bought back the finished articles at an imposed low price, and resold them at the highest prices possible. The Pasha established a number of new industries, mainly to supply goods for the public service or for export. They were conducted on the whole at a loss, on account of the high cost of imported machines and spare parts, the lack of suitable overseers and engineers, the apathy and discontent of the workers, dragged from their field and workshops to labour in 'dark satanic mills', the waste of raw material, the breakage of machinery, delays, confusion, even deliberate sabotage and obstruction in the working of the factories. A British observer found in 1838 that cotton cloth produced in Egypt cost 16 per cent. more than imported English cloth of the same quality. By 1840 the strain of the accumulated losses on these undertakings had become unbearable, and the ultimate failure of the industrial enterprise had become evident even to the Pasha. During the Second Syrian War many factories were closed to save expense, and thousands of the workpeople were conscripted into the army. Orders were given that all factories that could not show a profit on their operations were to be closed down. Many of them were closed immediately, others dragged on for a few years. Their ruin was completed in 1842 when, as part of the settlement of the Syrian War, the British Government compelled the Pasha to accept the application to

Egypt of the Anglo-Ottoman Commercial Treaty of 1838, by which British merchants were given the right to enter any part of the Ottoman dominion and buy from the natives the products of the soil and of the industry of the country. A few years later all that remained of the vast industrial structure, which had cost millions to create, was a quantity of rusting machinery in old, deserted buildings, scattered throughout the country. The attempt to make Egypt an industrial country had failed.

'Its failure was perhaps inevitable. The attempt to impose upon a primitive agricultural and guild economy a totally new system of industrial production was bound to meet with very great obstacles. . . . The managers of the factories were for the most part salaried government officials, ignorant and unenthusiastic about the work they were called upon to do. The machines imported were still novelties and enormously expensive, while very few in Egypt had mastered the new machine technique. . . . The attempt to stimulate agricultural production was no more successful. The low prices which were paid to the farmers for their crops took away their incentive to work. . . . They had to be literally driven to the fields and obliged to work by threats and punishments. Thousands of them deserted their farms. From time to time the fugitives were rounded up, in the towns and marshes in which they had taken refuge, and were sent back to the villages. . . . The monopoly system did not help in the production of new wealth. Its only effect was to keep down the standard of living of the farmers, and to divert into the hands of the government the additional wealth created by higher prices and increased production.'[1]

The experience of our own day has shown how difficult it is to bring about the rapid modernization and industrialization of an undeveloped agricultural economy by imposing a bureaucratic collectivized régime. The resistance which the Soviet government has encountered in this respect is well-known; and Mohammed Ali, despite his great energy and iron determination, lacked a popular ideological appeal which could evoke the co-operation of thousands of assistants. He was dealing, not merely with a backward peasantry, but with one exceptionally apathetic by reason of

---

[1] Crouchley, op. cit., 74 f., 103 f. The similarity to the labour-situation created by the bureaucratic control attempted by the Greek and Roman rulers of Egypt is very striking.

its isolation in the closed environment of the Nile Valley[1] and its debilitation by endemic disease; and he had no instrument for the execution of his plans comparable for energy, devotion, training, powers of leadership, and ruthlessness towards opposition or incompetence, with the Communist party in the U.S.S.R.[2] Another instructive comparison is with the Westernization of the Japanese economy in the second half of the nineteenth century. Here again the initial advantages were all with the Japanese since, although their economic and social system was already being undermined by degenerative processes, Japan even in her isolation was a far more healthy organism than decayed and depopulated Egypt. The Emperor was an institution with divine attributes that could be used as a focus for the absolute loyalty and fanatical devotion of a people who had learnt by tradition to regard these as the supreme virtues of their race. The ruling-class, while enjoying prestige and self-confidence, was not rigidly separated from the rest of the population, but provided opportunities for men of talent to rise into its ranks. 'In every class there was a capacity for co-operation and organized effort which was in part the product of a long experience of group action in the family, the clan, and the guild.'[3]

In the light of these comparisons, so unfavourable to the exhausted condition of Egypt at the accession of Mohammed Ali, the cause for surprise is not that he failed to achieve his plans for material re-organization, but that he was able to effect what must have seemed impossible fifty years before, the lifting of Egypt out of the morass in which centuries of misrule were smothering her. He permanently increased the agricultural productivity of the country by the introduction of perennial irrigation, though at the cost of thereby lowering the natural fertility of the soil, formerly enriched annually by the Nile mud but now requiring the addition of fertilizers. It is some index of the improved agricultural productivity that, after centuries in which the population of Egypt had declined to perhaps only one-third or one-quarter of its ancient maximum, it should, according to estimates, have increased by some 75 per cent. in one generation between 1821 and 1847, not-

---

[1] This factor is well brought out by D. G. Hogarth, *A Wandering Scholar in the Levant* (1896), 156 ff.
[2] This comparison has been independently developed by Dr. A. Bonné, in *Journal of the Middle East Society*, I, No. 3–4 (Jerusalem, 1947), 40 ff.
[3] G. C. Allen, *A Short Economic History of Modern Japan*, 156.

withstanding the drain of war and conscription. Mohammed Ali moreover introduced to some thousands of young Egyptians the elements of Western education and culture.[1] And, not least, he left his country free from debt.

*   *   *

During his nine years government of Syria and Lebanon (1831–40), Ibrahim Pasha followed his father's example in encouraging education with a military and technical intention. While government elementary and secondary schools were opened for Muslims in the principal towns, he provided for the Christian majority in the Lebanon, a community outstanding in the Middle East for its combination of intelligence with application and adaptability, by encouraging the establishment of foreign missions. The French Jesuits were allowed to return in 1831 and rapidly opened schools, finally founding their Université de St. Joseph at Beirut in 1875. The American Presbyterian Mission which had first arrived at Beirut in 1820 established a printing-press in that town in 1834.[2] By 1860 they had thirty-three schools with a thousand children, and in 1866 they founded the Syrian Protestant College, subsequently renamed the American University of Beirut. While the Jesuits' printing-press produced from 1853 onwards a series of scholarly works in French or Latin, the Americans devoted themselves to the production of school-texts *in Arabic*. Thus, while the French Catholics made a valuable contribution to the progress of Syrian education in general, the Americans played the greater part in the revival of Arabic as a literary language, after three centuries of neglect in favour of the official Turkish, and so unconsciously inspired the first Arab nationalist aspirations, in the propagation of which some of their students and locally-recruited teachers played a leading part. What began as cultural societies came to assume an air of political conspiracy in the sacred name of liberty from Ottoman oppression. About 1880 a secret society of twenty-two members, including Muslims and Druze but founded by young Christians educated at the Syrian Protestant College, displayed a

[1] The number of students who passed through the government schools has been estimated at 10–12,000 (J. Lugol, *Le Panarabisme* (Cairo, 1946), 166 f., quoting A. Sammarco).
[2] While the first printing-press at Istanbul was set up in 1727, it was not until the arrival of Napoleon in Cairo that this instrument of intellectual awakening reached any of the cities of the Arabic-speaking East.
H

series of placards in the cities of Syria, demanding in increasingly violent language the adoption of Arabic as the official language, the freedom of the press from censorship, self-government for Syria in union with Lebanon, etc. About 1883, however, the young conspirators became so nervous of the ubiquitous Ottoman secret police that they closed down the society and destroyed their records, while several of the most active members found it prudent to retire to the tolerance of Egypt under its new British rulers. George Antonius, who alone records this first incident in the history of Syrian nationalism, has been at some pains to demonstrate, by eliciting after some fifty years the testimony of surviving participants or contemporary Arab observers, that the appeal of this 'enlightened elite' to Arab national sentiment had a widespread effect;[1] but in spite of his argument that their secret activities could not, in the nature of things, have been fully appraised by the British consular agents then resident in Beirut, his patriotism seems to have led him to exaggerate the influence of these pioneers, and the consuls' assessment of the movement as 'a damp squib which excited an apathetic population only to a faint show of curiosity' is borne out by the sequel. For the next twenty-five years Arab nationalist activity was conducted in the main from the safe remoteness of Cairo and Paris. In Syria, except for the temporary excitement provoked by an agitator who was imprisoned in the 'nineties for his outspoken denunciations of Ottoman tyranny, the movement 'lay prone as though in sleep, held down by Abdul Hamid's tyranny, and drugged by the opiates of his pan-Islamic policy'. The resourceful Sultan,[2] indeed, besides encouraging the revival of Muslim sentiment by such measures as the construction of the Hijaz Railway to Madina, had systematically bestowed benefactions on Arab learned institutions, had spent large sums on the Muslim Holy Cities, had employed large numbers of Arabs in his personal service, and had had an Arab battalion in his royal Guards. In these ways, and through his far-reaching spy-system, the incipient growth of political thought among his Arab subjects was diverted from a nationalist direction into the safer channel of pan-Islam. A number of Christian Arabs, on the other hand, and a few Muslim modernists, were seduced from their cultural tradition

[1] op. cit., 79 ff.
[2] He was still regarded by the townsmen of Iraq with 'very remarkable veneration' as late as 1925 (Longrigg, op. cit., 312, n. 1).

by the European education provided by the French mission-schools and became 'Levantines', 'living in two worlds or more at once, without belonging to either; . . . no longer having a standard of values of their own, unable to create but able only to imitate; and so not even to imitate correctly, since that also needs a certain originality', in the penetrating diagnosis of Albert Hourani.[1]

*   *   *

In Persia and Iraq the impact of Europe was much more lightly felt. While the coasts of the Levant and Egypt were directly exposed to the influences of Europe, they reached Tehran and Baghdad only after they had passed through the filters of Moscow, Bombay, or Istanbul, which greatly lessened their vitality and penetrating power. The influence of Christian missions was confined in the main to the small Christian minorities. More important was the impact of European commerce and techniques, the influence of European traders and mechanics, of travellers and archaeologists. In Persia the printing-press had reached Tabriz in 1812 and Tehran in 1823. Persian medical and other students were sent to England as early as 1810–15. In 1852 the Persian government granted a large subsidy to found and maintain the Dar al-Funun or House of Sciences, intended to educate a hundred boys, primarily as army-officers. The subjects taught included some sciences and French, English, and Russian; and there were European as well as Persian teachers. In 1855 the Persian Ministry of Education was set up, and three years later forty-two students were sent to Europe. However, during his long reign the policy of Nasir ud-Din Shah (1848–96) was to discourage his subjects from visiting Europe, and he did not as a rule allow the sons of notables to be educated abroad. Modernism had thus to come in trickles through the indirect and uncertain channels of mission-schools and hospitals, European military missions, consuls, bank and telegraph-company officials, and traders. In Baghdad schools and the first printing-press were established under Da'ud Pasha (1817–32), and by the middle of the century the efforts that were being made in Istanbul to modernize the Ottoman administration were beginning slowly to take effect even in this remote and neglected province. 'If government be judged by the freedom and

[1] *Syria and Lebanon*, 70 f.

happiness of its subjects, the new era showed no great advance on the old: security was as low, justice as rare, exaction as cruel, policy as foolish. In certain aspects indeed there was progress. . . .Increasingly officials appointed to high office had something of modern education. There was greater specialization of function. There were, in fact, the bones of reasonable government into which the rare ability and goodwill of a governor might yet infuse life.'[1] For example, the 'honest, vigorous, and liberal' Mohammed Rashid Pasha, who governed for five years from 1853, re-opened a score of disused irrigation-canals and founded a company for river-navigation; and he was only the precursor of Midhat Pasha who in three short years 1869–72 began to organize for the first time a system of land-registration, in an attempt to put an end to tribal lawlessness. He made plans for river-reclamation, river-navigation, industrialization, town improvements. He founded municipalities and administrative councils, enforced conscription, tried but failed to suppress corruption, and in Baghdad started a newspaper, military factories, a hospital, an alms-house, an orphanage, and numerous schools whereby the literacy-rate among townspeople rose from perhaps $\frac{1}{2}$ per cent. in 1850 to some 5 to 10 per cent. by 1900. In this mass of projects completed or attempted 'it is not difficult to find traces of hastiness, of economic considerations mistaken or ignored, of excessive confidence in the catchwords of progress, of a preference for the spectacular to the judicious. . . . Yet his vision, his patriotic energy, his absolute integrity performed greater works than his imperfect education could mar', and as recently as twenty years ago his name was still 'constantly on the lips of townsmen and tribesmen, and always as an enlightened innovator'.[2] Midhat applied in its entirety the modernized Ottoman administrative system. 'A numerous class of regular officials, the Effendis, stepped into the place of the old arbitrary Pashas. Literate but not otherwise educated, backward but decorous in social habit, uniform in a travesty of European dress, exact and over-refined in the letter of officialdom, completely remote from a spirit of public service, identifying the body-public with their own class, contemptuous of tribe and cultivator, persistent speakers of Turkish among Arabs and, finally, almost universally corrupt and venal—such were the public servants in

[1] Longrigg, op. cit., 281.
[2] Longrigg, op. cit., 298 ff.

whose sole hands lay the functions of government.'[1] The period is marked by 'the change of turban to fez, of flowing beard to the stubble of the half-shaven, of careless medieval rule to corrupt sophistication'.[2] In spite of the coming of steamship and telegraph and a rudimentary postal-system, the historian of modern Iraq concludes: 'The country passed from the nineteenth century little less wild and ignorant, as unfitted for self-government, and not less corrupt, than it had entered the sixteenth; nor had its standards of material life outstripped its standards of mind and character. Its resources lay untouched, however clearly indicated by the famous ages of the past and by the very face of the country. Government's essential duty of leading tribe and town together in the way of progress had scarcely been recognized, barely begun . . . ; in the yet clearer task of securing liberty and rights to the governed, however backward, it had failed more signally perhaps than any government of the time called civilized.'[3]

★   ★   ★

The discretion, the judgment, the basic financial soundness which, in spite of many errors and miscalculations in detail, characterized the work of Mohammed Ali, were lacking in his successors in Egypt. When Sa'id Pasha died in 1863 he left debts of about £12,000,000, composed of his obligations to the Suez Canal Co. for his 44 per cent. share of the capital issue, of public works of various kinds, personal loans, etc. But whereas the keynote of Sa'id's character had been easygoing indolence and complacency, his thirty-three-years-old successor Isma'il was a man of large and ambitious ideas which had been stimulated by his education in Paris. Moreover, he came to the throne at the height of the American Civil War, when the interruption of the supply of American cotton to Lancashire led to a tremendous boom in Egyptian cotton. Between 1861 and 1864 the export of cotton increased threefold and its value more than fourfold. Consequently Isma'il was led by prosperity into extravagant dreams of expanding and modernizing his country's economy. He began by taking exception to some of the more audacious terms of the Suez Canal Co.'s concession which De Lesseps had foisted upon his complacent pre-

[1] Longrigg, op. cit., 281 f.
[2] Longrigg, op. cit., 277.
[3] Longrigg, op. cit., 321 f.

decessor, and to indemnify the Company and meet other liabilities Isma'il raised in 1864 his first foreign loan, a matter of £5,700,000 from the 'British' banking-house of Frühling and Goschen.[1] In the years 1863–5 an outbreak of cattle-disease swept Egypt; in order to restore the herds and carry out a plan for extending the railways, Isma'il went to Frühling and Goschen again in 1866 for another loan of £3,000,000. Heavy expenditure on the army and public works—railways, telegraphs, canals, etc.—caused his budget for 1867 to be in deficit by some £4,000,000. He accordingly contracted with the 'British' bank of Oppenheim & Co. a new loan of £11,900,000, which was so discounted by the bank that he actually received only £7,200,000. The end of the American Civil War having been followed by a fall in the sale of Egyptian cotton, Isma'il had attempted to redress the economic situation by encouraging the planting and processing of sugar on a large scale. To finance this he went in 1870 to the firm of Bischoffsheim for a new loan of £7,000,000, which discounting reduced to about £5,000,000 in ready cash. He conceived an ambitious scheme for opening up the Sudan to modern influences and suppressing the slave-trade 'throughout Central Africa', an enterprise in which he was enthusiastically abetted by the British soldier Sir Samuel Baker, who promised him that he would place the Egyptian flag 'at least one degree south of the Equator'. The total cost of this, and other expeditions to extend Egyptian dominion along the Somali coast to Cape Guardafui and as far south as Kisimayu (from where he was warned off by the British government, on behalf of its protégé the Sultan of Zanzibar) is not known; but Baker's four-year expedition to the Equatorial Sudan cost about half-a-million. Baker himself received £10,000 a year and all expenses; he was accompanied by his wife and nephew; and his successor Gordon was amazed to discover the superb china, the Bohemian glass, fine cutlery, damask linen, and the best French wines which had alleviated the rigours of the expedition. With the lavish expense on such enterprises, on railways and irrigation-canals, the Suez Canal, on European-style schools, harbours, bridges, shipping, urban development, telegraphs, water-works, and lighthouses, on the Army, on presents to the Sultan and bakhshish to his ministers and courtiers, on personal display, pageantry, and self-indulgence, on

---

[1] Sa'id had already three times taken the insidiously tempting bait of foreign loans, but for smaller sums.

interest and sinking-fund payments on the loans which never amounted to less than 12 per cent. per annum on the principal, it is not surprising that, despite a great increase in the taxes levied on the fellahin, expenditure during Isma'il's reign amounted to nearly double the total revenue for the period. In 1873 the floating debt had risen to £23,000,000; and in order to gain temporary relief from this burden the Khedive[1] contracted with Oppenheim & Co. a new loan of £32,000,000, but at a disastrous discount: after discount, interest and commission had been deducted, he received less than £20,000,000 in hard cash. In order to execute his ambitious programme of public works, moreover, Isma'il had had recourse to large numbers of European contractors (by 1871 the foreign population had increased to about five and a half times its size in 1836), and many of these were un-scrupulous adventurers who undertook concessions only in order to find some alleged breach-of-contract on the part of the Egyptian government and extract an exorbitant indemnity in the appropriate consular court to which the Capitulations gave them access. When the Mixed Courts were set up in 1873 to regulate foreign litigation, there was £40,000,000 in foreign claims outstanding against the government: one case is on record in which the courts awarded £1,000 to a claimant who had sued for £1,200,000. So accustomed was the Khedive to victimization by these sharks from Europe that he is reported to have remarked sarcastically in the presence of one of them, 'Shut that window; if this gentleman catches cold, it will cost me £10,000'. Lord Milner, a far from sympathetic critic of the extravagance of Isma'il, summed up the situation: 'The European concession-hunter and loan-monger, the Greek publican and pawnbroker, the Jewish and Syrian moneylender and land-grabber, who could always with ease obtain the protection of some European Power, battened on the Egyptian Treasury and the poor Egyptian cultivator to an almost incredible extent.'[2]

By the end of 1875 Ism'ail, whose debts now amounted to £91,000,000, was four millions short on his next payment of interest. In this plight he decided to dispose of his 44 per cent. share in the capital of the Suez Canal Co.; and, as is well known, Disraeli bought these shares for Britain for just under £4,000,000. Isma'il's

---

[1] He had purchased this impressive but empty Persian title from the Sultan in 1866.
[2] *England in Egypt*, thirteenth ed., 15; cf. also 176 ff.

rueful comment was, 'This is the best financial and political trans-action ever made even by a British government; but a very bad one for us'.[1] The end could not now be long delayed. By April 1876 the state was bankrupt; and an international Caisse de la Dette Publique was set up, with British and French commissioners to receive the Egyptian revenues, supervise the railways and the port of Alexandria, and maintain the payments due to the creditors. 'In short, the bailiffs were in', and the Dual Control, British and French, had begun to regulate the public life of Egypt.

Egyptian nationalists in our own day have claimed that Isma'il was an enlightened ruler actuated primarily by the desire to develop his country, and that it was his misfortune, due to inex-perience of the pitfalls in international finance, that submerged him and Egypt under the burden of debt.[2] Closer examination of his character, however, fails to exonerate him to this extent. He was the first of his dynasty to be superficially Europeanized in education and tastes. To instal in Egypt all the external evidences of European material civilization, regardless of the cost, was for him to be in the forefront of progress, to be hailed by the world as a truly illustrious prince. He was actuated by personal ambition and an inordinate love of display, rather than by prudent regard for the lasting improvement of his country's economy. Vast and costly development-schemes were embarked on after entirely inadequate study of their practicability. Intoxicated by the showers of gold which descended on him so frequently in the first ten glorious years of his reign, it was all one to the Khedive whether they were expended on public works or an agricultural scheme, the annexa-tion of some remote Equatorial province, or on a new palace and lavish entertainments; Milner doubted whether the portion of Isma'il's loans devoted to works of permanent utility, excluding the Suez Canal, equalled 10 per cent. of the amount of debt which he contracted; and meanwhile his agents drove and pillaged the peasantry without mercy.[3]

[1] In 1871 Gladstone had refused to discuss an offer to buy a share in the Canal Co., regarding it as purely a matter for private financiers, and unbefitting a government; but Disraeli with Levantine tuition grasped its imperial implica-tions, and immediately on coming to power in 1874 had sent Baron Lionel de Rothschild to Paris to try to re-open negotiations for a purchase.

[2] This is the case put forward by P. Crabites: *Ismail, the Maligned Khedive*, and by M. Rifaat Bey, op. cit., ch viii, 'Ismail the Magnificent'.

[3] Milner, op. cit., 179. For a summary of the impressions of an unofficial and sympathetic British resident in Egypt, cf. Gordon Waterfield, *Lucie Duff Gordon*, ch. XLIII.

The European penetration of Egypt in the previous fifty years and the inauguration of a system of education along formally European lines, had created a small class of young men with a modern outlook, the Effendis. These young men, who through their education had imbibed some of the liberal and nationalist ideas of contemporary Western Europe, were further stimulated by the agitation of the Saiyid Jamal ud-Din al-Afghani, a propagandist for the liberation of all Islam from European influence and exploitation, and its union under a strong Caliphate; expelled from Istanbul in 1871, he lived and taught in Cairo for eight years. Moreover, while Isma'il's public-works schemes had greatly improved Egypt's communications, production, and trade,[1] they had brought little profit to the masses who bore the main burden of the heavy taxation, which had risen by 1875 to five times its figure in 1861. Thus a strong undercurrent of popular discontent was added to the nationalists' criticism of Isma'il for his favouritism for Europeans, his ruinous financial policy, and the preference he showed for the Turco-Circassians, who survived from Mamluk times as the ruling-class over the native Egyptians. The inferior position of the native element in the army especially excited their indignation. The first nationalist newspapers appeared in 1877, and the slogan 'Egypt for the Egyptians' began to be heard.

In 1878 a ministry led by the Armenian Nubar Pasha, and containing a British Minister of Finance and a French Minister of Public Works, ordered, among other measures for reducing expenditure and so furnishing sums to meet Egypt's creditors, the drastic reduction in the size of the army to 11,000 men from a previous maximum of 80,000. Two thousand officers were placed on half-pay without settlement of their year-long arrears of pay. This naturally caused the greatest indignation, and in 1879 a riot of officers forced the resignation of the government. The British and French Controllers suspected that this demonstration had been instigated by Isma'il himself, who resented the Nubar government as an encroachment on his own authority. Accordingly the Powers obtained from the Sultan the deposition of Isma'il in favour of his

[1] The railway-system was increased to nearly five times its size at the beginning of Isma'il's reign, telegraphs to nearly ten times, and postal services were greatly improved. Egyptian exports rose by 50 per cent. The population of Egypt as a whole increased between 1848 and 1882 by 50 per cent., and that of Alexandria, which had already grown about ten-fold between the beginning of the century and its middle, jumped by another 60 per cent. between 1848 and 1882.

more amenable son Tawfiq, and the restoration with greater powers of the Dual Control, whose financial policy was based on the principle, financially orthodox but extremely callous when applied to the poverty-stricken masses of Egypt, that 'no sacrifice should be demanded from the creditors till every reasonable sacrifice had been made by the debtors', i.e. by the fellahin who paid the bulk of the taxes. The nationalist unrest grew, unchecked by the weak-willed new Khedive, until in September 1881 a military demonstration headed by Colonel Arabi, an Egyptian of fellah origin who had played a minor part in the officers' riot of 1879 and was now the accepted leader of the native-Egyptian junior officers against their Turco-Circassian seniors, forced the Khedive to accept a nationalist government with Arabi as Under-Secretary for War. Encouraged by this nationalist success, the Chamber of Notables, a body previously without political authority, had the temerity to claim the right to vote the Budget without heeding the representations of the foreign financial Controllers. Concerned at this intransigence the French government, zealous as always in its protection of the interests of the bond-holders who were mainly French, proposed to the British government a joint armed intervention in Egypt.

   The British Liberal government showed itself reluctant to interfere so drastically in the affairs of a nominally sovereign state, but as the situation in Egypt showed no signs of improvement it finally accepted the French suggestion in January 1882. Before any action could be taken however, the French government fell on a domestic issue, and its successor proved singularly irresolute on the subject of Egypt. In February a full-blooded nationalist government came into power in Cairo with Arabi now Minister for War. He made plans to expand the army and place the effective political power in the hands of the native-Egyptian officers. The British and French governments, now thoroughly alarmed at the course of events, joined in despatching naval squadrons to Alexandria, and in sending a note to the Khedive demanding the dismissal of the nationalist government. At the same time the British government invited the Ottoman government to intervene, and was willing to refer the whole Egyptian question to an international conference composed of the ambassadors of the Great Powers at Istanbul; gestures which appear to rule out any idea of a pre-conceived British plan to annex Egypt. The dismissal of the nationalist government was followed by anti-foreign disorders, the worst of which occurred at Alexandria and caused the deaths of 57 Europeans and 140 Egyptians. Arabi began to strengthen the military defences of Alexandria, presumably to meet the threat of a landing from the British and French squadrons. On 5 July, the British government decided to demand the cessation of these military works at Alexandria, with the threat that the fleet would otherwise destroy them. The French government, however, declined to co-operate, and withdrew its ships the day before the British on 11 July, having had no reply to their ultimatum, destroyed Arabi's defences by a heavy bombardment. The commander of the British force disembarked at Alexandria, faced by the Egyptian army in prepared positions twelve miles away, resolved on an outflanking movement from the Suez Canal. The French government now proposed to concert with Britain action limited to safeguarding the neutrality of the Canal; but the Opposition overwhelmingly defeated the motion, arguing the impossibility of separating the Canal from the general Egyptian question. While the French chamber debated, British troops were landed at Port Said. They shattered the Egyptian army at Tell el-Kebir on 13 September and entered Cairo two days later. In the following month Britain informed France of her intention to withdraw from the Dual Control. In the following July a Khedivial decree abolished it altogether, and Evelyn Baring, later Lord Cromer, became for twenty-four years the de facto ruler of Egypt. The French historian Driault claimed that the abstention of France was due to 'her desire not to conflict with Egyptian national sentiment, which she had believed capable of more energetic resistance'. French public opinion had, however, made no objection to the systematic exploitation of the inexperience of Egypt's rulers to the profit largely of French investors in the previous twenty-eight years, nor to the pitiless spoliation of the Egyptian fellahin to meet the payment of usurous interest.[1] The abstention of France was due to her government's indecision, the besetting weakness of her political system under the Third Republic. But French public opinion has never forgiven Britain for taking action when she hung back, and for twenty-two years she bitterly obstructed every constructive British effort to restore and improve the economic condition of the Egyptian people.

[1] Lord Cromer, *Modern Egypt*, 28 ff.

With the trial and exile of Arabi the first Egyptian nationalist movement collapsed utterly.[1] It had originally been the genuine intention of the British government, with the concurrence of Baring, to withdraw from Egypt as soon as the authority of the Khedive had been restored. This is clearly demonstrated by telegrams exchanged between the Foreign Office and Baring as late as January 1884.[2] As late as 1887 the government negotiated with the Ottoman government for a withdrawal at the end of three years, provided that at that time the security of Egypt was not threatened either from within or without. This proposal was however brought to nothing, mainly (ironically enough) by the opposition of France to the conditions imposed. The principal factor behind the continued British occupation was the rising in 1881 of the Sudanese Muslims, under the religious leadership of the self-styled Mahdi Mohammed Ahmed of Dongola, against grievous Egyptian oppression and misrule, and their destruction of Egyptian armies under British command sent to repress them. It was felt that Britain could not allow this fanatic horde to overrun Egypt, as it might well have done in view of the collapse of authority there, and threaten Britain's imperial communications. The killing of General Gordon at Khartoum in 1885 let loose a surge of patriotic sentiment in Britain and finally made it impossible for the government to withdraw from Egypt.

The collapse of the nationalist movement gave Cromer some twenty years to re-organize the finances and promote the economic development of Egypt with the passive co-operation of the Egyptians, except for some opposition from the headstrong young Abbas II, who succeeded as Khedive in 1892, and his advisers, jealous of Cromer's power. The restoration of Egypt's solvency, the extension of the crop-area by nearly one-fifth in the 'nineties as a result of the completion of the Delta Barrage and the extension of perennial irrigation, and the abolition of the age-old institution of compulsory unpaid labour (the corvée), which thus gave the

---

[1] The most recent Egyptian historian, a former Director-General of the Ministry of Education, roundly condemns Arabi and his associates, but in terms highly significant of the present-day Egyptian political outlook. They were 'a handful of adventurers who *knew nothing about war*, statesmanship, or even decent government. . . . Had a death-sentence been pronounced against them . . ., their crime would not only have been treason and rebellion, but also *ignominious failure and incompetence in battle*.' (M. Rifaat Bey, op. cit, 213; italics not in the original.)

[2] Lord Zetland, *Lord Cromer*, 88 ff.

fellahin the first rudimentary rights of free men: these elements of progress, which form one of the finer chapters in the history of British imperialism, were possible only because of Cromer's creation of an administrative machine which was summed up as consisting of 'British heads and Egyptian hands'. The Egyptian upper and middle classes were not yet capable of the necessary administrative efficiency and integrity to occupy positions of responsibility in so complicated a machine. The Khedive and the Prime Minister had continually to accept the 'advice' of the august and masterful British Agent and Consul-General. Each Egyptian minister and his British adviser, and each provincial governor his British inspector, who through their direct access to Cromer wielded the effective power of government. Hence the Turco-Egyptian upper-class resented the British encroachment on their freedom to manipulate the governance of their country to their own advantage, and the growing literate middle-class (the number of newspapers published in Egypt increased more than four-fold from 1892 to 1899) envied the British their control of the best positions in the administration,[1] and was humiliated by that chilly reserve which afflicts so many Englishmen in the presence of strangers and foreigners. These grievances were to some extent fanned by the French, for it was to France that progressive Egyptian fathers continued to send their sons to finish their education, and the Egyptian secondary-school system, such as it was, was still modelled on the French pattern. The necessity for keeping the capitulatory Powers acquiescent towards Britain's de facto position in Egypt by interfering as little as possible with the international status quo there prevented Cromer from entering into effective competition with the French virtual monopoly of higher education and cultural and political propaganda, even had the *laissez-faire* attitude towards education of successive British governments admitted such an idea. When Cromer did at length come to organize an educational system, it was for the utilitarian purpose of training Egyptian junior officials for the administration, and served no cultural or political end.[2]

Thus it was in anti-British circles in Paris that the apostle of the second phase of Egyptian nationalism, the consumptive young law-student Mustafa Kamil, was encouraged to make

[1] cf. the rather naive comments of M. Rifaat Bey, op. cit., 225 f., 234.
[2] cf. Lloyd, op. cit., Vol. I, ch. xi.

his first inflammatory speeches against the British occupation. On his return to Egypt about 1895 he formed the Nationalist Party, al-Hizb al-Watani, founded a newspaper, and set up a school for propagating his political creed among the young men. The Anglo-French Entente of 1904 was a setback for the Nationalists, since the French could no longer actively support Britain's enemies in Egypt. But the defeat by Asiatic Japan of Russia, the European Great Power that had encroached so extensively and so consistently on the Dar ul-Islam, encouraged them greatly; and they were fanned to fury in 1906 by the 'barbarity dictated by panic' with which the British-controlled administration, during Cromer's absence on leave, punished the villagers of Dinshawai for a murderous attack on British officers who had mistakenly shot their tame pigeons. In the following year Lord Cromer retired from his long proconsulship. He was not a man who sympathized with the pretensions of mediocrities nor, as he grew older, with the headstrongness of youth; and his final Annual Report did not spare the weaknesses of the Nationalist movement: 'It can be no matter for surprise that the educated youth should begin to clamour for a greater share than heretofore in the government and administration of their country. Nothing could be more ungenerous than to withhold a certain amount of sympathy for these very legitimate aspirations. Nothing, on the other hand, could be more unwise than to abstain, at this early period of the National movement, from pointing out to all who are willing to listen to reason the limits which, for the time being, must be assigned to those aspirations. . . . The programme of the National Party is quite incapable of realization at present, and it may well be doubted whether, in the form in which it is now conceived, it can ever be realized. . . . In any case I must wholly decline to take any part in furthering proposals, the adoption of which would in my opinion constitute a flagrant injustice, not only to the very large foreign interests involved, but also to those ten or twelve millions of Egyptians, to the advancement of whose moral and material welfare I have devoted the best years of my life.' While Cromer did not reject the idea of self-government as the ultimate goal of Egypt's political evolution, he had many doubts of Egyptian administrative capacity, and the 'very large foreign interests' he had in mind comprised not only the $2\frac{1}{2}$ per cent. of the population that was foreign, but the fact that 78 per cent. of the Egyptian public debt and joint-stock capital was in foreign hands. Hence his preference, underestimating the emotional forces which national sentiment generates, for 'a constitution which will enable all the dwellers in cosmopolitan Egypt, be they Muslim or Christian, European, Asiatic, or African, to be fused into one self-governing body'. He gave his encouragement to the newly-formed reformist party Hizb al-Umma, inspired by the distinguished theological reformer Sheikh Mohammed Abduh, probably the first great thinker that Eastern Islam had produced since al-Ghazzali; and he had recently approved the appointment of one of the most promising members of that party as Minister of Education: his name was Sa'd Zaghlul.

Cromer's successor Sir Eldon Gorst had served under him with considerable distinction; but he returned to Egypt in 1907 with 'strong, if not very precise instructions' to introduce political reforms. The British general-election landslide of 1906 had brought into power after twenty years in the political wilderness a Liberal government which contained a considerable proportion of humanist Radicals who regarded constitutional representative government as something of a panacea for the ills of the world. The kind of directive which Gorst received has been summarized as to 'relax British control and give the Egyptian government greater freedom of action in matters of policy and administration, even at the cost of less efficiency; to help the Egyptian people to learn for themselves the first lessons of self-government which some measure of responsibility, however slight, alone could teach them'.[1] It was, however, to be no programme of headlong surrender to the Nationalists, though it was represented as such by diehards among the official and unofficial British colony in Egypt. Gorst declared in his first Annual Report that 'until the people have made a great deal more progress in the direction of moral and intellectual development, the creation of representative institutions, as understood in England, would only cause more harm than good, and would give a complete setback to the present policy of administrative reform'. He accordingly sought to win the co-operation of the Khedive Abbas II, now a man of thirty-five, in the hope of moulding him into a constitutional monarch, who would provide stability at the apex for the pyramid of the Egyptian polity; and he planned to strengthen the base of the pyramid by a constructive extension of the very limited powers of the Provincial

[1] Chirol, op. cit., 108.

Councils. Thus, underpinned from below and held in place from above, there was a prospect that the central Legislature might grow in responsibility and wisdom.

It was not to be. The Young Turk Revolution of 1908 had forced the Sultan to restore the constitution which he had suspended in 1876; and in an access of emotional liberalism it had declared equal all the races of the Ottoman Empire. The sympathetic enthusiasm generated among the Egyptian Nationalists was great, and found expression in violent and unrestrained agitation. The campaign reached its climax in 1910 in the murder of the Coptic[1] Prime Minister Butros Ghali, who had given the Nationalists some reason on three occasions in his career to regard him as a Quisling of the British. His murderer was characteristic of the type that commits such political crimes: a physically weak, bankrupt young chemist of fair education, moody and introspective.

In 1911 Sir Eldon Gorst retired, fatally stricken with cancer and disappointed by the failure of his experiment in the gradual introduction of representative institutions. He stated in his last Annual Report: 'We have to make the Egyptians understand that the British government do not intend to allow themselves to be hustled into going further or faster in the direction of self-government than they consider to be in the interests of the Egyptian people as a whole. Institutions really representative of the people are obviously impossible in a country in which only 6 per cent. of the population can read and write.' A critic might have asked why Britain persisted in imposing her rule on this people whose vocal elements were so ungrateful. The fact was, of course, that since the German Drang nach Osten had become a serious factor in her Middle East policy, the control of the Suez Canal was more than ever vital to her imperial communications; and in addition, her prestige and a large sum of British capital were now committed in Egypt. But it was not the British way to admit openly these material *arcana imperii*. Instead, the *Spectator* could write, 'It would be an inhuman devolution of our duty in the world to sacrifice the *poor* Egyptians, to allow them to become once more the prey of extortioners and bullies', and *The Times* could declare with less than its customary objectivity,

---

[1] There had never been an Egyptian-Muslim Prime Minister since the British occupation in 1882: one was Armenian, one a Turkish Jew, two Turkish Muslims, and now the Copt Butros Ghali.

'The real object (of the Nationalists) is a return to the old system of class-privilege, oppression, and corruption'.[1]

In choosing a successor to Sir Eldon Gorst the British government made one of those sharp reversals of policy which are not uncommon when a previous policy has proved unsuccessful. After consulting Lord Cromer, whose scepticism of the Egyptian capacity for self-government had hardened in view of the events which had followed his retirement, it appointed that formidable soldier Lord Kitchener, who regarded Western political institutions as an unqualified danger to Oriental peoples. 'Party spirit', he once said, 'is to them like strong drink to uncivilized African natives. . . . The future development of the vast mass of the inhabitants depends upon improved conditions of agriculture which, with educational progress, are the more essential steps towards the material and moral advance of the people.' He declared in his Annual Report for 1912 his strong disapproval of any encouragement of the 'so-called political classes', and in his Organic Law of 1913 he sought to re-organize the existing legislative bodies so as to secure adequate representation for the agricultural population: 'Noisy extremists and outside political influences must be eliminated if the Assembly is really to represent the hardworking, unheard masses of the people.' At the same time the administration provided additional irrigation-water for agriculture by raising the height of the Aswan Dam, and sought to protect the small proprietor from the seizure of his holding for debt through the Five Feddan Law. The prestige attaching to Kitchener's past career, and the strength of his personality did restore a measure of political tranquillity, and his vigorously prosecuted agricultural policy engendered prosperity and confidence. Nevertheless the Legislative Assembly, as elected after the passing of the new Organic Law, continued its factious obstruction. A clash between the administration and Zaghlul who, after losing his ministerial office as a result of his incurring the enmity of the Khedive, had become leader of the Nationalist opposition with a solid group of followers, was averted only by the outbreak of the First World War. Moreover, the administration had deteriorated in quality owing to Kitchener's

[1] J. Alexander, *The Truth About Egypt* (1911), 209, 92; this work is an excellent example of contemporary 'Egyptophobia'. As late as 1934 Lord Lloyd could write, 'From 1889 to 1922 our *foremost concern* had been to secure the humane and stable administration of the affairs of the Egyptian masses.' (*Egypt since Cromer*, II, 354; the italics are mine.)

high-handed methods, unwillingness to accept advice, and personal prejudices. Some valuable British servants of the Egyptian government had resigned in consequence, and had been replaced by men with poorer qualifications. Thus, while the number of British officials had rapidly increased since Cromer's time, their standard had steadily deteriorated. It was said also that Kitchener's choice of Egyptian advisers and assistants was not always of the happiest.[1] A contemporary appreciation clearly saw the dangers which lay below the surface: 'The superficial quiet is that of suppressed discontent—a sullen, hopeless mistrust towards the government of occupation. The government has not yet succeeded in endearing, or even recommending, itself to the Egyptian people, but is on the contrary an object of suspicion, an occasion of enmity. Nationalist feeling is very strong in spite of determined attempts to stamp out all freedom of political opinion. The wholesale muzzling of the press has not only reduced the Muslim majority to a condition of internal ferment, but has seriously alienated the hitherto loyal Copts.'[2] However, the entry of the Ottoman Empire into the War was followed by the declaration of martial law in Egypt, and the whole political question was suspended, and discontent driven still further underground, to fester until the end of the world conflict.

★   ★   ★

Meanwhile, although Arabs were not strongly represented in the Young Turk Committee of Union and Progress, the nationalists of Syria had been greatly encouraged by the Turkish Revolution, and in September 1908 they formed at Istanbul the Arab-Ottoman Brotherhood, al-Ikha al-'Arabi al-'Uthmani, whose objects were to unite all the races of the Empire in loyalty to the Sultan, to protect the new liberal constitution, to promote the well-being of the Arab provinces on a footing of real equality, etc. However, following an attempted counter-revolution promoted by Abdul Hamid in 1909, the Young Turks introduced new security measures, one of which was the prohibition of all societies founded by non-Turkish groups. The Ikha was shut down, and the Arab Nationalists were driven underground to continue their

---

[1] Amin Yusuf, *Independent Egypt*, 53.
[2] *Asiatic Review* (April, 1914), quoted by Lothrop Stoddard, *The New World of Islam*, 154 f.

political activities in secret. The first of their secret societies, the Qahtaniya, was dissolved after one year for fear that it had been betrayed to the Turks. In Paris seven Muslim students, who included Jamil Mardam (in 1948 Prime Minister of Syria) and Awni 'Abdul Hadi (now a Palestine Arab 'elder statesman'), founded the Young Arab Association, al-Jam'iya al-'Arabiya al-Fatat, with the object of securing Arab independence from Turkish or any other foreign rule. The society grew and in 1913 organized in Paris a six-day congress attended by twenty-four delegates, eleven of them Christians, drawn mainly from Syria and Iraq (the Iraqi delegates included Tawfiq as-Suwaidi, Prime Minister of Iraq during part of 1946). The congress expressed a general desire to remain within the Ottoman Empire, provided that home-rule could be secured, and stressed the importance of preventing European Powers from meddling in the question. In the same year al-Fatat moved its headquarters to Syria. By this time its membership had risen to over 2,000, mainly Muslim, and included Shukri al-Quwwatli and Faris al-Khuri (who in 1948 are respectively President of Syria, and Syria's representative on the Security Council of UNO).

Nor was Iraq without its local nationalist stirrings. A Patriotic Society, founded at Baghdad to expel the Turks and establish an autonomous government, numbered among its members more than a hundred army-officers and many local notables; among those who came to the unfavourable notice of the Turkish authorities were Hamdi al-Pachahji (who was Prime Minister of Iraq early in 1946). In March 1913 a conference of Arab notables of Lower Iraq and neighbouring territories was held at Muhammara, in Persian territory, to work for the independence of Iraq and Turkish Arabia. In November the Iraqi nationalists made overtures to the young Amir Abdul Aziz ibn Sa'ud, who had by now made himself master of Najd with an outlet on the Persian Gulf. He expressed his sympathy for their cause, but could at present do no more, neutralized as he was strategically by his ancestral enemy, the pro-Turkish Amir of the Jebel Shammar to the north. The Turks were partly aware of this growth of nationalist sentiment, and attempted to disrupt both the Syrian and the Iraqi movements by offers of high political positions to some of their leading figures; but though some few were seduced in this way, the Turks were not prepared to offer any such concessions in the direction of local autonomy as would disarm the politically-ambitious Arab notables who were as yet the sole exponents of nationalism.

Meanwhile Aziz Ali al-Misri, a young Arab officer who had distinguished himself in the Ottoman service, but who had resigned his commission feeling that his services had been unworthily rewarded by the Young Turks, founded early in 1914 as a substitute for the defunct Qahtaniya a society called al-'Ahd, the 'Solemn League and Covenant'. It consisted almost entirely of Arab army-officers and consequently contained a preponderance of Iraqis, since they were the most numerous regional group of Arabs in the Ottoman Army. Branches of the society were founded at Baghdad and Mosul, and it is said to have recruited 4,000 members throughout the Empire. It became to the Arab army-officer what al-Fatat was to the civilian upper-class intellectual; but neither society knew as yet of the existence of the other, and contact between them was not established till early in 1915. In January 1914 the Young Turks had Aziz al-Misri arrested in Istanbul on charges of trying to set up an Arab kingdom in North Africa, of receiving bribes from the Italians during the Tripolitanian War of 1911, etc. He received a death-sentence, but was reprieved and finally released only on the intervention of the British Ambassador, as a result of representations from Lord Kitchener in Egypt.

An index of the spread of intellectual, and consequently of political, interest in the Arab world at this time is provided by the great increase in the numbers of newspapers published between 1904 and 1914. They rose in Lebanon from twenty-nine to 168, in Syria from three to eighty-seven, in Palestine from one to thirty-one, in Iraq from two to seventy, in the Hijaz from none to six, a ten-fold expansion over the entire area. In addition, nationalist newspapers published by Arab emigrés abroad were smuggled in through the foreign post-offices which existed under the Capitulations. The nationalist movement was, however, still confined to a very small group of army-officers and upper-class intellectuals, and touched the masses hardly at all; and behind the façade of the secret societies one may without prejudice infer the interplay of 'personal rivalries, religious differences, and sectional animosities, arising out of the essential individuality of the Arab character.'[1] Their disunity was of course aggravated by the lack of liaison occasioned by the slowness of communications. Of the capitals of states and the chief

[1] Ireland, op. cit., 237.

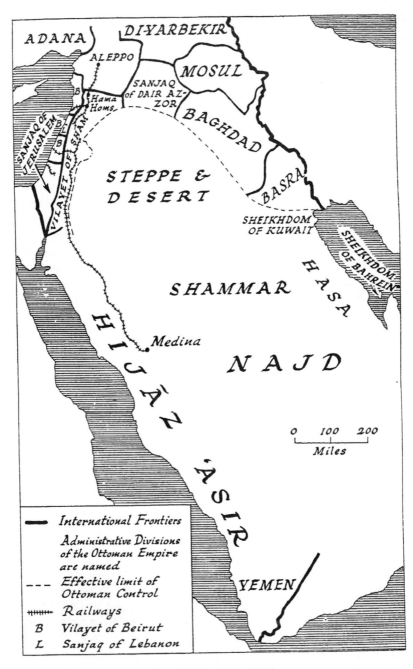

ADANA

DIYARBEKIR

ALEPPO

MOSUL

SANJAQ
of DAIR AZ-
ZOR

B

Hama
Homs.

BAGHDAD

SANJAQ OF
JERUSALEM

VILAYET OF SHAM

STEPPE &
DESERT

BASRA

SHEIKHDOM
OF KUWAIT

SHEIKHDOM
OF BAHREIN

HASA

SHAMMAR

HIJĀZ

Medina

NAJD

'ASIR

0   100   200
Miles

─ *International Frontiers*

*Administrative Divisions
of the Ottoman Empire
are named*

─ ─ ─ *Effective limit of
Ottoman Control*

━━ *Railways*

B   *Vilayet of Beirut*

L   *Sanjaq of Lebanon*

YEMEN

II.   ARAB ASIA, 1914

towns of the vilayets, Damascus alone was connected by rail with Beirut and Aleppo; but between Cairo and Jerusalem, Jerusalem and Damascus, Damascus and Baghdad, Aleppo and Mosul, there was as yet no conveyance more rapid than the horse-carriage and the camel-caravan. This physical factor was, however, less an obstacle to the national movement than the immoderate and unpractical character of the Arab imagination was in the long run to prove. Their aim of reconstituting an independent Arab kingdom was inspired by the memory of the far-off Arab caliphate of history, and in its ambitious and unpractical flights bore little relation to the hard facts of the present. Regarding the European Great Powers only as interlopers to be kept at arm's length, the nationalists failed to realize to what extent, in the impending dissolution of the Ottoman Empire, their prospects of attaining self-government would be determined, not by grandiose aspirations and utopian and wordy manifestoes, but by the relative amounts of material pressure and influence which they and the interested Powers could respectively bring to bear on the situation. National freedom meant primarily to them, as members of leading Arab families, access to positions of power and authority for which under the Ottoman Empire they had to compete at a disadvantage with Turkish aspirants. There is no evidence that the desirability of improving the economic and social conditions of the poorer classes of the population played at this stage any part in their programme; indeed, since so large a proportion of them derived their wealth from landed property, such a programme would, by inevitably disturbing the present relation of tenant and landlord, have been contrary to their interests.

★   ★   ★

In the uncertain interval between August and October 1914, in which the Ottoman Empire was still neutral, the Arab nationalists sought to exploit the situation to win guarantees of their independence, but their tactics remained cautious. The Higher Committee of al-Fatat added to a resolution in favour of independence the following reservation, 'In the event of European designs appearing to materialize, the society is bound to work on the side of Turkey in order *to resist foreign penetration of whatever kind or form.*' Similarly Aziz al-Misri, who was now living in Egypt, issued a warning to the leading members of al-'Ahd not to be tempted into hostile action against the Ottoman Empire, as her entry into the war would expose the Arab provinces to European conquest; they were to stand by Turkey until effective guarantees against European designs were obtained. These nationalist suspicions of European intentions are important in the light of the conflict with Britain and France that was to develop after the War.

Meanwhile, Kitchener and his Oriental Secretary Ronald Storrs had been in correspondence since February 1914 with the Sharif Husain of Mecca, who ruled the Muslim Holy Cities on medieval theocratic lines and heartily disliked the efforts of his Ottoman suzerain to centralize provincial administration and thus subordinate him to the Turkish wali appointed from Istanbul. This threat to his hereditary authority had become acute with the advent of the Young Turks, and had been held off only by Husain's skill in tortuous and non-committal diplomacy. He had, however, found it prudent to seek the support of the British in Egypt, though his sons Abdullah and Faisal were anxious not to commit themselves to the 'Franks' and make an open breach with the Turks prematurely. The British negotiators were similarly cautious as long as Turkey remained neutral, but in October 1914 they did commit themselves in general terms to 'the emancipation of the Arabs' and 'an Arab nation' in return for Arab support against Turkey. At the same time Storrs and Gilbert Clayton of the military Intelligence approached Aziz al-Misri and others concerning the possibility of starting an Arab revolt; but these nationalists insisted as an indispensable preliminary on guarantees of Arab independence which the British spokesmen were not empowered to give. In January 1915 a member of the prominent Bakri family of Damascus, travelling to Mecca on Turkish official business, took with him a message from al-Fatat to the Sharif, asking him to concert measures with them for an Arab rising. The Sharif accordingly sent his son Faisal to Istanbul, ostensibly on official business, but really to sound the disposition of both the Ottoman authorities and the Syrian nationalists. On his northward journey he visited the Bakris, met members of both al-Fatat and al-'Ahd, was admitted to both societies, and informed them of the Sharif's parleys with the British. On his return to Damascus in May he found that in the meantime the two secret societies had prepared a joint Protocol requiring, as a condition of an Arab revolt against the Ottoman

Empire, that Britain should recognize an independent Arab kingdom comprising Arabia (except Aden), Palestine, Syria and Iraq.

In July, after Britain had announced her intention of recognizing an independent Arab state in the Arabian Peninsula, the Sharif sent to Sir Henry McMahon, the British High Commissioner in Egypt, a note which repeated the requirements of the Damascus Protocol brought back by Faisal. The British Arab Bureau in Cairo had still only vague knowledge of the existence of the two secret societies, and the notion consequently became established in British minds that the Sharif's demands for a Greater Arab Kingdom were solely the product of his own personal ambition, whereas in fact they faithfully represented the views of the nationalist movement, (except that its Syrian exponents did not necessarily regard Husain as a suitable King of the whole Arab world). Husain's note inaugurated the famous Husain-McMahon Correspondence, the interchange of which continued till January 1916. In the course of it the British negotiators made reservations on behalf of French interests in those parts of the Levant 'west of the districts of Damascus, Homs, Hama, and Aleppo', as not being wholly Arab; another reservation was made for British interests in Lower Iraq. The Sharif, who insisted that he was waiting only for an opportunity to revolt ,suggested that the solution of both these problems should be left till the end of the War. The British agreed, but warned him that 'when victory is attained, the friendship of Britain and France will be stronger and closer than ever'.

Meanwhile the policy of the Turkish governor and commander-in-chief under martial law in Syria, Jamal Pasha, had hardened against the Arabs since the failure of the first Turco-German attack on the Suez Canal in February 1915. Before that he had seized French consular documents incriminating various Syrian and Palestinian personalities with treasonable conspiracy with France before the War: the French Consul-General Picot had failed to destroy these highly secret documents, but had left them in the charge of the American Consul, who innocently supposed that the Turkish police would respect the inviolability of the consular seals.[1] During 1915 and the early part of 1916 Jamal Pasha held a series of treason trials: thirty-four nationalists, of whom twenty-seven were Muslim, were executed and hundreds of prominent

[1] In view of French designs on Syria, which were not compatible with Arab nationalism, Picot's negligence may not have been entirely unmotivated.

persons deported to remote parts of Anatolia. In the spring of 1916 the Turkish High Command despatched a picked force of brigade strength with German staff-officers attached to reinforce their troops in the Yemen, which had driven back the small British garrison in the Aden Protectorate almost to the narrow confines of Aden Colony itself. This Turkish force travelling south by the Hijaz Railway arrived at Madina in May 1916. Its arrival greatly alarmed the Sharif, who feared that his correspondence with the British might have become known to the Turks, and that the force had been sent to deal with him. In addition, the recent news from Syria of the last and largest crop of political executions had finally convinced the sceptical Faisal that nothing was to be gained by further procrastination and haggling with both sides. The Arab Revolt was accordingly begun on 5 June 1916. Lord Wavell has commented, 'Its value to the British commander was great, since it diverted considerable Turkish reinforcements and supplies to the Hijaz, and protected the right flank of the British armies in their advance through Palestine. Further, it put an end to German propaganda in south-western Arabia and removed any danger of the establishment of a German submarine base on the Red Sea. These were important services, and worth the subsidies in gold and munitions expended on the Arab forces.'[1]   That the Revolt did not succeed in raising the civil populations of the Arab provinces is partly due in Syria to the effectiveness of the Turkish repression, and in Iraq to the unsympathetic attitude of the Indian Army authorities, who withheld or minimized the news of the progress of the Revolt in order not to encourage ideas of independence in the local Arab population. The Government of India, aiming at an outright British annexation of Lower Iraq, regarded the Cairo Arab Bureau policy of encouraging Arab independence as visionary, and its support of an Arab rising against the Ottoman Sultan-Caliph[2] as liable to cause unrest among the ninety million Muslims of India, whose sentimental attachment to the Caliphate was magnified by their immunity from the realities of Ottoman rule. The Viceroy of India actually described the Arab Revolt as 'a displeasing surprise whose collapse would be far less prejudicial to us

---

[1] *The Palestine Compaign*, 56.
[2] Later Ottoman sultans, and especially Abdul Hamid II with his pan-Islamic policy, had elaborated a fiction that the medieval Caliphate had passed from the last Abbasid to them in 1517. cf. T. W. Arnold, *The Caliphate*, ch. XIV.

than would our military intervention in support of it'. Sir Ronald
Storrs declared that the passive resistance of the civil population of
Syria and Palestine to the Turks following the Revolt was worth
almost nothing to the British forces; on the other hand, the German commander Liman von Sanders has recorded that after the
successful Third Battle of Gaza 'the British advancing towards
Jerusalem found themselves fighting in friendly country, while
the Turks were faced with a decidedly hostile population'. We
may, however, ask how far this was due to their enthusiasm for the
Arab Revolt, and how much to a natural desire to be in on the
winning side: Allenby now had a superiority in fighting strength
over the enemy of more than two to one. But whatever the
limitations of the value of the Arab Revolt as a military operation,
its importance in stimulating the aspirations of politically-minded
Arabs cannot be overstated, with effects that were to be immediately felt after the end of the War.

CHAPTER VI

The Struggle for Independence (1918–39)

THE WAR OF 1914–18 was the first total war in modern times, in which the peoples of even the 'victorious' countries are left more or less exhausted, and disillusioned about the ideals which, they were given to believe, they went to war to defend. The reaction that followed was consequently all the more acute because it had not been anticipated by most political thinkers. In Britain the strong current of imperialist sentiment that had flowed towards the end of the nineteenth century had already been greatly reduced by the sordid motives and material setbacks of the South African War. The 'Great War' left in the public mind a strong disinclination for any foreign or imperial policy which would call for further efforts from the war-weary people; and there was thus everywhere support for a policy of 'appeasement', which was strong enough to affect the judgments of statesmen. Furthermore, the statesmen themselves had been overworked and over-driven during four years of deadly struggle. They had had to subordinate, even more than is normal, any long-term considerations of policy to the short-term aim of securing immediate tactical advantages over the enemy. They had been driven by force of circumstances into making a number of contradictory commitments—in the Middle East, for example, to the Arabs on the one hand, and to the French, the Zionists, and to British self-interest on the other. In addition, an important section of informed British opinion, which may be labelled 'liberal' in the wider, non-party sense, regarded self-government for all peoples as the ultimate ideal of imperial politics, however remote the attainment of that ideal might be.

The English people had fought for their independence of the Spaniard and the Pope, of royal absolutism, and of the French; they had looked with sympathy on the struggles for independence of the Greeks, the Italians, and the peoples of the Balkans; they had acquiesced in the British Dominions' gradual acquisition of the right to manage their own affairs; and many of them regarded the political aspirations of nationalist Indians or Egyptians as having greater moral force than the interests of Britain in those lands. Such idealists were only a minority; but for the reasons previously stated, the majority of the British people were reluctant to resort to any extreme measures to maintain the imperial status-quo unchanged. The nationalists of the Middle East and elsewhere were consequently able from 1918 onwards to obtain greater concessions by pressure and violence than reasoned argument would probably have achieved; and not being aware of the symptoms in the British public mind which favoured their own violent course, they attributed their success solely to that violence and were encouraged to continue in it.[1]

In the flush of their victorious power in the immediate post-war period Britain and France extended and intensified their interests in the Middle East at the expense of the nationalist movements which were rising there. Britain sought from 1919 to 1921 to make permanent her direct protectorate over Egypt, which had been proclaimed as a temporary expedient at the outbreak of war· to replace the undefined proconsulship of Cromer. British and French pre-war cultural and economic penetration of the Fertile Crescent crystallized into the imposition of their direct rule over the whole region, Palestine and Transjordan, Syria and Lebanon, Iraq. Nor was this imposition mitigated in fact by the invention of the Mandates system as much as might appear on the surface. The Mandates system was little more than a polite fiction created in order to satisfy President Wilson and the idealists who had inaugurated the League of Nations. Britain and France arrogated to themselves their mandates over the Middle East by the Treaty of San Remo in April 1920, and the League dutifully subscribed to their will. In June 1920 Lord Curzon, then Foreign Secretary, could tell the House of Lords, 'It is quite a mistake to suppose that under the Covenant of the League or any other instrument the gift of a mandate rests with the League of Nations. It rests with the Powers who have conquered the territories, which it then falls to them to distribute.' The Permanent Mandates Commission of the League could in theory recommend the withdrawal of a mandate from an offending Power, but this authority was never exercised. It could, and sometimes did, animadvert critically on the conduct of a Mandatory; but it had no powers to inspect

[1] cf. A. J. Toynbee, *The Islamic World since the Peace Conference*, 11 f.

on the spot the conditions in a mandated territory. It failed
to induce the French to make timely concessions to nationalism
in Syria. It could not order the adoption, nor the reversal,
of a policy unless it could be shown to be contrary to the original
mandate; and in the special case of Palestine the Mandate,
framed to give legal sanction to a political experiment whose
components had received insufficient preliminary study, was
found in the next twenty years to be incapable of sufficiently
flexible interpretation to meet rapidly changing conditions.[1]

It was not surprising that the reaction of the growing nationalisms
of the Middle East to this intensifying of foreign control, this virtual annexation by Britain and France, should be a violent one.
Examined from this standpoint, the inter-war period falls into two
unequal parts, with the dividing line between them varying by
several years from one country to another. In the first period, the
post-war settlement, the efforts of the nationalists to throw off the
European imperialisms were violent, and they resorted in some
countries to armed rebellion. In the second, or inter-war period
proper, the agitation was more constitutional in character, though
armed action still sometimes occurred. In Palestine, owing to the
special local circumstances, the violence was spread over both
periods, and was actually more intense in the later one; but even
here there was a pause of seven years, from 1922 to 1929, which
makes the division into two periods applicable here also. It is convenient in both periods to examine the subject country by country,
since it was only toward the end of the second period that the
co-ordination of nationalist activity between the various Arab
countries, which was to culminate in 1944 in the creation of the
Arab League, became of any significance.

A. The Post-War Settlement

In Egypt, while the imposition of martial law had ensured a
respite from political agitation during the War, the exigencies of
the campaign combined with a considerable measure of British

---

[1] After the 1929 Riots in Palestine, which were a direct result of the clash of
the Zionist and Arab nationalisms, the Permanent Mandates Commission, ig-
noring the realities of the situation, commented that, had the Mandatory more
vigorously carried out a constructive programme in the interest of the peaceful
masses of the population, it 'would have enabled them to convince the fellahin
more easily of the *undeniable material advantages* that Palestine has derived
from the efforts of the Zionists'.

ignorance did much to aggravate the grievances of the Nationalists. The country was flooded with inexperienced British army officers and civil officials who treated Egypt, now proclaimed a British protectorate, almost as an occupied territory in which the rights and wishes of the inhabitants counted for little. The shortage of man-power and of transport for the Palestine campaign led to the conscription of thousands of fellahin for the Labour Corps and the Camel Transport Corps, and the requisitioning of their draught-animals. Although such measures were theoretically regulated to cause the minimum hardship—the conscription period, for example, was limited to six months—their execution was largely left, owing to the heavy demand on British personnel for the Army, to Egyptian provincial and local officials, who naturally. applied them with a view to their own profit: the fellah who paid the necessary bakhshish to the village 'umda was exempt from conscription or requisitioning; the fellah who could not or would not pay found himself included in the conscription-list for one six months' period after another, and his camel or donkey carried away by the requisitioning authorities. The fellahin were thus filled with a strong sense of injury, and blamed the British all the more because, under their rule, they had acquired some measure of personal liberty and had lost some of their servile respect for authority and the patient endurance of oppression. The urban population was made discontented by the shortage of imported supplies, especially of cereals in a country whose profitable cotton-growing had to a great extent supplanted grain; and they were offended by the tactless collection of subscriptions for the Red *Cross*, from a predominantly Muslim population and by methods which locally sometimes approximated to compulsion. Politically-minded Egyptians were further irritated by the establishment of the Protectorate, which seemed to make the prospect of self-government more remote. The kind of post-war constitution which senior British officials in Egypt envisaged was exemplified by a Note on Constitutional Reform drawn up by the Judicial Adviser, which leaked out to the Cairo press despite the censorship. It 'entirely ignored the existence of the national sentiment which the War had stimulated . . . and did not spare the deficiencies of the politically-minded classes in an incisive review of their past activities. It proposed the creation of a new legislature in whose upper chamber, the Senate, not only British Advisers and

Egyptian Ministers were to have seats, but also representatives of the large foreign communities, chosen by special electorates, to voice their commercial, financial, and professional interests. . . . The opinion of the Senate was to prevail in all matters of essential policy . . . clearly with a view to securing the passage of whatever the British government might consider necessary for the maintenance of their controlling authority.'[1]

In this atmosphere of discontent it is not surprising that, as the war drew to an end, Zaghlul was able to recruit strong support for his campaign to bring about a radical change in the political status of Egypt. Two days after the Armistice he headed a delegation (Wafd) to the High Commissioner, informing him 'on behalf of the whole Egyptian people' of the desire for complete independence, and requesting permission to go to Europe to lay Egypt's case before the Peace Conference. The Egyptian Prime Minister then asked permission for a ministerial delegation to go to London, which the High Commissioner urged the Foreign Office to receive; but Lord Curzon, the acting Foreign Secretary, refused, feeling that it would raise hopes in Egypt which it would be impossible to satisfy, especially as the government was preoccupied with the greater problems of the settlement of Europe and would prefer to postpone consideration of the Egyptian question until the pressure of more urgent business was relieved. To the Egyptian nationalists, however, their case was the most urgent matter in the world. They saw Syrians, Arabs, and even Cypriots sending delegations to the Conference, and interpreted the Foreign Office refusal as proof that Britain intended to impose her own solution by force. Zaghlul began a nation-wide campaign for independence. The Foreign Office then reversed its decision and agreed to receive the ministerial delegation; but Zaghlul's campaign had already gathered so much momentum that the Egyptian Prime Minister now insisted that Zaghlul should be included in the delegation and share its responsibility; otherwise he knew well that whatever the delegation achieved in London would be repudiated by the nationalists at home. But Lord Curzon was not prepared to accept Zaghlul; as late as 24 February 1919 he continued to receive optimistic reports from the Residency in Cairo: 'The agitation which the Nationalist leaders have organized is dying out, or is at any rate quiescent in the country at large. . . . Zaghlul is trusted by

[1] Chirol, op. cit., 145 f.

no one. . . . The agitation has from the beginning been entirely pacific in character. . . . The present movement cannot be compared in importance with that of Mustafa Kamil, and there seems to be no reason why it should affect the decisions of H.M. Government on constitutional questions and the proper form to be given to the protectorate.'

The Egyptian Prime Minister, denied permission to plead his country's case at the Peace Conference, resigned on 1 March 1919, and strikes, disturbances and riots followed. The Residency counselled firmness: four nationalist leaders, three of whom—Zaghlul, Isma'il Sidqi, and Mohammed Mahmud—have made their mark in subsequent politics, were deported to Malta. This was followed by a widespread insurrection among the fellahin, inspired by the middle-class nationalists. Railways and telegraph and telephone communications was extensively cut, and Cairo was isolated from the rest of the country, where British authority had ceased to be effective. Provincial 'republican governments' were proclaimed and even villages set up their own independent authorities. Isolated parties of British troops and some European residents were massacred. By 23 March however railway communication between Cairo and the north had been restored, and three weeks later the army had re-imposed order almost everywhere.

The Residency subsequently tried to explain the revolution by allegations that the hand of Bolshevist, Young Turk and even German agents had been 'clearly discernible'; but the Milner Commission placed these hypotheses in their true perspective: 'The Anglo-Egyptian authorities appear to have been so greatly out of touch with native sentiment that such statements must be accepted with reserve. They have shown a complete lack of foreknowledge for which it is almost impossible to account.' The internal organization of the Residency had in fact become far from adequate for its increased responsibilities; the duties of the various senior officials had never been clearly defined, and it had no sound system for obtaining and assessing intelligence.

Meanwhile Lloyd George had recalled the High Commissioner and appointed in his place Lord Allenby, the victor of the Palestine campaign, 'to maintain the Protectorate on a secure and equitable basis'. The new High Commissioner adopted a conciliatory policy towards the nationalists. The four deported deputies were released, and Zaghlul went off to Europe to lay Egypt's case before the Peace Conference; but his intransigence and rigid inability to compromise made a poor impression there, and his case was weakened by the fact that President Wilson had given his recognition to the British Protectorate. The British Government set up, under the chairmanship of the Colonial Secretary Lord Milner, a commission 'to enquire into the form of government which, *under the Protectorate*, will be best calculated to promote peace and prosperity, the progressive development of self-governing institutions, and the protection of foreign interests'. In the same document British policy was defined as seeking 'to defend Egypt against all external danger and the interference of a foreign power, and to establish constitutional government, under British guidance as far as may be necessary, so that the Sultan[1] and his ministers and the elected representatives of the people may in their several spheres and in an increasing degree co-operate in the management of Egyptian affairs'. The Mission was met by a complete boycott; their residence was picketed by the Wafdists (as the followers of Zaghlul now called themselves), and any Egyptian who ventured to call upon them was pursued by menaces. On the return of the Mission to London Milner continued negotiations with the Egyptian Prime Minister and with Zaghlul, and finally in August 1920 produced a memorandum proposing a definite settlement provided that Zaghlul would urge its acceptance upon his followers. It recommended 'a treaty of alliance under which Britain will recognize the independence of Egypt as a constitutional monarchy with representative institutions, and Egypt will confer upon Britain the rights necessary to safeguard her special interests and to enable her to give foreign Powers guarantees which will secure the relinquishment of capitulatory rights. Britain will defend the integrity of Egyptian territory, and Egypt will in case of war render Britain all assistance in her power within her own borders. Egypt will not adopt an attitude inconsistent with the alliance, or enter into any agreement with a foreign power prejudicial to British interests. Egypt will confer on Britain the right to maintain a military force on Egyptian soil for the maintenance of her imperial communications. ... Egypt will recognize the right of Britain to intervene, should legislation operate inequitably against foreigners. The British representative

---

[1] The Khedive had been made to adopt this title in 1914 when Ottoman suzerainty was renounced with the Turkish entry into the War.

K

will enjoy a special position and precedence', etc. This memorandum, which provided the basis for Anglo-Egyptian relations until
1946, was received not unfavourably in Egypt, though Zaghlul
had made the significant counter-proposal that British troops
should be specifically limited in number and confined to the Canal
Zone. The main opposition came from the British cabinet, parliament, and public, 'many of whom had come to regard Egypt as an
integral part of the British Empire and were beyond measure
astonished that Milner, whose imperialism was unimpeachable,
should have proposed what they regarded as the surrender and
abandonment of British territory'.[1] Milner, however, showed
how untenable historically this unaccommodating attitude was:
'Unless all our past declarations have been insincere and all our
professions hypocritical, the establishment of Egypt as an independent state in intimate alliance with Britain is the goal to which
all our efforts have been directed. It may indeed be argued that the
goal has not yet been reached, that Egypt is not yet strong enough
to stand on her own feet. Such arguments are entitled to respectful
consideration. But what cannot be maintained, with any regard
for historical accuracy, is that these changes in themselves are not
absolutely in accordance with the constantly declared policy of
Great Britain.'[2]

During 1921 the British government carried on negotiations
with moderate Egyptian ministers drawn from the Turkish
ruling class; but these broke down on the Egyptian insistence that
the British garrison should in peace-time be confined to the Canal
Zone, where it could not be used so readily to exert pressure upon
Egyptian internal politics. The British Army, on the other hand,
apparently insensible of the constant irritant presented to Egyptian
susceptibilities by the presence of a British garrison in their capital,
stubbornly opposed its withdrawal from Cairo. A familiar theme
of those who opposed any concessions was that 'the real fellahin, if
their voice could be heard, preferred British rule to that of their
own leaders; yet all the evidence conclusively proved that these
misguided peasants preferred indifferent government by their own
compatriots to the efficient and honest administration of an alien
power'.[3] The Cabinet, dependent on an unstable coalition in the

[1] *Round Table*, December, 1936,110 ff.
[2] Preface to the thirteenth edition of *England in Egypt*, October, 1920.
[3] N. G. D., reviewing Lord Wavell's '*Allenby in Egypt*' in *Royal Central Asian
Journal*, XXXI (1944), 213.

House of Commons, and fearful that it would be attacked by the imperialist wing of the press if, after its recent surrender to Sinn Fein in Ireland, it now made concessions to militant nationalism in Egypt, followed the lead of the Colonial Secretary, Winston Churchill, who characteristically was much more alive to the broad bearing of the question on imperial strategy than to the intensity of feeling in Egypt itself. Finally Allenby, realizing the hopelessness of trying to get any agreement in Egypt without some concessions and holding that Britain was pledged by the Milner Report to offer a measure of independence, forced the government's hands by tendering his resignation with that of the four principal˙British advisers to the Egyptian government. The Cabinet yielded and Allenby was allowed to proceed with his policy of granting conditional independence. On 28 February 1922 the Sultan was informed that the Protectorate was terminated, and Egypt declared to be an independent sovereign state. The following four points were however absolutely reserved to the discretion of H.M. Government pending the reaching of agreement on them: (1) The security of imperial communications; (2) the defence of Egypt against all foreign aggression or interference direct or indirect; (3) the protection of foreign residents and minorities; (4) the Sudan. This unilateral declaration was followed by a Note to the foreign Powers warning them that Britain would not admit any questioning or discussion of her special relations with Egypt, and would regard as an unfriendly act[1] any attempt at intervention in Egyptian affairs. Egypt was not proposed for admission to the League of Nations; and in November 1924 the Conservative government which had newly come to power informed the League that, should Egypt sign the Geneva Protocol for the Pacific Settlement of International Disputes, H.M. Government would not admit that the act entitled her to invoke the intervention of the League in any matter covered by the Four Reserved Points. As Toynbee commented, the granting of independence to Egypt was so limited by these reservations that it amounted in fact to less than Dominion Status. Egyptians received it without gratitude as merely an instalment of independence; as the Iraqi soldier Ja'far al-'Askari had remarked, 'Complete independence is never given; it is always taken.'

★   ★   ★

[1] The diplomatic euphemism for an act which would be resisted by force.

As Iraq was progressively occupied during the War, it came under a military administration whose tone, set by the Indian Army and the Government of India, was unsympathetic to the new idea of Arab nationalism as fostered by the British Arab Bureau in Cairo. An interim compromise plan produced by the British government in March 1917 provided for the annexation of the Basra vilayet, while that of Baghdad was to be administered as far as possible by Arabs, but to be in everything but name a British protectorate having no relations with foreign Powers. A new factor was introduced by an Anglo–French Declaration of 7 November 1918 which stated that: 'France and Britain agree to further and assist the setting-up in Syria and Iraq of indigenous governments and administrations, deriving their authority from the free exercise of initiative and choice of the indigenous populations. The only concern of France and Britain is to offer such support and efficacious help as will ensure the smooth working of these governments and administrations.' This Declaration caused great excitement among the young nationalists of Baghdad, but, in the opinion of the distinguished Arabist and traveller Gertrude Bell who was serving on the staff of the Administration, 'the prematurity of the national movement has so clearly been manifest that it has found no support among the stable elements of the population.'

At this stage the Chief Civil Commissioner, Sir Percy Cox, a man of great experience and personal prestige, was transferred as British Minister to Tehran, and was succeeded by his assistant Colonel Arnold Wilson. This thirty-four-year-old Indian Army officer had rapidly come to the fore for his energy and vigour; but his previous acquaintance with Arabs and his knowledge of their character was limited to his experience in the Persian Gulf and on the Lower Tigris. He had no experience of or sympathy with the Ottomanized effendi of Baghdad, whose political aspirations were those of al-'Ahd. More than this, his admirable positive qualities were offset by a strong vein of self-righteousness and self-justification. On taking over from Cox he advised the Foreign Office that 'There is an almost entire absence of political, racial, and other connexion of Iraq with the rest of Arabia. . . . The average Arab, as opposed to the handful of amateur politicians of Baghdad, sees the future as one of fair dealing and material and moral progress under the aegis of Britain. Iraq should not be assimilated politically to the rest of the Arab and the Muslim world, but should remain insulated as far as may be, as a wedge of British-controlled territory'; and he comments in his apologia *Loyalties*: 'A small independent state of under three millions seemed a retrograde, almost anarchic step. . . . My imagination envisaged some form of protectorate which might develop ere long into a fully-fledged Arab state with Dominion status under the British crown.' Having determined in November 1918 to obtain confirmation for his thesis by holding a plebiscite, he was at some pains to ensure that it produced the desired result. His instructions to his Divisional Officers stated, 'When public opinion appears likely to take a definitely satisfactory line, you are authorized to convene an assembly of all leading notables and sheikhs . . . informing them that their answers will be communicated to me for submission to the Government. Where public opinion appears likely to be sharply divided, or in the unlikely event of its being unfavourable, you should defer holding a meeting and report to me for instructions.' The effect on the British cabinet of the plebiscite so conducted was less serious than its effect on Wilson himself, since it led him increasingly to find reasons for disregarding the views of those with whom he disagreed. Thus, characterizing the Iraqi nationalist officers with the Amir Faisal in Syria as 'such small fry' and regarding the Shi'i mujtahids and other religious dignitaries with much justification as 'spiritual tyrants whose principal ambition was to stem the rising tide of emancipation', he 'underestimated the influence of the Nationalists, and the susceptibility to their propaganda and that of the dissident 'ulama of the mass of the people on the Middle Euphrates', as he himself later admitted.[1] He was not, however, averse to cautious constitutional progress; he proposed to the Interdepartmental Committee on Eastern Affairs in April 1919: 'The legitimate demand for active participation in the government and administration can best be met, not by creating central legislative and deliberative councils, but by giving carefully selected Arabs of good birth and education from the very outset positions of executive and administrative responsibility. I would propose to instal selected Arab officials as governors of (the principal towns) with a specially chosen British official of ability and character as principal commissioner and adviser to the governor.' The Allied Powers were, however, still fully occupied with imposing terms on Germany, and had not yet approached the

[1] *Loyalties*, II, 254.

problem of the disposal of the Ottoman Empire. Consequently the Foreign Office replied to Wilson that it was premature to attempt constitutional experiments pending the decision of the Peace Conference on the Mandatory Power for Iraq and the nature of the Mandate. In these circumstances it is not surprising that Arab notables who were approached as possible governors of Basra declined to accept the responsibility and commit themselves until the future of their country became clearer.

Meanwhile there had existed in Damascus since its liberation in October 1918 an autonomous Arab government under the Amir Faisal, assisted by British officers who had taken part in the Arab Rebellion and were sympathetic to the Sharifian form of Arab nationalism. Among the officers on Faisal's staff were many Iraqis, members of al-'Ahd, who ardently desired to see their country similarly placed under Arab rule. In 1919 one of these visited Baghdad and was offered the post of Assistant Military Governor of the city. He apparently imagined that he had been invited to assist in setting up a national government; but on finding that he was merely to be an Arab unit in the British administration hurriedly resigned. 'This incident evidently confirmed in the minds of the Iraqi officers in Syria the impression that the British military administration in Iraq was intended to be permanent, and that it regarded them as active enemies who were trying to undermine British influence there.'[1] The Iraqis in Syria thereupon organized a rising wave of political feeling in the towns of Iraq, and brought about a rapprochement between Sunnis and Shi'is. In October 1919 Gertrude Bell remarked in an official Note: 'When we set up a civil administration in this country, the fact that a responsible native government has existed for a year in Syria will not be forgotten by the Iraqi nationalists; and if we seek to make use of those Iraqis who have done best in Syria, they will claim great liberty of action, and will expect to be treated as equals. . . . Local conditions, the vast potential wealth of the country, the tribal character of the rural population, the lack of material from which to draw official personnel, will make the problem harder to solve here than elsewhere. I venture to think that the answer to such objections is that any alternative line of action would create problems whose solution we are learning to be harder still.' Wilson, however, still did not fully grasp the strong, intimate, and constant influence exerted

[1] Sir Hubert Young, *The Independent Arab*, 292, 297.

on Iraqi nationalism by the autonomous Arab government in Syria, and sought to nullify Gertrude Bell's conclusions in his covering despatch: 'The fundamental assumption throughout this Note . . . is that an Arab state in Iraq and elsewhere within a short period of years is a possibility, and that the recognition or creation of a logical scheme of government on these lines would be practicable and popular. . . . My observations in this country and elsewhere have forced me to the conclusion that this assumption is erroneous. . . . I believe it to be impossible in these days to create a new sovereign Muslim state . . . out of the remnants of the Turkish Empire. . . . It is my belief that the Arab public at large would after a very few years prefer the return of the Turks to the continuance of an amateur Arab government. . . . For some time to come the appointment of Arab governors or high officials, except in an advisory capacity, would involve the rapid decay of authority, law and order, followed by anarchy and disorder, and the movement once started would not be checked.' Long afterwards he admitted, 'It is easy to see after the lapse of ten years that I was perhaps unduly sceptical.'

In May 1920 the British government at last obtained by the abortive Treaty of Sèvres the mandate for Iraq, and instructed Wilson to consult the recently-created Divisional Councils on proposals for the development of national life. Wilson and his advisers objected, since the Arab government in Damascus, subsidized with gold from the British treasury, had during the long delay carried on a violent nationalist propaganda with considerable success among the middle-class younger generation, who had been greatly encouraged by the proclamation of Faisal's brother Abdullah as King of Iraq by the 'Ahd in Damascus in March. Wilson's advisers produced a draft constitution: there was to be a Council of State, consisting of British and Arabs in equal numbers, and a Legislature. The members of the Council could, however, be removed at will, and its resolutions over-ruled, by the British High Commissioner. The powers of the so-called Legislature were to be confined to the passing of resolutions without the force of law and the putting of questions to the government. Although Wilson claimed that 'leading Arabs regarded these proposals as revolutionary and as a generation ahead of the times', Lord Curzon critically commented: 'This is not an Arab government inspired and helped by British advice, but a

British government infused with Arab elements. . . .' Meanwhile nationalist activity had passed from agitation to open defiance. Already early in the year Arab irregulars with encouragement from the Arab government in Damascus had forced the British to withdraw from Dair az-Zor, their furthest outpost in the direction of Syria.[1] In June a force under the Iraqi officer Jamil Midfa'i[2] seized the post of Tell Afar, thirty miles west of Mosul and massacred its small British garrison, but was driven back before it could reach Mosul itself. In the months of May and June £7,000 in gold was reported to have reached extremists at Karbala.

The British government announced on 20 June that Sir Percy Cox would return in the autumn as Chief British Representative in anticipation that the Mandate, when finally promulgated, would constitute Iraq an independent state. But this gesture came too late. Owing presumably to the severe climate and the steady drain of demobilization, the Civil Administration was staffed mainly by very young and inexperienced men, who shared the somewhat headstrong views of their Chief.[3] 'It seems probable that had the Civil Administration been less anxious to justify its continued existence' (with generous pay and allowances, be it noted, at a time of rising unemployment and wage-cuts in Britain) 'by proving its superiority over the previous régime and all other possible régimes . . . had it been staffed by men older and more experienced in dealing with the Arab character and temperament, or had it shown itself more sympathetic to the idea of Arab government instead of merely paying it lip service as a possibility in some remote or indefinite future, many of the classes who hardened their hearts against the once-popular British régime would have continued to support it.'[4] The revenue collected in 1920 was three and a half times that received by the Turks in 1911. Taxation, which was enormously heavier than in India, tended to press most heavily on the fellahin, but was vexatious also to the landlords and dignitaries and to the tribes, who had formerly largely escaped paying taxes. The Iraqis had no say in the objects on which these revenues

[1] Under the Ottoman Empire this part of the Euphrates valley had not belonged to any of the vilayets of Iraq, but had formed an independent sanjaq.

[2] He has subsequently been Prime Minister of Iraq, and is now (April 1948) Minister of the Interior.

[3] In the autumn of 1919, out of a total of 233 officers only four were over forty-five years of age. On 1st June 1920 two-thirds of the Divisional Political Officers were under thirty, and almost one-quarter were only twenty-five or less.

[4] Ireland, op. cit., 252. cf. Ph. Graves, *Life of Sir Percy Cox*, 262 f.

were expended. In the financial year 1919-20 16 per cent. of all expenditure was devoted to Headquarters and the costs of administration, and this marked a reduction from previous years; another 11 per cent., nominally for public works, was largely applied to improving the amenities of British and Indian officials. Wilson had expressed the view that the interests of the country would be served by having a large proportion of British personnel in all branches of the administration. The Divisional Advisory Councils, composed of Arabs, had no influence on policy. Less than 4 per cent. of the senior-grade officials were Arab, and on the railways there were nearly five times as many Indian as Iraqi personnel. After the Rebellion had already begun Gertrude Bell wrote, 'On the whole, the wonder is that there are so many moderates and reasonable people. I try to count myself among them, but I find it difficult to maintain a dispassionate calm when I reflect on the number of blunders we have made.'

The garrison consisted of 80,000 troops, nearly half the size of the standing army of India with a hundred times the population. The general situation had long been known to be threatening; but Army H.Q. had tended to place little faith in the reports of the Political Officers of the Civil Administration. When the Rebellion broke out at the end of June, the C.-in-C. and the bulk of his staff were at their Persian hill-station; only 4,200 British troops, almost all new to the country and without previous military experience, and 30,000 Indians were available for service in Iraq; and only 500 British and 2,500-3,000 Indians were available as a mobile force. The main centre of the Rebellion was the tribal area of the Middle Euphrates, and though the moderate nationalists held aloof it lasted from July to September, when it was put down by heavy reinforcements. Over 400 British and Indian troops were killed, and the rebels were estimated to have suffered 8,450 casualties. It cost Britain £20,000,000, and in Iraq the damage to railways and loss of revenue amounted to more than £400,000.

Sir Percy Cox arrived on 1 October to take back the supreme authority from Wilson with the new title of High Commissioner. He had the advantage of his great personal prestige, and handled the situation in a more sympathetic spirit than his predecessor. A provisional Council of State was set up, consisting of Arab ministers, who were, however, subject to the advice of their British Advisers and, in the last resort, to the High Commissioner whose decision was final in all matters. There was no intention of transferring the administration to the Iraqis any faster than practical considerations demanded. The situation was very comparable with that of Cromer's Egypt: British heads and Iraqi hands; and in fact the country was at about the same stage of development. But at least a concession had been made to national aspirations by appointing Iraqi ministers. The Iraqi officers stranded in Syria after the French suppression of Faisal's government in July 1920 were encouraged to return to Iraq. The garrisoning of Iraq was in 1921 handed over to the R.A.F., and its cost progressively reduced in three to four years to one-seventh of its former figure. Nevertheless the extreme nationalists were not appeased, and it was alleged that they were receiving material help from nationalist Turkey and Bolshevist Russia. Gertrude Bell wrote, 'If we hesitate in appointing a king, the tide of public opinion may turn overwhelmingly to the Turks.' At the Cairo Conference called by the Colonial Secretary, Winston Churchill, in March 1921 the choice finally fell on Faisal, for whom Cox's staff and especially Gertrude Bell began to make active propaganda in Iraq.[1] The popular reception on his arrival was lukewarm, but the administration made every effort to secure a favourable vote in the projected referendum. A printed form containing a resolution in his favour was sent to the Divisional Officers to obtain the signatures of the notables. Annexures asking for the continuance of British control were encouraged, while any addition of a nationalist character was punished, and the mutasarrif of Baghdad was forced to resign for permitting them. The majority-vote of a town or district was regarded for the purpose of enumeration as unanimous.[2] As Gertrude Bell remarked with her curious mixture of cynicism and ingenuousness, it was 'politics running on wheels greased with extremely well-melted grease'. The official return gave Faisal 96 per cent. of the votes, while independent observers were disposed to give him two-thirds.[3]

---

[1] St. John Philby, then Adviser to the Ministry of the Interior, who favoured a republic, was dismissed for obstructing the official policy.

[2] Similarly in the United States, the party in each state which gains a majority, however small, fills the whole of that state's seats in the electoral college that elects the President.

[3] The Kirkuk liwa with its Turcoman population voted against him, and the Kurdish liwa of Sulaimaniya boycotted the referendum. The Shi'is, who constitute a majority in the whole country, demanded the end of foreign control, as did over 80 per cent. of the poll in Baghdad.

The nationalists hoped that the creation of the monarchy meant the end of the Mandate, and the establishment of full independence sweetened with British financial support. The British, on the other hand, proposed to retain control of Iraq's foreign relations and 'such measure of financial control as might be necessary'. The King was to agree to be guided by the advice of the High Commissioner, and British officials were to be appointed to specified posts. Negotiation over the terms of the Treaty to define Anglo-Iraqi relations was protracted through most of 1922 owing to Iraqi reluctance to make such large concessions as Britain required. The King was inclined to associate himself with the nationalist attitude. Five nationalist leaders were deported, including Hamdi al-Pachahji, and unrest in the provinces called for the use of R.A.F. bombers on four occasions. In September Cox delivered an ultimatum to the King: H.M. Government could not further tolerate his connexion with the nationalist agitation nor the delay in ratifying the Treaty. At this moment the King had a very opportune, though entirely genuine, attack of acute appendicitis, and in October the Council of Ministers ratified a twenty years' Treaty, subject to its subsequent ratification by the Naional Assembly. Every royal Act or ministerial order was to receive the previous approval of the High Commissioner or British Adviser respectively. If a minister refused to yield to his Adviser's disapproval, the High Commissioner had the power eventually to 'advise' the King that the measure should not receive the Royal Assent.

The National Assembly did not meet to ratify the Treaty till March 1924. The High Commissioner had taken pains to 'make' a pro-Treaty majority. The Opposition objected to the appointment of British advisers; it claimed that the financial stipulations, which required one-quarter of the revenue to be allotted to national defence and imposed on Iraq a heavy share of the Ottoman Public Debt, constituted an excessive burden; and it complained that Britain had given Iraq no guarantee over the question of the vilayet of Mosul, whose ownership was being vigorously contested by the nationalist Turkey of Mustafa Kemal. As the Assembly proved unexpectedly obstructive, the High Commissioner finally gave the King a fortnight's warning that, if the Treaty were not ratified in time to place it before the next session of the League of Nations Council, H.M. Government would put its own alternative proposals before the League. With only twenty-four hours to go, the High Commissioner refused to grant an extension of the time-limit. The Treaty was finally ratified with about an hour to spare by thirty-seven votes to twenty-four, with eight abstentions and thirty-one absentees out of a total of 100 members. Britain had with difficulty safeguarded her essential interests, and the nationalists had 'gone down fighting'. The immediate obstacle had been cleared, and the process of historical evolution could go on without bloodshed.

★   ★   ★

The special position of Palestine as the Holy Land of three great religions had been not unsatisfactorily met during the nineteenth century by the Ottoman creation of the Sanjaq of Jerusalem taking its orders direct from Istanbul, and by allowing a large measure of civil autonomy to the multiplicity of foreign religious communities. Though Sir Henry McMahon stated twenty years afterwards that in his mind Palestine was always excluded from the territories promised to the Arabs by the Husain-McMahon Correspondence in 1915, there is no direct reference to Palestine in that Correspondence.[1] In 1916, with a large-scale invasion of the Levant contemplated from Egypt, it was necessary to reconcile the interests of Britain in that region with those of France, who ever since 1860 had regarded Syria as her special preserve, had continued to expand her schools, had built the railways and obtained other commercial concessions. Some French publicists at this time even insisted that the French special interest extended to Palestine; but such a claim was not tenable in view of the variety of religious interests there other than those of the Church of Rome. In the secret Sykes-Picot Agreement of 1916 it was decided that, while French interests should be paramount in Syria, in the eventual

---

[1] It has been argued that Palestine was implicitly included in the area 'west of the *wilayât* of Damascus, Homs, Hama, and Aleppo', which was excluded from the proposed Arab kingdom, since the *wilaya* (vilayet) of Damascus extended south as far as Aqaba and consequently Palestine lay immediately to the west of it. This interpretation breaks down on the immediately-following reference to Homs and Homa: there were no 'vilayets' in the strict administrative sense of Homs and Hama, since these towns lay within the vilayet of Damascus. It would therefore follow that the word was intended in its alternative general sense of 'district'; and as the four cities mentioned all lie well to the north of Palestine, to argue that an area to the west of them was intended to include Palestine is as unprofitable as to argue that an area 'west of the districts of Warwick, Sheffield, Leeds, and Newcastle' includes the counties of Hereford and Monmouth.

partitioning of the Ottoman Empire Palestine should come under an international administration.

So far, not a word had been officially said about any special rights for the Jews. In all the centuries that had elapsed since the destruction of Jerusalem in A.D. 70, there had probably never been a time when there was not a small Jewish community in Palestine; and pious Jews of the Dispersion had always dreamed of the restoration, by the will of God, of the Temple and the Kingdom. In 1799, when Napoleon invaded Palestine from Egypt, he issued a manifesto to the Jews of the world offering them 'the patrimony of Israel'. Of more practical importance was the sentiment entertained by many British Protestants in the nineteenth century that the fulfilment of the Scriptures entailed the restoration of the Jews to Palestine. This view was held by the philanthropist Lord Shaftesbury, who as a kinsman of the great Palmerston had some indirect influence on British policy. Both Russia and France, whose activities in the Middle East Palmerston regarded with equal suspicion, were using the benevolence of Ibrahim Pasha in the 1830's to expand their respective Orthodox and Catholic missions in Palestine; and Palmerston therefore sought the opportunity of using some other community to offset their influence. In 1838 he appointed the first British Vice-consul in Jerusalem, and instructed him as part of his duties 'to afford protection to the Jews generally; and you will take an early opportunity of reporting . . . upon the present state of the Jewish population in Palestine'. They were found to number some ten thousand souls, nearly all of them from the Mediterranean countries. In 1840, at the height of the crisis of the Second Syrian War, Palmerston wrote to the British Ambassador in Istanbul, 'It would be of manifest importance for the Sultan to encourage the Jews to return to, and settle in Palestine; because the wealth which they would bring with them would increase the resources of the Sultan's dominions; and the Jewish people, if returning under the sanction and protection and at the invitation of the Sultan, would be a check upon any future evil designs of Mohammed Ali or his successor. . . . Bring these considerations confidentially under the notice of the Turkish government, and strongly recommend them to hold out every just encouragement to the Jews of Europe to return to Palestine.'[1]

This project, however, came to nothing, and there was little

[1] cf. A. N. Hyamson, *The British Consulate in Jerusalem.*

change in the numbers or status of the Jews in Palestine till the 'eighties, when the nationalist reaction in Russia, then the home of two-thirds of world-Jewry, to the murder of the Tsar was followed by an outbreak of anti-Jewish outrages, in which hundreds were killed and thousands ruined, while discriminatory anti-Jewish legislation was enforced over a period of three years. There was a large-scale exodus of Jews from Russia, finding ready admission into North America and Britain in those easygoing and liberal days. A small proportion of the emigrants went to Palestine, where some of them settled on the land with the financial help of Baron de Rothschild, and readily employed the Arab fellahin to cultivate the lands for them. By the outbreak of the First World War the Jewish population of Palestine was over 80,000. The growth of their agricultural settlements, despite many material difficulties, to the number of forty-four with a total population of about 12,000 had already provoked some Arab opposition. The American geographer Ellsworth Huntington, who was in Palestine in 1909, wrote: 'The fellahin of the Plain of Sharon and of other fertile parts of Palestine, such as Carmel and parts of the Jordan Valley, see in the Jew their greatest enemy. . . . Around Jaffa the Jewish colonies are undoubtedly successful, so much so that the native population is sorely jealous. In enmity towards the colonists they steal the fruit and break the branches in the orchards, turn horses into the grain-fields and break down hedges.'[1] In 1912 there was an angry scene in the Ottoman Chamber of Deputies, when Arab deputies protested against the Jewish acquisition of large areas of arable land in the Plain of Esdraelon from absentee landlords and the threatened dispossession of the tenants.[2]

Meanwhile the growing anti-Jewish prejudice in Europe, which reached flash-point in France in the Affaire Dreyfus, had had a profound effect on a Viennese journalist Theodor Herzl, 'one on whom his Jewish origin lay so lightly that it is probable that . . . he often completely forgot it.' But stung now by the sense of helplessness and homelessness of the Jews faced by unreasoning persecution, he

[1] *Palestine and its Transformation* (1911), 87.
[2] Geo. Antonius, op. cit. 259. In the early years of the British mandate these lands were transferred to the Jews. Twenty-one Arab villages disappeared from the map of Palestine, and it has never been definitely established what happened to their inhabitants. The tenants (but not the landless labourers) are said to have been compensated by the Jewish purchasers to the extent of about 4 per cent. of the purchase-price. The landlords, a wealthy and cosmopolitan Beirut Christian family, gave them no compensation. (Barbour, op. cit., 117 f.)

produced in 1896 a pamphlet *The Jewish State*, in which he proposed the creation of a Jewish national territory. It fell on fertile soil among Jewish student-societies in European universities, and others whose dream of the return to Zion had been given urgency by the persecution of Jewry in Russia. The three motifs: religious Zionism, the need of asylum from persecution and discrimination, and Herzl's political idea, fused. 'Almost overnight he found himself the head of a great party in Jewry: political Zionism had been born. . . . Jewry was to be divested of its peculiar attributes and made "as other nations", bound together politically and self-conscious.' After seven years of failure of the Zionist Organization to interest any Great Power in their plans 'to establish for the Jewish people a home in Palestine secured by public law', it received in 1903 an offer from the British government to establish an autonomous Jewish settlement in what was then called British East Africa. Herzl himself, who had never been wedded to Palestine as the only land for his prospective state, was attracted by this so-called 'Uganda Scheme'; but before anything could be finally settled he died, and the Zionist Congress of 1905, dominated by Eastern European Jews imbued with the traditional religious Zionism, resolved on the fundamental principle of the colonization of 'Palestine and the adjacent lands' and nowhere else.[1]

The outbreak of the First World War transferred the centre of gravity of the growing Zionist movement from the continent of Europe to Britain and the U.S.A. In these two countries the principal protagonists of Zionism were respectively Dr. Hayyim Weizmann, born in Poland but for some years lecturer in chemistry at Manchester University, where he had 'converted Prime Minister Balfour to Zionism in the middle of the East Manchester election'[2] (!): and the lawyer Louis D. Brandeis, who actively supported Woodrow Wilson for President of the U.S.A. and was rewarded by being made a Judge of the Supreme Court.[3] A 'British Palestine Committee' formed on Weizmann's inspiration, issued a periodical under the slogan 'To reset the ancient glories of the Jewish nation in the freedom of a new British dominion in Palestine'. The only non-Jewish member of this committee, the journalist Herbert Sidebotham of the *Manchester*

---

[1] Hyamson, *Palestine: A Policy*, ch. V.
[2] Herbert Sidebotham, *Great Britain and Palestine*, 54.
[3] Rabbi Stephen Wise, in *The Jewish National Home, 1917–42* (Paul Goodman, ed.), 41.

Guardian, had in 1915 written a leading-article advocating the permanent British occupation of Palestine for the defence of Egypt.
This had attracted the interest of Weizmann, who had asked Sidebotham to write a memorandum to the Foreign Office, proposing
a Jewish state in Palestine for the defence of Egypt and the Canal.
Sidebotham claimed that it was the needs, political and strategic,
of British policy that definitely inclined the scales in favour of
Zionism.[1]

Balfour had become Foreign Secretary in 1916. The influential
and enthusiastic Sir Mark Sykes,[2] who had helped to make the
Sykes-Picot Treaty, had become a temporary convert to Zionism.
With the gradual exhaustion of both Russia and France as effective
military powers in 1917 it had become imperative to ensure the
early armed intervention of the U.S.A., and President Wilson had
shown himself 'warmly responsive to the Zionist ideal'. In these
circumstances, after much interchange of opinion between
British and American Zionists, and while Zionists in Germany and
Turkey were conducting parallel negotiations with the enemy
governments,[3] a proposal was submitted in 1917 to the British
government for the 'recognition of Palestine as the National Home
of the Jewish people' with internal autonomy, freedom of immigration, and the establishment of a Jewish National Colonizing
Corporation for the resettlement of the country. This bold and
uncompromising phraseology was not however acceptable either
to the Foreign Office or to some influential British Jews who were
concerned about its possible effect on their status as British subjects.
After some months of redrafting it finally received official approval
as the famous Balfour Declaration of 2 November 1917: 'H.M.
Government view with favour the establishment in Palestine of a
national home for the Jewish people, and will use their best
endeavours to facilitate the achievement of this object, it being
clearly understood that nothing shall be done which may prejudice
the civil and religious rights of other non-Jewish communities in
Palestine, or the rights and political status enjoyed by Jews in any
other country.' There is thus a fundamental distinction between
the original Zionist proposal and the finally approved Declaration,
the one all-embracing, the other ambiguous and hedged with

[1] op. cit., chs. IV–V.
[2] T. E. Lawrence described him as 'the imaginative advocate of unconvincing
world-movements' (*Seven Pillars of Wisdom*, 58).
[3] Barbour, op. cit., 54 f., 64 f.

reservations. The Zionists have always persisted in interpreting the Declaration in the terms of their original proposal: as recently as August 1946 an official Jewish Agency spokesman claimed that 'the promise to the Jews of the whole of Palestine on both sides of the Jordan was implied in the Balfour Declaration'.[1]

The Army authorities in Palestine did their best to keep the news of the Declaration from the 'non-Jewish communities', i.e. the Arabic-speaking Muslims and Christians who then constituted 90 per cent. of the population; but a report of it reached the Sharif Husain, who with some concern asked Britain for an explanation. The government informed him that its support of the Zionist aspirations went only 'so far as is compatible with the freedom of the existing population, both economic and political'. This promise satisfied the Sharif, and early in 1919 his son Faisal reached with Weizmann a provisional agreement over Zionism in Palestine, subject however to the confirmation by the Powers of the Arab kingdom in Syria; 'but if the slightest modification or departure is made', wrote Faisal, 'I shall not then be bound by a single word of the present agreement.' At this stage the Palestine Arabs had never been consulted; they had given no mandate to Faisal to negotiate on their behalf; and his agreement with the Zionist leader could not be considered binding on anyone but himself and his father.

At the end of the War the political aspirations of the Zionists, kindled by the realization at last of their ancient hopes of returning to the Land of Promise, were heightened by the pressure exerted on Jews to emigrate in large numbers from the highly nationalistic Eastern European states which had emerged from the wreckage of the Austrian and Russian empires;[2] and they were still further encouraged by the pronouncements of such responsible statesmen as President Wilson, Lloyd George, Smuts, and Balfour in favour of an eventual Jewish state or commonwealth. The ignorance of these statesmen with regard to the rise of Arab nationalism was profound, and they apparently thought of the Arabs of Palestine (in so far as they were aware of their existence) as mere Bedouin, as little worthy of consideration as the American Indians, the Bantu, or any other politically unorganized and inarticulate race

[1] *Palestine Post*, 2 August, 1946. It has been well said that Zionism is not to be judged in terms of logic and politics, but as an intense emotional force. (Sir Harry Haig, in *International Affairs*, XXII (1946), 557.)
[2] *Round Table*, 1939, 259.
L

of 'natives', whose destiny it was to give place to the colonization of more 'progressive' peoples. At the Peace Conference, Dr.
Weizmann could state his movement's aspirations in the unequivocal words, 'To make Palestine as Jewish as England is
English or America American'; and a volume issued by the
promoters of the Zionist Foundation Fund (Keren ha-Yesod)
declared: 'The object of the modern Jewish pioneer in Palestine is
to prepare room and work for the thousands and millions who wait
outside.' 'The potency of Zionism swept like a tide over all the
types of Jew on whom Britain's original assumption (the recon-
cilability of Jew and Arab) had been based—the religious Jews who
had always lived unobtrusive lives in the holy cities of Palestine;
the pre-war agriculturalists who spoke Arabic and employed
Arabs; and the farseeing scholarly Jews who thought that the
surest way of fulfilling the Messianic promise was to join with the
local population in forming a covenant of peace. Zionism
brushed aside every consideration that did not contribute to the
immediate increase of the National Home.'[1]

The Arab reaction to the exuberance of the Zionist 'invasion'
was swift. Mark Sykes, who revisited the country in 1919 was,
in spite of his earlier enthusiasm, 'shocked by the intense bitterness
provoked there'. The King-Crane Commission, which toured
the Fertile Crescent in 1919 on the instructions of President
Wilson to test the reactions of the population to the proposed
mandatory arrangements, 'began their study of Zionism with
minds predisposed in its favour. . . . They found much to approve
in its aspirations and plans, they had warm appreciation for its
devotion, and its success by modern methods in overcoming great
natural obstacles. . . . Nevertheless, actual facts drove them to
recommend a serious modification of the extreme Zionist programme of unlimited immigration. . . . The fact came out re-
peatedly in the Commission's conference with Zionists that they
look forward to a practically complete dispossession of the present
non-Jewish population of Palestine by various forms of purchase.
More than 72 per cent. of the petitions received by the Commission in the whole of Syria were against the Zionist programme.
The whole non-Jewish population of Palestine was emphatically

[1] Elizabeth Monroe, *The Mediterranean in Politics*, 58. The pre-war Zionists
had had a characteristically self-centred and misleading slogan, 'The people
without a land for a land without a people' (James Parkes, *The Emergence of the
Jewish Problem*, p. vii).

against the entire Zionist programme. No British officer consulted by the Commission believed that the Zionist programme could be carried out except by force of arms. Officers generally thought that a force of not less than 50,000 soldiers would be required even to initiate the programme.' The American government pigeon-holed the Commission's Report, and it was published unofficially only after Wilson had relinquished the Presidency.

In their intense and passionate enthusiasm and zeal to rebuild their National Home the Zionists in Palestine struck out wildly against anyone who made objections to their extreme demands, anyone who imposed a brake on their dynamic career. Sir Ronald Storrs who became Military Governor of Jerusalem in 1918 with a sincere sympathy for Zionism, has written, 'From the beginning we encountered a critical Zionist press, which soon developed into pan-Jewish hostility. We were inefficient, ill-educated; those with official experience strongly pro-Arab, violently anti-Zionist, even anti-Jewish.'[1]   Their incomprehension and intolerance for the British officers who were administering the country extended also to its Arabic-speaking inhabitants. The Anglo-American Committee of 1946 has impartially summed up their attitude: 'Too often the Jew is content to refer to the indirect benefits accruing to the Arab from his coming, and leaves the matter there. Passionately loving every foot of Eretz Israel, he finds it impossible to look at the issue from the Arab point of view, and to realize the depth of feeling aroused by his "invasion" of Palestine. He compares his own achievements with the slow improvements made by the Arab village always to the disadvantage of the latter; and forgets the enormous financial and educational advantages bestowed upon him by world Zionism. When challenged on his relations with the Arabs, he is too often content to point out the superficial friendliness of everyday life in town and village—a friendliness which indubitably exists. In so doing, he sometimes ignores the deep political antagonism which inspires the whole Arab community; or thinks that he has explained it away by stating that it is the "result of self-seeking propaganda by the rich effendi class". It is not unfair to say that the Jewish community in Palestine has never, as a community, faced the problem of co-operation with the Arabs. It is, for instance, significant that, in the Jewish Agency's

[1] *Orientations*, 359 ff.

proposal for a Jewish State, the problem of handling one and a
quarter million Arabs is dealt with in the vaguest of generalities.[1]
As a shrewd observer had concluded earlier, 'Seeing the Jews and
hearing their arguments in Palestine, even an admirer of their great
gifts is forced to the conclusion that they are politically an obtuse
people—that the very characteristics which give them such force as
preservers of a race, a religion, or a business are a hindrance in
social intercourse, or in the give-and-take of democratic politics.'[2]

From the beginning they have never been prepared to concede
any validity to the growing Arab nationalist movement. Though
provincial Palestine had played a smaller part in the movement
than the cities of Syria, the young Awni Abdul Hadi, members of
the Nashashibi family of Jerusalem and other Palestinian notables
had been prominent in the nationalist secret societies, and some had
suffered death under Jemal Pasha. The Muslim community was
divided into two great clan-partisanships, the Husainis and the
Nashashibis. 'In the face of Zionism Husainis might be said to
represent Church and extreme Arab nationalism, Nashashibis
State and making the best of a bad job.'[3] Sir Herbert Samuel as
High Commissioner sought to moderate the Husainis by appointing the most active of their younger members Mufti of Jerusalem
and head of the Supreme Muslim Council; 'and in fact Hajj Amin
was for years denounced by extremist Arab politicians as a British
agent.'[4] The Nashashibis, in spite of holding for years the
Mayoralty of Jerusalem, were conscious that their influence in the
country as a whole was less than that of the Husainis, and sought to
redress this inferiority by a loose alliance with the Zionists, receiving some encouragement from their middle-class elements.
The Zionist leftists, however, sought from the first to drive a wedge
between the Arab ruling-class as a whole, stigmatizing them as
'feudal exploiters', and the unorganized and inarticulate fellahin[5]
and town-labourers, holding out promises of material benefits to
the former and trade-union organization to the latter. The Arab
Rebellion of 1936–9 showed the Zionists that their efforts to
divide the Arabs had almost completely failed, and they have

[1] Ch. VIII, paras. 4–5.
[2] Eliz. Monroe, op. cit., (1938), 59 f.
[3] Storrs, op. cit., 401 f.
[4] Barbour, op. cit., 130.
[5] F. H. Kisch, *Palestine Diary* (1938), Index, s.vv. Nashashibi; Dajani;
Peasants' Party.

subsequently tended to speak plainly to the Arabs as a whole. At a May-Day rally in 1946 the labour-leader Mrs. Golda Meyerson, now head of the Jewish Agency's Political Department, 'told the Arab labourers and fellahin that no force would swerve the Jewish people from their goal'. Three months later the Zionist Labour party Mapai, the strongest Jewish party in Palestine, passed a resolution at its annual conference 'appealing to the Arab people and assuring them that the Jewish people were ready to co-operate as equals for the peaceful development of Palestine. At the same time, all measures intended to destroy the Zionist programme would be fought.'[1] The Zionists may be perfectly right in supposing that the only language the Arabs understood is the language of force. They are behaving as colonists have always behaved towards an indigenous population less well equipped with material and intellectual resources. But the fact remains that this *is* the language of force, not the language of conciliation; and it contrasts curiously with Dr. Weizmann's habitual gesture of 'stretching out his hands to the Arabs in friendship'.[2]

Finding that the Arab masses still preferred to follow their own ruling-class rather than their Zionist mentors, and that their efforts to divide the Arab community met with little success, the more moderate Zionists criticized the Palestine Government for not suppressing the Arab extremists.[3] The extreme Zionists, however, reacted by creating a myth, which they still ventilate with assiduity and versatility, that there is at bottom no clash of interests between Arab and Jew, and that the discord between them is entirely a product of British machinations. While Zionist allegations of British hostility to their aims have been levelled principally at the Administration in Palestine, military and civil alike,[4] they have more recently, since Britain's official policy became less favourable and their own demands more extreme, attacked official circles at home also. The London correspondent of the *Palestine Post* has pilloried the 'official caste, deeply committed to policies which treat the East as an area hitherto unspoilt by the hideousness of the twentieth century, and if possible to be kept in a state of pristine purity for the benefit of all that is most decorative in Arab and most

[1] *Palestine Post*, 10 September, 1946.
[2] e.g. *Palestine Post*, 19 June, 1946.
[3] Kisch, op. cit., 19, and Index, s.v. Officials, Attitude of British.
[4] Storrs, op. cit., 362, makes a frank appreciation of anti-Zionist sentiments in the Military Administration.

snobbish in British, society.'[1]   A more candid admission comes, as
so often, from a Jewish Revisionist:[2] 'It is to be assumed that a
clash between Jews and Arabs in Palestine would have taken place
even without any prompting from the British administration.
The Jews wanted Palestine for a Jewish state.   The Arabs would
sooner or later object to that. . . . . There had to come a psychological clash between the Jew and the Arab, a clash between the
Jewish immigrant and the British colonial official. . . . A clash
between Jewish dynamics and dormant Arabia was inevitable.'

From the outset, the atmosphere of total lack of understanding
and sympathy, mistrust and suspicion, steadily darkened. Denied
the independence which they believed had been promised to them,
the Arab ruling-class was not slow to retaliate against the Jews
whom they held responsible. The scene was set for the agitator and
the killer; and at Easter 1920 occurred the first of the many communal riots that have disgraced the Holy Land. The Chief Ad-
ministrator reported, 'I can definitely state that when the strain
came the Zionist Commission did not loyally accept the orders of
the Administration, but from the commencement adopted a
hostile, critical, and abusive attitude. It is a regrettable fact that,
with one or two exceptions, it appears impossible to convince a
Zionist of British good faith and ordinary honesty. They seek, not
justice from the military occupant, but that in every question in
which a Jew is interested, discrimination in his favour shall be
shown. . . . In Jerusalem, being in the majority, they are not
satisfied with military protection, but demand to take the law into
their own hands; in other places where they are in a minority they
clamour for military protection. . . . The representative of the
Jewish community threatens me with mob law, and refuses to
accept the constituted forces of law and order. . . . My own
authority and that of every department of my Administration is
claimed or impinged upon by the Zionist Commission. . . . This
Administration . . . has strictly adhered to the laws governing the
conduct of the military occupant of Enemy Territory, but that has
not satisfied the Zionists, who appear bent on committing the
temporary military administration to a partialist policy before the
issue of the Mandate. It is manifestly impossible to please partisans

[1] George Lichtheim, 4 June, 1946.
[2] Eliahu Ben-Horin, The Middle East: Crossroads of History, 132. For an explanation of the term Revisionist, see below, p. 179f.

who officially claim nothing more than a "National Home", but in reality will be satisfied with nothing less than a "Jewish State".' The Zionists promptly countercharged that, on account of the sympathy of some members of the military administration for the Arabs, there had been dilatoriness in suppressing the outbreak. The Lloyd George government abolished the military administration and replaced it by a civil one, with the Mandate as its charter.

It is illuminating that in the Mandate the only reference to the predominantly Arabic character of the population was still merely indirect, in the article which recognized Arabic as one of the three official languages.[1] The first High Commissioner Sir Herbert Samuel was, if not himself a Zionist, very sympathetically disposed to Zionism as he then understood it.[2] It must be said, however, that during his tenure of office he was conspicuously impartial, to the point of being strongly criticized by extreme Zionists for being pro-Arab. In 1921 he was violently denounced by the Zionist Congress for having recommended immigration 'within the limits fixed by the numbers and interests of the present population' to develop the country 'to the advantage of all its inhabitants'.[3] Another and more serious outbreak of Arab violence in 1921, arising out of a May-Day riot between two Jewish labour factions, was followed by the first of the many Inquiry Commissions which have visited Palestine. This Haycraft Commission declared that the Zionist Organization had 'desired to ignore the Arabs as a factor to be taken into serious consideration, or else has combated their interests to the advantage of the Jews', and that it had 'exercised an exacerbating rather than a conciliatory influence of the Arab population of Palestine, and has thus been a contributory cause of the disturbances'. In reply to Zionist arguments that Arab antagonism was directed more against British rule than against themselves, and had been artificially stimulated among the uneducated mass of the Arab population by the effendis, it declared that 'feeling against the Jews was too genuine, too widespread, and too intense to be accounted for in the above superficial

---

[1] Elsewhere the Arabs were described as 'the existing non-Jewish communities' (in the Preamble, quoting the Balfour Declaration); 'the inhabitants of Palestine, irrespective of race and religion' (Art. 2); 'other sections of the population' (Art. 6).

[2] Hyamson, op. cit., 131.

[3] Storrs comments, 'I cannot conceive that any Gentile High Commissioner could have weathered the storms of Zionist public opinion for five years.' (op. cit., 358, 392).

manner. If it means that had it not been for incitement by the notables, the effendis and the sheikhs, there would have been no riots, the allegation cannot be substantiated. . . . Any anti-British feeling on the part of the Arabs that may have arisen in the country originates in the association of the Government with the furtherance of the policy of Zionism.'

Concerned at the continued unrest, the Cabinet resolved to make a new definition of its policy, which appeared in the 'Churchill White Paper' of 1922. While affirming that the place of the Jews in Palestine was 'of right and not on sufferance', it marked a definite recognition of the hard facts of the situation, in that it did for the first time acknowledge the existence of the Arabs as such. It remarked that 'unauthorized statements have been made to the effect that the purpose in view is to create a wholly Jewish Palestine. . . . H.M. Government regard any such expectation as impracticable and have no such aim in view. Nor have they at any time contemplated . . . the disappearance or the subordination of the Arabic population, language, or culture in Palestine. They would draw attention to the fact that the terms of the (Balfour) Declaration referred to do not contemplate that Palestine as a whole should be converted into a Jewish National Home, but that such a home should be founded *in Palestine*.' The White Paper introduced for the first time the principle of 'economic absorptive capacity' as a regulator of immigration. It proposed to set up a Legislative Council, but this was boycotted by the Arabs, who refused to recognize the validity of the Mandate. The composition of the proposed Council was indeed distinctly weighted against the Arabs, since, though Muslims and Christians combined still constituted 89 per cent. of the population, their ten elected members could be outvoted by the ten official members and the two elected Jewish representatives. A proposal to set up an Arab Organization with an official status comparable with that of the Zionist Organization was also rejected by the Arabs, 'since its members were to be nominated by the High Commissioner, himself a Zionist, and the offer was conditional on its being understood that acceptance signified the settlement of all Arab claims, together with Arab recognition of the Balfour Declaration.'[1]

For the next six years a sullen but superficially quiet status quo was maintained. By 1926 it had been possible to reduce the gar-

[1] Barbour, op. cit., 111.

rison, and entrust internal security to the R.A.F., to disband the British gendarmerie, and cut down the police. By 1928 the Jewish population had risen to 150,000, about two and a half times what it had been at the end of the War, and now amounted to 16 per cent. of the population. Jewish agricultural settlement had made marked progress, thanks to the boundless enthusiasm and devotion of the Pioneers; but funds for development were scarce, the economic situation difficult, unemployment rife, and in 1927 Jewish emigration exceeded immigration by 2,300. The Arab population also had rapidly increased in numbers, thanks to the very high birthrate, the cessation of the Turkish conscription which had taken many young men never to return, the lowering of the high deathrate for which the Public Health Department of the Government may claim at least some credit, and to some illegal immigration from neighbouring Arab countries. Beneath the superficial order and progress, however, 'a conflict had been created between two national ideals, and under the system imposed by the Mandate it could only be solved if one or both of these ideals were abandoned'.[1]

★   ★   ★

The lands east of the Jordan, which had been little more than nominally administered by the Ottoman government, were administered from 1918 by Faisal's Arab government at Damascus. However, at the San Remo Conference of April 1920 this region was assigned to Britain as part of the mandate for Palestine, with the proviso, however, that 'in the territories between the Jordan and the eastern boundary of Palestine as ultimately determined, the mandatory shall be entitled, with the consent of the Council of the League of Nations, to postpone or withhold application of such provisions of this mandate as he may consider inapplicable to the existing local conditions, and to make such provision for the administration of the territories as he may consider suitable to those conditions'.[2]   Soon after the collapse of the Damascus Arab government before the French in July 1920, therefore, the High Commissioner for Palestine convened the local Arab notables at as-Salt, then the principal town of the region, and informed them

[1] *Royal Commission Report* (1937), 61.
[2] Mandate, Art. 25.

that H.M. Government intended to grant them immediate self-government with the help of a few British advisers. Local councils were accordingly set up in the four principal towns; but before any coherent administrative system could take shape, the Amir Abdullah arrived in February 1921 with an Arab force at Ma'an, which had been provisionally left within the boundaries of his father's kingdom of the Hijaz, and announced his intention of raising a rebellion against the French in Syria. He advanced to Amman, was welcomed by the local councils and unopposed by the British, and took over the effective administration. At the close of the Cairo Conference in April, the Colonial Secretary, Mr. Churchill, agreed to recognize him as *de facto* ruler of Transjordan, provided that he abandoned his aggressive intentions against the French and accepted British protection and financial help in setting up a modern administration. In September 1922 Britain secured the consent of the Council of the League, as provided for in Art. 25 of the Mandate, to the exemption of Transjordan from all the clauses of the Mandate concerned with the establishment of a Jewish National Home, including the Mandatory's obligation to facilitate Jewish immigration and land-settlement. In 1923 Britain recognized the existence of an 'independent government in Transjordan under the rule of the Amir Abdullah, provided that such government is constitutional.'·

The Zionists have never accepted the exclusion of Transjordan from their potential embrace. In 1921 Dr. Weizmann told the Zionist Congress, 'The question of the eastern frontier . . . will be better answered when Cisjordania is so full of Jews that a way is forced into Transjordania';[1] and in March 1946, shortly before the announcement of the treaty in which Britain terminated the Mandate and recognized the independence of Transjordan, the Jewish Agency Executive objected to the Colonial Office that 'the Jewish people had a contingent interest in the retention of Transjordan within the scope of the Mandate'; while previously Moshe Shertok, then head of the Agency's political department, had commented: 'We have looked forward to arrangements that would make Jewish settlement in Transjordan feasible and permit joint development with Palestine, which the Jewish Agency could initiate and implement together with the Arabs of Transjordan. This would make it possible for Jewish settlement to be fostered and to improve

[1] Barbour, op. cit., 104, n. 1.

the conditions of the inhabitants. . . . We have never excluded from our considerations those great, desolate, and uncultivated stretches of land across the river which are capable of settlement and development.'[1]

*   *   *

During the war Britain had sought to protect her pre-eminent position in the Arabian Peninsula by agreements with France and Italy by which these powers undertook not to acquire, nor to consent to a third power acquiring, territory in Arabia or a naval base in the Red Sea. Britain had also from the beginning been on friendly terms with the young Wahhabi Amir Abdul Aziz ibn Sa'ud. Early in the War she, like the Arab nationalists, had sent emissaries to him to enlist his support for an Arab rising against the Turks; but the pro-Turkish Amir of the Jebel Shammar to the north, his ancestral enemy, was too nearly a match for him to give more than moral support. It was psychologically difficult for him to make common cause with the Sharif Husain, the ruler of Mecca and Madina, those centres of what the strict Wahhabis regarded as idolatrous and corrupt saint-worship unauthorized by the Qur'an and Sunna; and the Sharif made matters worse by his assumption in 1916 of the title of King of the Arabs. With his Ottoman culture and his overweening personal ambition he evidently regarded Ibn Sa'ud as a barbarian upstart, and behaved to him with 'a show of studied condescension and even discourtesy' combined with 'somewhat highhanded methods'.[2]

Turkish support for the Shammar having ceased with the collapse of the Ottoman Empire, Ibn Sa'ud was able to annex their territory in 1921, and was now in a position to settle scores with King Husain. He had already for some years been making Wahhabi propaganda among the tribes on the Hijaz border to win them away from Husain, and when Abdullah had led a force against him in 1919 had severely defeated him. He was at that time deterred from invading the Hijaz by the British government, which was still supporting Husain. But the old King, with greater consistency than worldly wisdom, broke with Britain, mainly over the political disability imposed on the Arabs of Palestine by the Balfour

[1] 24 January, 1946.
[2] Antonius, op. cit., 329,

Declaration and the Mandate. Refusing to compromise on this point, he forfeited Britain's support and subsidy. At the same time he had been misguided enough to intrigue against Ibn Sa'ud with such enemies or potential rivals of his as the Shammar, tribal chiefs of outer Najd, and the Imam of the Yemen. He became involved in an unnecessary quarrel with Egypt about the medieval sanitary conditions of the Holy Places; and in 1924 he alienated what remaining support he had in Islam by having himself proclaimed Caliph. Ibn Sa'ud invaded the Hijaz. Husain abdicated in favour of his eldest son Ali; but the Wahhabi prince in the following year drove out Ali and annexed the Hijaz. His former 'semi-vassal' relationship to Britain was now clearly out-of-date; and in 1927 by the Treaty of Jidda Britain recognized him as sovereign and independent King of the Hijaz, Najd, and its Dependencies, which were later fused as the Kingdom of Sa'udi Arabia. Ibn Sa'ud in return undertook to maintain friendly relations with the British-protected sheikhdoms of the Persian Gulf. He had already acknowledged the presence of Husain's two sons Faisal and Abdullah on the thrones of Iraq and Transjordan, and allowed Britain to determine his frontiers with these two states; but in respect of his frontier with Transjordan he has always maintained mental reservations which may yet disturb relations between the two kingdoms.

★   ★   ★

The Sykes-Picot Agreement of 1915 had arranged that the Fertile Crescent should be divided into four areas, two to be directly administered by France and Britain respectively, while the other two should be administered by Arab governments under the guidance and protection of France and Britain respectively. France's direct share was to be the Syrian coastlands and Cilicia, while her protectorate was to consist of the hinterland of Syria including the vilayet of Mosul. By 1919 British troops had however occupied the Mosul vilayet after driving out the Turks; and Lloyd George succeeded with great difficulty in persuading Clemenceau to give up the French claim, so that this oil-bearing district could be added to Iraq. The French were compensated by the transfer to them of the German quarter-share in the Turkish Petroleum Co., now renamed the Iraq Petroleum Co., and the promise that France should have a quarter-share of its output.

Britain handed over to her the military occupation of the Syrian coastlands, while the independent Arabs under Faisal still governed the cities of the interior. The situation was very unstable. The Arabs resented and feared the very presence of the French: France's part in the campaign against the Turks had been confined to the presence of a small token-force, and the Arabs could not be expected to agree that her enormous sacrifices on the Western Front entitled her to claims on Syria. The French, on the other hand, had no sympathy for the Arab Revolt or for Arab nationalism in general, having in mind their millions of Arabic-speaking subjects in North Africa; they regarded these phenomena as a British manoeuvre to trick France out of her rightful legacy in Syria. Her claim was carried back to the Crusades, in which France had played a preponderant part, and was reinforced by the educational missions, and railways and other public utilities she had established in the country. Nevertheless, over 60 per cent. of the petitions presented to the King-Crane Commission in 1919 protested directly and strongly against a French mandate.

In April 1920, one month after a 'General Syrian Congress' of nationalists had proclaimed an independent kingdom of Greater Syria, including Lebanon and Palestine, with Faisal as King, the San Remo Conference awarded France the mandate for the whole of Syria. The French now had legal authority to deal with the unfriendly Arab administration in the interior, whose troops had unofficially attacked French military positions near the demarcation-line between the two zones, while the Arab authorities had carried on anti-French propaganda, and obstructed French commerce; the French in their turn were not guiltless of counter-provocation. In July 1920 General Gouraud sent Faisal an ultimatum demanding satisfaction on all these points, and the unqualified acceptance of the French mandate for the whole country. While Faisal was attempting to negotiate, there were armed clashes between his troops and the French. The latter then occupied Damascus and expelled him from the country. Masters of the situation, they could now reshape the prostrate bulk of Syria at their will. Conscious that their main support lay in the Maronites of the Lebanon, that the other Christian communities were only lukewarm, and that they were cordially disliked by the bulk of the Muslims, they decided to ease their task by an unashamed policy of 'divide-and-rule', by exploiting and widening the religious divisions with which Syria, more than any other Middle Eastern country, is vexed. Sunni Muslim Arabs constitute about 53 per cent. only of the population of Syria and Lebanon combined. Some minorities form more-or-less compact geographical blocks: the 340,000 Maronites in the Mountain Lebanon; the 325,000 Alawis or Nusairiya[1] in the Jebel Nusairiya (Ansariya) along the northern half of the coast; the 160,000 Druze, mainly in the Jebel Druze but also in Lebanon; perhaps as many as 200,000 Kurds in the Jazira of the north-east. The separatist tendencies of all these minorities, which had un-doubtedly suffered discrimination at the hands of the Sunnis under Ottoman rule, were encouraged. In 1920 the old sanjaq of Lebanon was expanded to three times its size by the inclusion of the predominantly Muslim towns of Beirut, Tripoli, and Saida (Sidon); South Lebanon down to the Palestine frontier, with a predominantly Shi'i population; and the fertile Biq'a, with a mixed population consisting mainly of Muslims and Orthodox Chris-tians. In this enlarged Lebanon the Maronites no longer had an absolute majority as in the old sanjaq, and Christians of all sects constituted only a precarious majority.[2] This weakening of the Christian position was perhaps designed to make them more dependent on French protection and less inclined to follow a nationalist line of their own. In 1921 the Jebel Druze, and in 1922 the Territory of the Alawis, were recognized by the French as in-dependent. The remainder of Syria was divided in 1920 into the two states of Damascus and Aleppo, in an attempt to exploit the traditional rivalry between the two great cities but this experiment did not last, and in 1924 the two states were united.

Having thus dismembered the country, the French set to work to impose their cultural pattern on it in a fashion which was pas-sively accepted by the inarticulate majority, but was bound to estrange further the minority that had political aspirations. The pinning of the Syro-Lebanese currency to the French franc, though logical, had the unfortunate effect of causing it to follow the franc's severe devaluation. The teaching of French was carried to such a pitch that it was reported that in some districts children

[1] Their religion is a curious amalgam of Shi'i Islam, with early Christian and pagan elements; cf. Encyclopaedia of Islam, art. Nusairi.
[2] This they are now losing, owing to the higher Muslim birth-rate, and the disproportionate amount of emigration by Christians. (Pierre Rondot, Les Institutions Politiques du Liban (Paris, 1947), 25 ff. and sketch map, p. 32 bis.)

who could scarcely read Arabic were taught the Marseillaise. Specially-prepared history-books were at pains to demonstrate that the Syrians were not ethnically Arab. The administrative machine was frequently abused to further the interests of French companies and concession-holders. As instruments of their policy the French made great use of two minority communities foreign to Syria and without any defined habitat in the country: the Circassians, who had been introduced by the Turks fifty years before when their homeland was annexed by Russia; and the Armenians who had escaped the Turkish massacres during and after the War. The former made useful if undisciplined soldiers, especially apt for punitive expeditions and for garrisoning restive districts; the latter, with their keen intelligence and sense of superiority to other Levantines, gave good service as informers.

By 1925 the ruling families of the Jebel Druze, who had not originally been averse to French rule in preference to Sunnis from Damascus, had grown restive under their impetuous French local governor, who may be described as a French equivalent of Arnold Wilson: 'sincere, disinterested, energetic; extremely effective in putting his immediate aims into action, especially when they were related to the production of material results; but he was tyrannical in his methods, and psychologically blind in his dealings with human beings, to a degree which made it inevitable that his well-meant efforts should end in disaster. During twenty months he forced upon the outraged but intimidated Druze a host of material benefits which they neither dreamt of nor desired.'[1] Protests to the French High Commissioner met with a discourteous rebuff and the four principal Druze leaders were arrested as conspirators. This was followed by a general rising in the Jebel, landlords and tenants together, which completely overpowered the French garrison. The revolt spread to the cities of Syria, the rebels being well-organized and led by members of the great families and ex-Ottoman officers with military experience.[2] By November 1925 the French began to gain the upper hand by greatly increasing their garrison, but they did not penetrate the Jebel Druze till the early summer of 1926, and peace was not finally restored for another year. The rebellion had been even more costly in lives and

---

[1] Toynbee, *Islamic World after the Peace Conference*, Part III, sec. vii.
[2] Such as Fawzi al-Qawuqji, who was to lead the Palestine Arab rebels in 1936 and served the Axis during the Second World War.

money than the Iraq Rebellion, and the French had twice found it necessary to bombard the centre of Damascus by artillery and air-craft, killing over a thousand persons. The revolt had, however, taught the French that it was impossible to hold down Syria in-definitely by martial law. The series of military High Com-missioners was ended in November 1925, and in 1926 the first High Commissioner with civil administrative experience was ap-pointed. The Lebanese Republic had been proclaimed in 1926, and an attempt was made to reach an understanding with the more moderate Syrian nationalists, but without success; the first two nominal Presidents of Syria were both aliens, a Turk and a Cir-cassian.

★   ★   ★

B. *The Inter-War Period*

The unilateral British declaration of Egyptian independence in 1922 did not immediately bring about the end of violent agitation, since the Wafd refused to accept the limitations imposed on Egyptian sovereignty by the Four Reserved Points. Encouraged by the successes of the Turkish nationalists in extorting major con-cessions from Britain and France by armed force, the Wafd con-ducted a murder campaign inspired by well-educated fanatics and executed by weak-minded students and a number of professional killers. In Cairo four British subjects and two Egyptian moderates were murdered, and nine British wounded. The Egyptian public, intimidated by the terrorists, gave no help to the police, and it was left to a special force under British direction to track them down: three students were executed and ten imprisoned.

At the beginning of 1924 general elections had produced the combination of the first Wafdist government in Egypt and the first Labour government in Britain, some of whose members when in Opposition had shown sympathy for Wafdist aspirations. Zaghlul was invited to London to negotiate, but demanded in effect complete independence, with the withdrawal of all British troops, the return of the Sudan to Egypt, etc. This was far too much for the British government which observed that, while British troops would not interfere in the functioning of the Egyptian government nor encroach on its sovereignty, no British govern-ment could divest itself of all interest in the defence of the Canal, nor could the good administration and development of the Sudan be jeopardized. Zaghlul showed himself as inflexible as ever in negotiation, and returned to Egypt without achieving anything. Meanwhile his government had made gestures hostile to the presence of the British garrison and the position of the Sirdar, the British commander-in-chief of the Egyptian Army. On 19 November the Sirdar, Sir Lee Stack, was murdered in the streets of Cairo. On his own initiative Allenby presented to the Egyptian government an ultimatum in which the following were the principal demands:

(1) The withdrawal from the Sudan of all Egyptian officers and purely Egyptian units, which had been inciting the Sudanese troops to mutiny, with some effect.

(2) Egyptian consent to the unlimited irrigation of the Sudanese cotton-growing district of the Gazira, which had previously been limited to ensure adequate water-supplies to Egypt.

(3) Payment of a fine of £500,000.

The British colony in Egypt, prone as ever to 'Egyptophobia', was indignant at the 'weakness' of Allenby's ultimatum; but the Foreign Office instructed him to moderate the second and third of the above demands; and there is no doubt that the threat to divert Nile water from Egypt for unlimited irrigation in the Sudan has, in spite of subsequent agreement on this vital subject, left Egyptians with the uncomfortable realization that the water supplies on which their economy depends are at Britain's mercy as long as she remains in control of the Sudan.

The Lee Stack murder was the culmination of the murder-campaign, in which a number of the younger Wafd leaders[1] were charged with criminal complicity. The Wafd government fell, leaving the ground free for King Fuad to take a more active part in the country's politics. The son of Isma'il and now in the prime of his life, he had inherited enough of the autocratic spirit of his line not to accept tamely the limited authority of a constitutional monarch. As a Europeanized Turk who spoke but indifferent Arabic, he despised the middle-class Egyptian politicians of the Wafd, and their demagogic appeal to the city-rabble and the ignorant rural masses. The greatest landowner in Egypt, he mis-

---

[1] These included Mahmud Fahmi an-Nuqrashi, now Prime Minister. They were acquitted by a majority of two Egyptian judges to one British judge, who resigned in protest.
M

trusted the radical and republican tendencies of the younger Wafdists; and he was therefore ready to exploit to the full the considerable powers left to him under the constitution, especially those of nominating a third of the Senate and dissolving at will the Chamber of Deputies. Even before the Wafd came to power in 1924, he had had an unsuccessful struggle with the moderates in an attempt to enlarge his powers; and now he dissolved the Chamber of Deputies with its overwhelming Wafdist majority and ruled without a parliament through a newly-formed group of 'King's friends', the Ittihad party.[1] So unpopular was this régime, however, that the moderate Liberal party joined the Wafd in a coalition against it; and early in 1926 the new British High Commissioner pressed the King to permit the holding of a general election. It returned the Wafd to power with over 70 per cent. of the seats.[2] In view of the murder-campaign under the previous Wafd government, Britain refused to accept Zaghlul as Prime Minister; and a compromise was reached by which the Liberal leader headed a cabinet of six Wafdists, three Liberals and an Independent, with Zaghlul President of the Chamber.

In 1927 Sarwat Pasha, now Prime Minister in this coalition, came to London and the Foreign Office put forward for negotiation a draft treaty closely following the recommendations of the Milner Report. The Foreign Secretary, Sir Austen Chamberlain, described it as 'the high-water mark of British concessions to Egyptian nationalism'. The difference of views between the two sides was narrowed down to two points: (1) the British personnel in the Egyptian Army, whom Britain was prepared to convert into a military mission, and (2) the maintenance of British officials in the Departments of Police and Public Security pending the reform of the Capitulations. On this point Britain undertook to support an Egyptian appeal to the League of Nations if the reform had not been effected within five years.

At this stage, however, Mustafa an-Nahhas, who had just succeeded to the leadership of the Wafd on the death of Zaghlul, took the party into opposition to the draft treaty because it did not

---

[1] Its founder Hasan Nash'at became Egyptian Ambassador to Britain in the earlier years of the Second World War.

[2] The Wafd was, in fact, and has remained the only party in Egypt with a permanent party-machine covering the whole country: the other parties are little more than small groups centred round certain personalities without any apparent positive principles other than personal hostility to the Wafdist leaders.

amount to a complete British evacuation of Egypt. A majority of Sarwat's coalition cabinet voted against the treaty and he resigned. Nahhas now headed an entirely Wafdist cabinet, and soon came into conflict with both the High Commissioner and the King. In June 1928, three months after the formation of the Wafd government, some Egyptian newspapers published an alleged agreement by which, before they came into office, Nahhas and the new vice-president of the Chamber of Deputies were stated to have undertaken to secure the handing-over of the insane prince Saif ud-Din's estate, now being administered by the King, to the prince's mother in return for the payment to them of £150,000. The King dismissed Nahhas and issued a royal decree dissolving both Houses of Parliament and legalizing the postponement of elections for three years.

The High Commissioner, Lord Lloyd, whose conception of the British position in Egypt was as conservative as his handling of affairs was masterful, had several times come into conflict with successive Egyptian governments. The Foreign Office came to feel that their representative was in danger of over-stressing Britain's position, and in May 1929, therefore, he was sent a redefinition of British policy, which contained the following important passage: 'Because the interests at stake are of supreme importance to the safety and well-being of the Empire, H.M. Government reserved by the Declaration of 1922 certain matters for its own determination, but even in these cases it is the desire of H.M. Government to act with, and where possible through, the Egyptian Government, respecting in the largest possible measure the liberties and independence which by the same Declaration they conceded to Egypt.

'It is not in the interest of H.M. Government to intervene in the internal affairs of Egypt further than is necessary to secure the political objects defined above. The influence which they must ever possess in the councils of Egypt will be best secured by ensuring that the closest harmony shall always govern the relations between the Residency and the Government, and these conditions can only obtain if the interventions of H.M. Government into the purely internal affairs of Egypt are reduced to a minimum. . . .'[1]

[1] On three occasions between 1927 and 1930 British warships were despatched to Alexandria, twice to exert political pressure on the Egyptian government and once to be in readiness in case political disturbances got out of hand. (*Survey of International Affairs*, 1936, 663, n. 1.)

The advent to office of the second Labour government in 1929 brought the Egyptian Liberal Prime Minister Mohammed Mahmud to London to reopen negotiations, hoping for greater consideration than Sarwat had received from the Conservatives. While these were in progress, however, a general election in Egypt produced once again a sweeping victory for the Wafd, and Nahhas came to London in 1930 to take the place of Mohammed Mahmud. The Sudan proved a stumbling-block, since Nahhas insisted that, pending a final agreement, there should be no restriction on Egyptian immigration into the Sudan, while the furthest concession Britain would make was that 'the Governor-General would not exercise unreasonably the right which any government has to control immigration in the interests of its own nationals'. The Wafdist press had created the impression in Egypt that the Labour government was prepared to concede anything, and Nahhas thus had to justify himself in the eyes of the extremists by obtaining terms conspicuously better than those offered to Mohammed Mahmud. When a report did reach Cairo that Nahhas might be disposed to compromise, he was violently attacked as a traitor.

Meanwhile, mindful of his humiliating dismissal from office by the King in 1928, he had drafted two bills which would prevent the King from ruling without parliament in future. The King refused to give the royal assent to these, holding that, inasmuch as the Wafd was the only party with a country-wide organization, the diminution of the powers of the Crown would amount to the creation of a permanent Wafd dictatorship. Nahhas resigned in protest, and the King invited Isma'il Sidqi, now one of the wealthiest men in Egypt and a bitter opponent of the Wafd, to form a government. Thus driven into opposition, Nahhas began a campaign for non-co-operation with the government and refusal to pay taxes. There were serious disorders all over the country, and Sidqi dissolved parliament and prepared to 'make' an election, returning to the pre-1924 system of voting in two stages as a check on demagogy and providing for the nomination by the King of three-fifths of the Senate. He banned Wafdist newspapers and prohibited the holding of the annual Wafdist congress. This was too much for the Liberal-Constitutionals, to which party Sidqi himself belonged, and they joined the Wafd in boycotting the elections. Nothing daunted,

Sidqi formed round himself a new party, which he cynically called the Sha'b or People. At the election in May 1921 the Sha'b and the Ittihad 'King's Friends' won a comfortable majority. The Wafd tried to organize the growing Trades Union movement to make political difficulties for the government, to which Sidqi replied by dissolving the unions. In 1933, however, he had to resign, as his health had been impaired by overwork. There followed what amounted to the virtual dictatorship of the Director of the Royal Estates. Palace rule did not prove to be appreciably better for Egypt than so-called democratic rule, since public money was now poured out on an enormous civil list and other expenditure without much value to the public.[1]

The Italian invasion of Abyssinia in the summer of 1935 brought a new note of urgency to the question of an Anglo-Egyptian settlement. In December a united front composed of Nahhas, Sidqi, and Mohammed Mahmud sent a note to the High Commissioner declaring their readiness to conclude the draft treaty of 1930. The British replied, however, that in the light of the Abyssinian War the military clauses needed revision, and that it was desirable to reach a preliminary agreement on the status of the Sudan. Negotiations began in March 1936 with an all-party delegation consisting of seven Wafdists and six non-Wafdists. There was still a considerable gap to be bridged between the views of the British and the Egyptian negotiators, and the unaccommodating attitude of the British service advisers, unsympathetic as ever towards Egyptian national aspirations, called forth a reproof from *The Times*: 'It is natural enough that the technical advisers of H.M. Government should recommend such a military agreement as would achieve an ideal security for this country's interests for ever ... but the military ideal of 100 per cent. security takes no account of the political side of the question. ... An alliance, if it is to have any real value, must be based on respect for national feeling. It must be freely negotiated, not dictated; and one of its primary conditions ... is that it should be inspired by a spirit of mutual trust. This spirit will hardly be encouraged by efforts to persuade the delegates to make concessions for which their countrymen would never forgive them, in the hopeless quest for the unattainable ideal of a perfect military security for all time and in all circumstances. An alliance based upon common interests and confidence is surely worth

[1] *Round Table*, December 1936, 110 ff.

minor military risks, some of which are likely to prove imaginary on closer examination. . . .'[1]

In the end a Treaty was successfully negotiated, and signed in August 1936. It was for twenty years, but capable of revision any time after ten years. (1) Its principle was that of a close military alliance, which was to be maintained in any revised form of the Treaty until its final expiration. Each country was to aid the other in the event of war, and was to give Britain all facilities, including the imposition of martial law and an effective censorship, in the event of any threatened international emergency. Each country undertook not to conduct its foreign policy in any way inconsistent with the Treaty.

(2) Egypt recognized the vital interest to Britain of ensuring the liberty and entire security of navigation in the Canal, and accordingly granted Britain the right to retain troops in the Canal Zone, to the number of 10,000 land-troops and 400 R.A.F. pilots with the necessary ancillary services, until it should be agreed that the Egyptian forces could themselves assume full responsibility for the Canal. Egypt was to build specified strategic roads, and to improve the railways in the Canal Zone and the Western Desert. As soon as all these works were sufficiently advanced, British troops would be withdrawn from Cairo. The British Navy might continue to use Alexandria for not more than eight years. Britain would provide a military mission to the Egyptian army, which would obtain its equipment from Britain and send its specialists there for training.

(3) Egyptian troops, officials, and immigrants were once again to be admitted to the Sudan, though the Egyptian government recognized that the primary purpose of the Condominium was the welfare of the Sudanese, and that the Sudan government would appoint British or Egyptian officials only if qualified Sudanese were not available (an important recognition, for the first time, of the growing Sudanese claim to manage their own affairs).

(4) The Egyptian government would henceforth be responsible for the protection of the foreign communities, and Britain undertook to support its approaches to the capitulatory Powers to remove the restrictions on the application of Egyptian legislation to foreigners. Egypt undertook not to impose on foreigners legislation inconsistent with modern principles or to discriminate

[1] Quoted by *Survey of International Affairs*, 1936, 687 f.

against them. The abolition of the Capitulations was finally negotiated in the Montreux Convention of 1937.

(5) Britain was to be represented in Egypt by an Ambassador taking precedence over all foreign representatives.

Thus after seventeen years of fruitless negotiation, the gap that separated the Egyptian demand for complete independence and the British conception of what powers it was necessary to retain in Egypt in the interests of imperial security was bridged by concessions from both sides. But these concessions were made only because both parties were acutely aware of the menace to their respective interests from Italy, now an aggressive Mediterranean and Red Sea Power; and there was no reason to suppose that, if this menace were removed, Egyptian nationalist sentiment would not once more compel its leaders to seek to achieve complete independence by obtaining the evacuation of the British forces, freedom to follow a foreign policy untrammelled by the alliance with Britain, and the reassertion in fact of Egypt's sovereignty over the Sudan.

★   ★   ★

In Iraq the final ratification of the Treaty of 1924 was followed by a marked reduction in the number of British and Indian officials, but left in being a Dual Control whose proper working called for patience and tact on both sides. The nice relation between Iraqi officials and British advisers and inspectors was made more delicate by the fact that the British were paid more than their Iraqi nominal superiors, and that they were permanent while the Iraqis were liable to change with every government; and these changed far too frequently for good administration. Thus there was often friction between the Iraqis and British, leading to deadlocks which sometimes lasted for several months, impeding the administration and confirming the Iraqis in their opinion that the British officials were primarily interested in furthering imperial policy rather than in the welfare of Iraq. The Iraqi officials, on their side, were not yet ready to accept a western type of administration and fiscal system, democratic institutions, and the principle of government by the consent of the governed, in so far as these things varied from the methods and institutions time-honoured under the Ottoman Empire. The privileged ruling-class refused to give up the practices which they had found so lucrative under the Ottomans, and both the tax-system and the execution of the law were given a pronounced bias in their favour.

In 1925 the Council of the League of Nations was so doubtful about the fitness of Iraq for self-government that it recommended that the Mandate should continue for twenty-five years, unless she were previously admitted as a member of the League. Two years later the British government announced that it would propose the admission of Iraq in 1932 'provided that all went well in the interval, and the present rate of progress in Iraq was maintained'; it insisted, however, on a government 'friendly and bound by gratitude and obligation' to Britain. In 1928 the Iraqi government asked that it should be allowed to assume immediate responsibility for external and internal defence, and that British control of the army should cease. It rejected counter-proposals, and for three months Iraq was without a government. Sir Gilbert Clayton, the recently-appointed High Commissioner, urged the British government to break the deadlock by a declaration that would at least partially satisfy Iraqi aspirations. He died in 1929, but was the posthumous father of the Treaty of 1930, which was to come into force when Iraq was admitted to the League of Nations, and to last for twenty-five years: (1) Britain was to have air-bases at Habbaniya, in the desert west of Baghdad, and at Shu'aiba near Basra, and to have the right to move troops and supplies across Iraq by any means.

(2) In the event of war or the threat of war Iraq was to furnish Britain with all facilities and assistance, and place all means of communication at her disposal.

(3) Britain's diplomatic representative was to have precedence over those of all foreign Powers.

(4) Britain would continue to give military assistance to Iraq and send her a military mission. Iraqi service personnel sent abroad for training would normally go to Britain, and when engaging foreign experts Iraq would give preference to British subjects.

(5) Britain would sponsor Iraq's admission to the League of Nations.

The Treaty was ratified by a comfortable majority in the Iraqi parliament, and the progressive transfer of the administration to Iraqis was accelerated, though the High Commissioner had frequently to restrain an inclination to disregard British advice and cancel the contracts of British officials. When Iraq's application for admission came before the League of Nations, there was some scepticism about her fitness which was dissipated only by a British guarantee which stated that 'H.M. Government have never regarded the attainment of an ideal standard of administrative efficiency and stability as a necessary condition either of the termination of the mandate or the admission of Iraq to membership of the League; nor has it been their conception that Iraq should from the first be able to challenge comparison with the most highly-developed and civilized nations in the modern world.' Britain's argument was accepted and Iraq admitted.

In Faisal's reign 1921–33 Iraq had no fewer than fifteen governments, and twenty-one more in the four years 1933–36. All these were merely the reshufflings of a small and narrow group of professional politicians, well-to-do landowners and merchants, outside which there was no adequate class from which to draw responsible and public-spirited officials, and no substantial body of literate and informed citizens. 90 per cent. of the population was still illiterate. The government was not controlled by the Chamber of Deputies; instead it was the government that 'made' the Chamber, often during the mandatory period under pressure from the British High Commissioner. Confidential orders from the government to the provincial mutasarrifs were sufficient, except in Baghdad, to ensure the election of government candidates. In 1925 all but four of the government candidates were returned. In 1928 half of the twenty-two opposition deputies had previously been given the government coupon. Political parties were abolished as a sign of 'national unity' when Iraq became independent in 1932, and were revived only in 1946. Nuri as-Sa'id has described in an interview with an Egyptian newspaper how elections to the Chamber of Deputies have been managed: 'Nominations to the elections are arranged so as to include the names of all former prime-ministers, all ministers who were in office more than twice, the presiding officers of parliament, eminent ex-officials receiving government pensions, distinguished heads of communities and professional men, tribal chiefs, etc. These make up nearly 60 per cent. of the Chamber; the remainder depends for the most part on the will of the government in power, though such Iraqis as wish to put themselves forward may also submit their candidacy.'[1]

With the diminution and ending of direct British influence the only check on this narrow oligarchy, in which personal interest

[1] Quoted in *Middle East Times* (Jerusalem), 28 February, 1946.

prevailed over public spirit, was that of King Faisal. When the constitution was first promulgated, the King announced his withdrawal from direct participation in the affairs of state. But as time passed, acting on the advice of the British authorities, he not only resumed his place as the executive of the state but even exceeded his constitutional powers. Every Prime Minister had to choose ministers not only prepared to deal sensibly with relations between Britain and Iraq, but also with the King's personal wishes, likes and dislikes. As the point of balance between Britain and his people he had every encouragement to concentrate power within himself. The British used him as an instrument of their control and 'encouraged him to go beyond the strict interpretation of the constitution in order that their control might be more complete'. He manipulated his position adroitly to win concessions, sometimes encouraging the anti-British forces, and at others using his influence in the interests of moderation, e.g. to obtain the ratification of the Treaty of 1930. His influence was on the whole good. He initiated a scheme by which the oil-revenues were earmarked for definite development-projects, and favoured the settlement of the tribes, who still constituted about one-sixth of the total population. It is possible that if the King had not assumed the role of benevolent despot, the political system might have faltered and even collapsed entirely. Without his guiding influence it is probable that in their impatience the people would have refused to agree to the obligations imposed by Britain as the price of her assistance, in which case Britain would either have been forced to resume direct control or withdraw, delaying Iraq's achievement of independence.[1]

King Faisal died in 1933, and was succeeded by his twenty-one year-old son Ghazi. Almost immediately on his accession the country was plunged into the emotional crisis of the Assyrian incident. The Assyrians were Nestorian Christian mountaineers from the region of Lake Van, whom in their original habitat the Commission set up by the League of Nations to inquire into the incident described as 'in normal times just as truculent as the Kurdish tribes and no less savage'. In the Ottoman Empire they had been treated rather better than other Christian minorities, enjoying a fairly large measure of local autonomy under the rule of their hereditary Patriarchs. However, when the Russians invaded north-east Anatolia in 1915, the Assyrians rose in sympathy with

[1] Ireland, op. cit., 420 ff.

them as Christians. Abandoned by the Russians on the outbreak of the Revolution in 1917, some 20,000 fought their way south through the Turkish lines to join forces with the British in northern Iraq, losing twice that number en route. Some were now settled in northern Iraq and took some 'rather drastic steps' to clear the area of the existing Muslim population. In 1920 an Assyrian band attempted to establish a buffer-state on the Turco-Persian frontier, but the venture degenerated into an indiscriminate raid on both unfriendly and friendly Turks. In 1921 the British began to form the 'Iraq Levies' from their excellent fighting-men, as being the one element in the mixed population on whom they could rely for suppressing sporadic Kurdish risings and expelling Turkish irregulars from northern Iraq. In 1924 two companies of the Assyrian levies mutinied in Kirkuk, killing fifty of the Turkish townspeople. From this time onward their exploits were less remarkable, but they continued to be employed and favoured by the R.A.F. for their qualities as garrison-troops, and the Anglican Church encouraged them as a Christian minority which had suffered persecution and was, moreover, because of its ancient heresy, not protected by any other Christian church. Thus the patronage of Britain encouraged the young and inexperienced Assyrian Patriarch Mar Shimun[1] and some of their secular chiefs to presume too much, and to isolate themselves still further from the other inhabitants of Iraq. With the ending of the Mandate in 1932 the Iraqi government was ready to settle old scores with this uninvited and overweening minority. A party of 800 Assyrians crossed the Tigris into Syria in the hope that the French would allow them to settle, but recrossed and destroyed an Iraqi post. The Iraqi main body defeated this party, with wild excitement at having broken the Assyrian reputation for invincibility. The same Iraqi troops then attacked another group of 400 Assyrians, who were not at all in agreement with their leaders' hostile attitude towards the Iraqi government and had taken refuge in an Iraqi police-post. The Iraqis first disarmed them, and then murdered them in cold blood, before going on to sack and destroy twenty Assyrian villages and badly damage twenty more out of a total of sixty-four. There is little doubt that the massacre was, if not premeditated, at least arranged by the local army-officers and that some local civil officials must have connived at it. The news was

[1] He is now in the U.S.A.

received in Baghdad with savage rejoicing, as a national triumph over this Quisling minority.[1]

Young King Ghazi openly displayed his approval of the part played by Iraqi troops in this discreditable affair, decorated the colours of the regiments involved, and conferred on their Kurdish commanding-officer Bakir Sidqi the title of pasha. He thereby won immense popularity, which he tried to exploit for the manipulating of cabinets and governments after the manner of his father; but he lacked his father's personality, and government degenerated into the intrigues of political cliques. Between 1932 and 1936 cabinets rose and fell at an average of more than five a year. Then in 1936 Bakir Sidqi, who had in the meantime suppressed a tribal revolt with great ability and ruthlessness, advanced with a military force and air-support on Baghdad, demanding the dismissal of the cabinet 'with which the army had lost patience' and the formation of a cabinet of 'sincere citizens'. The existing government had suppressed newspapers, heavily bribed tribal leaders to keep the peace, curbed the opposition, and dismissed over 300 officials, many of them highly-placed. There was a general feeling that the country was making no progress; but Sidqi's principal grievance was that the army vote had been cut and that its organization was not being carried out according to his ideas. He was supported by many aspiring politicians who were out of office. In order to shake the morale of the cabinet he had Baghdad bombed from the air; and when the Minister of Defence, the honoured Ja'far al-'Askari, a veteran of the Arab Revolt, sought to negotiate, he had him treacherously murdered. There was no further opposition to the formation of a new government with Bakir Sidqi as military dictator. King Ghazi 'possibly connived at, and certainly did not disapprove' of this coup d'etat, but achieved no increase of power from it. The dictatorship showed itself no more effective than previous governments, and after the murder of Bakir Sidqi in 1937 constitutional government was outwardly restored under the same old round of politicians. But the army had tasted power and sought to hold on to it, backed up by

[1] This summary of the historical background of the Assyrian incident draws on the following sources:
Toynbee, *The Islamic World after the Peace Conference*, 483 ff.
Sir H. Dobbs, High Commissioner of Iraq, in *Gertrude Bell's Letters*, II, 551.
G. Antonius, op. cit., 365 ff.
J. Van Ess, *Meet the Arabs*, 152 f.

the young men whose imaginations and desires were kept at fever-heat by the Palestine Rebellion and the grievances of Syria against the French.

★ ★ ★

In Palestine the comparatively peaceful years that followed the 1922 White Paper were used by the two contending communities, not to seek an understanding with one another, but to improve their respective organization for further efforts, the one to establish their conception of the National Home, the other to destroy it. In 1921 the government had created the Supreme Muslim Council as an autonomous body for the administration of Muslim religious properties and the direction of the Shari'a courts; but on to this innocuous trunk there was grafted a multitude of political activities by its head, that indefatigable schemer Hajj Mohammed Amin al Husaini, a youngish man proscribed for his part in the 1920 Riots but pardoned and appointed Mufti of Jerusalem (an office heredi-tary in his family) by Sir Herbert Samuel. The Zionist Organiza-tion, which had been recognized by Article Four of the Mandate as the 'appropriate Jewish public body for the purpose of advising and co-operating with the Administration of Palestine, so long as its organization and constitution are in the opinion of the Manda-tory appropriate', had passed through some difficult years in the middle 'twenties owing to the inadequacy of its finances; but in 1928 Weizmann finally succeeded in putting through a plan for enlisting the large-scale financial support of American Jewry, non-Zionist and Zionist alike, by broadening the Zionist Organization into a Jewish Agency for Palestine. The constitutional change was more apparent than real, since executive powers were vested in the Zionist Executive with the addition of three non-Zionist mem-bers; and the latter have gradually withered away;[1] but it did have the important practical effect, once the American financial crisis of the early 'thirties was passed, of placing much larger sums at the disposal of the Zionist movement.

Meanwhile, there were some enthusiastic Zionists who were not satisfied with the pace set by their official leaders. These ex-tremists, who later crystallized as the Revisionist Party, so-called because they demanded a revision of the Mandate in favour of the

[1] Hyamson, op. cit., 121 f.

Zionists, had drawn up after the 1921 Riots comprehensive plans for an exclusively Jewish defence force to form part of the British forces in Palestine. The minds of these zealots were formed on a diet of ancient revolt—the Maccabees (whose name has been given to a widespread sport organization), the revolt of 66 A.D., and the desperate revolt in A.D. 132 of Bar Kokhba (whose memory was enshrined as a Zionist hero at least as early as 1910).[1] While these young extremists kept up their aggressive attitude, the desire of the Arab political leaders for independence was stimulated by the constitutional concessions which were obtained or foreshadowed in Egypt, Iraq, Transjordan, and Syria. The opposition of the two rival nationalisms came to a head in 1928 in the dispute over the Wailing Wall, that shrine of Orthodox Jewry which is yet Muslim property and the outer face of part of the wall of the chief Muslim sanctuary of Jerusalem, the Haram ash-Sharif, the third most holy spot in the Sunni world. While official Zionist bodies had given no offence, less responsible individuals among them had expressed their hope of ultimately winning back the Haram, the site of their historic Temple. The Muslims were therefore made even more than usually suspicious; and when some Jews began to encroach slightly on the status quo at the Wailing Wall they interpreted it as the thin end of the wedge, and the Mufti riposted with vigorous and provocative counter-measures. An attempt by the government to bring about agreement in the matter was baffled as much by Jewish reluctance to give way as by the Arabs.[2] In August 1929 there were provocative demonstrations by both Jews and Arabs. Meanwhile the Arabs had been whipping up fanaticism throughout the country, and at the end of the month there were massacres of Jews in all the mixed towns of the country. 133 Jews were killed and six agricultural settlements totally destroyed. The security forces in the country had been reduced to small proportions in the quiet years, and were now taken by surprise. There was little Jewish retaliation, though they killed seven Arabs at Jaffa and desecrated a mosque in Jerusalem. The Shaw Commission, set up to investigate the causes of the riots, emphasized the basic conflict of the two opposing nationalisms. 'Neither side have made any sustained attempt to improve racial relationships. The Jews, prompted by eager desire to see their hopes fulfilled, have

[1] Clara Boyle, A Servant of the Empire, 173.
[2] Royal Commission Report (1937), 67.

pressed on with a policy at least as comprehensive as the White Paper of 1922 can warrant. The Arabs, with unrelenting opposition, have refused to accept that document and have prosecuted a political campaign designed to counter Jewish activities and to realize their own political ambitions.' The Commission made four main recommendations: (1) A clear statement of policy with the least possible delay, including a definition of the meaning of the passages in the Mandate which purported to safeguard the interests of the 'non-Jewish' communities.

(2) A revision of the immigration regulations to prevent a repetition of the excessive immigration of 1925/6 which had resulted in considerable unemployment, and to provide for consultation with non-Jewish representatives with regard to it.

(3) An expert inquiry into the prospects of improving Arab agricultural methods, and the regulation of land-policy accordingly.

(4) A reaffirmation of the 1922 statement that 'the special position assigned to the Zionist Organization by the Mandate does not entitle it to share in any degree in the government of Palestine'.

Sir John Hope-Simpson, who was sent to Palestine to conduct the agricultural inquiry, reported very conservatively on the extent of lands suitable for development. He did agree that 'with thorough development there will be room, not only for all the present agricultural population on a higher standard of life than it at present enjoys, but for not less than 20,000 families from outside'; but pending the completion of this development he was opposed to the admission of any more Jews as settlers on the land, as tending to displace Arab cultivators. The Passfield White Paper of 1930, based on these two reports, restated the words used by Prime Minister Ramsay MacDonald a few months earlier: 'A double undertaking is involved, to the Jewish people on the one hand, and to the non-Jewish population of Palestine on the other', and added that much of the recent agitation had arisen from the failure, both by Arabs and by Jews, to realize the limits imposed on British policy by this double undertaking. A new Department of Development was to be given control of all disposition of land, and land-transfers would be permitted only in so far as they did not interfere with that authority's plans; any state land becoming available should be earmarked for the settlement of landless Arab cultivators.

It came just at a time when the reconstitution of the Jewish Agency with substantial financial support from the U.S.A. had raised Zionist hopes high. Dr. Weizmann protested that the White Paper was inconsistent with the terms of the Mandate, and resigned his presidency of the Jewish Agency and the Zionist Organization. In Britain prominent members of the Conservative opposition—Baldwin, Austen Chamberlain, Amery, Churchill—sought to make political capital out of the situation by supporting the Zionist complaints. 'The public ventilation of the controversy was an impressive demonstration of the political power the Zionists could mobilize in England.' Ramsay MacDonald, with the lack of firm resolution characteristic of the later stages of his career, capitulated to the Zionist pressure, invited the Jewish Agency to confer with the government, and eventually restated its policy to Weizmann in what the Arabs have nicknamed the 'Black Letter'. Defining itself as the 'authoritative interpretation' of the White Paper, it declared that H.M.G. did not intend to prohibit the acquisition of additional land by the Jews, since this could be done without prejudice to the rights and position of other sections of the population, nor to stop or prohibit Jewish immigration.[1]

'The first serious attempt to reduce the implications of the Balfour Declaration to terms compatible with our pledges to the Arabs had failed.'[2] The most important feature of the White Paper, the control of land-transfers, was never put into effect; for in January 1933 the Nazis came into power in Germany and a steadily increasing stream of Jewish refugees began to pour out of that country. Meanwhile the situation of the Jews in Poland and Roumania, where government and unofficial pressure to get rid of them had grown stronger since the creation of the National Home had offered an outlet, was growing steadily worse. The need of the Jews was more widespread, and in some respects more acute, than in the pre-war Russian pogroms. They naturally turned to Palestine as the only country they could enter 'as of right and not on sufferance'. Confronted with this demand for asylum the British government promptly pigeon-holed the Shaw Commission Report, with its admonition that the 1929 Riots were but a symptom of the dangerous and fundamental clash of the two rival

[1] *The Political History of Palestine under British Administration* (Jerusalem, 1947), 13.
[2] *Round Table*, 1939, 463.

nationalisms, and tacitly admitted a new principle not provided for in the Mandate, that Jewish refugees from persecution in Europe should be admitted to Palestine in unprecedented numbers. While Jewish immigration from the promulgation of the Mandate down to 1932 inclusive had averaged 9,000 a year, it rose in 1933 to 30,000; in 1934 to 42,000; and in 1935 to nearly 62,000; and these figures do not include clandestine illegal immigrants, who amounted to thousands per year. Immigrants from Poland continued to constitute over 40 per cent. of the total; but those from Germany, who had been negligible before 1929 and under 4 per cent. of the total in 1932, quadrupled themselves. Official estimates showed that by 1935 the Jewish population had more than doubled itself since 1929 and now amounted to one-quarter of the total. Statistical calculation demonstrated that if the rate of immigration of the last three years were allowed to continue, the Jewish population would equal that of the Arabs by 1952.

It was not surprising that in these circumstances the Arab nationalist leaders felt little sympathy for the persecuted Jews of Europe, failed to understand why their small country should be the principal asylum for them, and treated the nullification of the 1930 White Paper as a British breach of faith. As the Mufti later put it, 'We have had so many commissions; so much has been recommended by them in our favour; and what is the result? Over 60,000 Jewish immigrants in one year.'[1] Arab terrorists began to murder Jews, uproot their trees, maim their cattle, and herdsmen squatted on blocks of land to obstruct their sale to the Jews. The rapid increase of Jewish immigration in 1933 was followed by violent Arab attacks on government policy, alleging that its deliberate purpose was 'to drive the Arab nation away from its homeland'. Demonstrations against the government in several towns in October 1933 led to the deaths of twenty-six Arab civilians and one policeman. Meanwhile the Jewish Revisionists, who demanded the opening of Palestine and Transjordan to, not thousands but millions of Jewish immigrants, were becoming more extreme in their opposition both to Government and to the Jewish Agency, and were generally believed to have been responsible for the murder of Dr. Arlosoroff, a leading member of the Agency. In the following year Sir Herbert (now Lord) Samuel wrote, 'Everyone in Palestine agrees that the economic development is astonishing;

[1] Humphrey Bowman, *Middle East Window*, 335.

N

no one thinks that the political situation shows any appreciable improvement.' In the summer of 1935, with Jewish prospects in Poland worse and in the rest of Central and Eastern Europe no better, the Zionist Congress recorded its resolve 'to focus the energies of the Jewish people on the extension and acceleration of its resettlement in Palestine'. In November the five Arab parties, in an atmosphere of extreme political excitement stimulated by hopes of progress towards independence in neighbouring Arab countries, presented the High Commissioner with three main demands: (1) The establishment of democratic government; (2) the prohibition of land-transfers from Arabs to Jews;[1] (3) the immediate stopping of immigration.

The High Commissioner was authorized to announce that an Ordinance was to be enacted prohibiting the sale of land unless the owner kept a sufficient amount to provide for his family, and to offer the two communities a scheme for the constitution of a Legislative Council, in which the proportion of unofficial members was, as in the 1922 proposal, weighted somewhat against the Muslims and in favour of the Jews and Christians. The Council was not to be competent to question the validity of the Mandate, and the High Commissioner would be able to override the Council in certain circumstances. While the Arab leaders did not reject the proposal outright, the Zionist Congress denounced it as 'contrary to the spirit of the Mandate . . . at the present state of the development of Palestine', i.e. as long as the Jews were in a minority. In Britain both Houses of Parliament showed strong opposition, partly on general considerations of its inadvisability and partly because of the likelihood that it would operate to the disadvantage of the National Home. The Zionist press hailed the attitude of Par-

---

[1] Arab nationalist appeal has at no time had sufficient moral force to bring about, in the absence of legal sanctions, an effective voluntary refusal to sell lands to the Jews. 'Those who sold land, almost all at good prices, fell roughly into three classes: the landlord, very often an absentee, the sale of whose land raised the problem of ejected tenant occupiers; the industrious peasant, who sold part of his land and worked up the remainder on his profits; and the type who sold all his land at prices beyond his dreams of avarice, and who failed to use the substance thus acquired in a way that would keep himself and his family' (*Great Britain and Palestine, 1915–45*, 57). The Jewish Agency has generally paid compensation to the uprooted tenants, in addition to the purchase-money. Rumour adds that the Jewish organizations have made it worth the while of Arab moneylenders holding mortgages on land to foreclose and sell to them at a handsome profit, and that Arab lawyers prominent in the nationalist movement have not been above acting as brokers in land-transfers. Such venal Arabs have from time to time been murdered by extremists.

liament as 'a great Jewish victory', and indeed the debates were a 'striking illustration of the disadvantage which the Arabs suffer whenever the field of controversy shifts from Palestine to the United Kingdom'.[1] The Arabs interpreted the abandonment of the proposal as proof that they had no constitutional means of resisting their political subordination to the Jews who, at the present peak of immigration, would be in a majority within twelve years. It must have seemed to them, encouraged by the increase of violence in the whole world since the Japanese invasion of Manchuria four years before, that their only salvation lay in armed insurrection. Disturbances in mid-April 1936 began on a scale hardly greater than had been customary in recent months: two Jews were murdered by Arab bandits; on the following night two Arabs were murdered near a Jewish town, as an act of reprisal as the Arabs believed; the funeral of one of the murdered Jews led to angry Jewish demonstrations and a series of assaults on Arabs in Tel Aviv; excited by false rumours that Arabs had been killed there, Arab mobs in Jaffa murdered three Jews. At this moment an Arab National Committee proclaimed a general strike throughout the whole country until their demands of the previous November were met, and set up the Arab Higher Committee composed of all Arab parties. The strike was effective, and was accompanied by assaults on Jews and much destruction of Jewish trees and crops. The British government announced its intention to send out a Royal Commission to 'investigate the causes of unrest and alleged grievances' of both communities. Meanwhile Arab violence and sabotage increased, and armed bands appeared in the hills; among them were volunteers from Syria and Iraq. Attempts by the Amir Abdullah of Transjordan and Nuri as-Sa'id, then Foreign Minister of Iraq, to mediate between the Arab leaders and the government came to nothing. The activities of the Arab bands increased in scope and magnitude, they were joined by trained guerilla leaders from outside Palestine, and sabotage to communications became frequent and systematic. There were a few acts of reprisal by Jews, but they were quickly checked by their own authorities; and the government acknowledged the self-restraint of the Jewish community in the face of great provocation by enrolling nearly 3,000 as supernumerary constables and authorizing the acquisition of rifles as an addition to the permitted arms held in the Jewish settle-

[1] *Royal Commission Report*, 92.

ments. The British forces were reinforced to a total of about 20,000, and it became clear that the rebels could not long hold out. The civilian strikers were tiring of incurring financial losses, and the prospect of not participating in the profits of the impending orange season was an additional reason for calling a halt. In October, therefore, the strike was ended, the armed bands dispersed, and the Commission began its work. In all, eighty Jews and twenty eight British had been killed; the total Arab death-roll has been estimated at 800.

The Royal Commission's Report, published in July 1937, has been justly described as 'a great State Paper . . . direct, outspoken, incisive, showing remarkably sympathetic understanding both of the Zionism of the Jews and the nationalism of the Arabs'. After a penetrating analysis of the causes of the antagonism between them, it reached the conclusion that the promises made to Jews and Arabs were irreconcilable and the Mandate in its existing form unworkable. It therefore proposed the radical solution of a surgical operation, dividing the country into a Jewish and an Arab state, with a small residuary enclave from Jaffa to Jerusalem left in charge of the Mandatory. The proposed frontiers would have given the Jewish state (in addition to rounding off their existing holdings in the coastal plain, the plain of Esdraelon, and the upper Jordan valley) the whole of Galilee, which contained thirty times as many Arabs as Jews. It would have included initially 225,000 Arabs, or almost a quarter of all the Arabs in Palestine. The Jews would have had a precarious majority of 53.4 per cent.; but it was recommended that a part of the large Arab minority should be resettled, either voluntarily or compulsorily.[1] If, however, the Mandate were to be continued in its existing form, the High Commissioner should be empowered to prohibit the transfer to Jews of land in certain areas, and to subject immigration to a 'political high level' which should be 12,000 per year for the next five years.

The Zionist Congress authorized its Executive to enter into negotiations with the British government 'with a view to ascertaining the precise terms for the proposed Jewish state'. Ben Gurion, chairman of the Executive, explained to the press, 'The debate has not been for or against the indivisibility of Eretz Israel. No Zionist can forego the smallest portion of Eretz Israel. The debate was over which of two routes would lead quicker to the

[1] p. 391, para. 43.

common goal'; and Dr. Weizmann, defending the non-inclusion of Southern Palestine within the proposed Jewish frontiers, remarked, 'It will not run away.'[1] The Arabs, supported by the neighbouring Arab states, rejected the partition plan entirely, and asserted their right to independence in the whole of Palestine with an immediate stopping of Jewish immigration and land-purchase. The state of security deteriorated, and the Acting District Commissioner for Galilee and his police-escort were murdered by Arab terrorists; he was widely considered to have been one of the principal authors of the partition scheme. The Mufti was dismissed from his presidency of the Supreme Muslim Council; the Arab Higher Committee and all national committees were dissolved; and five prominent Arab leaders were deported. Jamal al-Husaini escaped to Syria, and the Mufti absconded in disguise to Beirut. But Arab terrorism increased, and some Jewish extremists also began to resort to terrorism, in spite of the restraint previously commanded by the Zionist leaders. In 1938 armed Arab gangs found a footing in all the main towns and rebel bands openly dominated the smaller towns. Communications were everywhere sabotaged. While heavy concentrations of British troops alone preserved a semblance of order in the northern and central parts of the country, Jerusalem and the south passed for a time entirely out of control. The active rebels probably amounted to no more than 1,000–1,500, split up in small bodies and mixed among peaceful citizens; but they had the sympathy and protection of a large part of the Arab population. Under the direction of the Mufti and the remnants of the Arab Higher Committee from outside Palestine, the Husaini faction carried on by intimidation and murder their traditional feud against the Nashashibi faction, the so-called moderates. In 1938 5,700 major acts of terrorism were recorded; casualties increased to fifteen times the figure for 1937; those killed included sixty-nine British, ninety-two Jews, 486 Arab civilians, and 1,138 armed Arab rebels. Some 100 Arabs were convicted by the military courts and hanged. Meanwhile the Woodhead Commission, sent out to prepare a detailed scheme of Partition, reported that it was unable to recommend any plan whatever: it was impossible to give the Jews a workable area without leaving an unfairly large Arab minority and the bulk of the Arab-owned citrus areas in the Jewish state, while the residual Arab state would not be economically self-

[1] Barbour, op. cit., 184 f.

supporting. They therefore suggested a scheme of economic federalism, by which the Mandatory would determine the fiscal policy for Arab and Jewish areas which would be otherwise autonomous. The British government then invited representatives of the Jewish and Arab communities and of the neighbouring Arab states, who had shown themselves increasingly concerned in the Palestine question in the past two years, to a Round-Table Conference in London early in 1939. Both parties rejected new British proposals, and the government was eventually left to announce a new policy in May 1939, when Hitler had occupied Czechoslovakia and the war-clouds were visible even to the most complacent eye.

The 1939 White Paper proposed to create an independent Palestinian state in treaty relations with Britain at the end of ten years. 75,000 Jewish immigrants were to be admitted in the first five years, after which further immigration was to be dependent on Arab consent. The High Commissioner would have powers to regulate or prohibit the transfer of land. The Paper 'declared unequivocally that it was not part of Government's policy that Palestine should become a Jewish State, regarding it as contrary to their obligations to the Arabs under the Mandate'.

The Zionists furiously condemned the White Paper as an outrageous breach of faith, claiming that it denied them the right to reconstitute their National Home in Palestine. Since its publication their vituperation of the Paper has never lessened.[1] They have never acknowledged how essential it was for Britain at this time to end the conflict with the Arabs of Palestine, and avert one with those of the neighbouring countries, in view of the impending World War.

The British parliament received the White Paper with little enthusiasm. The Labour opposition naturally opposed it wholeheartedly, and it was also strongly attacked by such strong imperialists as Churchill and Amery, presumably because they regarded a strong Jewish community as a better ally than the fickle Arabs.

In June the seven members of the Permanent Mandates Commission reported unanimously to the League Council that the

---

[1] Gershon Agronsky, the so-called moderate editor of the *Palestine Post* expressed the hope that the report of the Anglo-American Committee of Inquiry of 1946 would 'roll away the perfidy of the monstrous White Paper, a creature of funk spawned by a government dominated by a passion for appeasement'. (*Palestine Post*, 2 May, 1946).

White Paper 'was not in accordance with the interpretation which, in agreement with the Mandatory Power and the Council, the Commission had placed upon the Palestine Mandate'. It also considered whether the Mandate 'might not perhaps be open to a new interpretation which . . . would be sufficiently flexible for the policy of the White Paper not to appear at variance with it'; and the majority of four to three declared that 'they did not feel able to state that the policy of the White Paper was in conformity with the Mandate, any contrary conclusion appearing to them to be ruled out by the very terms of the Mandate and by the fundamental intentions of its authors'. The minority, consisting of the representatives of Britain, France, and Portugal, considered that 'existing circumstances would justify the policy of the White Paper, provided the Council did not oppose it'. The outbreak of the Second World War prevented the Council from discussing the White Paper, which thus remained *de facto* in force. Nevertheless the Zionists have continued to defend their opposition to it by the pretence that the disapproval of a majority of one of the Mandates Commission automatically rendered the White Paper illegal; this, although the Commission had no veto over the proposals of a Mandatory, but only the power to advise the League Council. The Mandatory could hardly afford to mark time without a policy till the end of the War. Indeed, as Dr. James Parkes, who cannot be accused of lacking sympathy for Zionism, has commented, the White Paper was not, 'as it might appear to be, a violent reaction against the policies of previous British governments. . . . From the moment when the Balfour Declaration stated that the rights of the existing population would be safeguarded, it was evident that no final solution was possible while these rights, as the population itself understood them, were ignored. The Arabs of Palestine stated their objection to the Declaration quite openly on the first occasion on which they were able. They have never wavered from that position. . . . This being so, then the only possible sequence of events was one in which the original encouragement given to the Jews was steadily whittled down in the face of Arab intransigence.'[1]

*   *   *

In Syria, after the suppression of the Rebellion of 1925/26, the French civilian High Commissioner made a genuine attempt to

[1] op. cit., 63.

allow the Syrian 'moderate' politicians to draw up a constitution. A draft was produced in 1928, but the High Commissioner objected to certain articles deemed to infringe the rights of France, and one which insisted on the political unity of Greater Syria. After many attempts to reach a compromise, the High Commissioner dissolved the Assembly in 1930, promulgating a constitution by his own act. Elections under this constitution were held in 1932, and negotiations begun for a Franco-Syrian Treaty modelled on the Anglo-Iraqi Treaty of 1930. But again no compromise could be found between French interests and the nationalist demands for a limitation in time and location on the French garrison and the inclusion in Syria of the governments of the Jebel Druze and Latakia; and again in 1934 the High Commissioner suspended the Chamber of Deputies *sine die*.

In 1936, after nationalist disorders causing sixty deaths had extorted from the French permission to send a deputation to Paris, the Front Populaire government came into power in France and immediately showed a more sympathetic attitude towards the Syrian demands, with the result that agreement was reached on a Draft Treaty closely modelled on the Anglo-Iraqi Treaty. It was to last for twenty-five years. There would be a close alliance between France and Syria, and France would support the admission of Syria to the League of Nations. The governments of Jebel Druze and Latakia would be annexed to Syria, but have special administrations. France would have two air-bases, and maintain troops in the districts of Jebel Druze and Latakia for five years. Syria would provide all facilities required by the French forces. France would be represented by an ambassador taking precedence over the representatives of all other powers. The existing monetary parity between the two countries would be maintained, and Syria would normally recruit foreign advisers and officials from France. A similar draft treaty was agreed between France and the more compliant Lebanon, the main difference being that no limitations were placed on the size or locations of the French forces there.

A government of the National Bloc party was elected in Syria, and exiled nationalists returned. 'It seemed as if the country were entering upon a new period of national construction under leaders whose patriotic energy had only been strengthened by disappointment, imprisonment and long years of exile . . . but the next two years saw the collapse of these hopes.' The Turkish government, which had agreed in 1921 to the inclusion under the French mandate of the sanjaq of Alexandretta with its large Turkish minority on condition that it had a special régime, now objected to its subjection to an inexperienced Arab nationalist government of Syria. A League of Nations Commission was set up in 1937 to supervise the election of a local assembly with seats allotted proportionately to the different communities. This placed the Turks in a difficult position since the population estimates showed only about 39 per cent. of Turkish-speakers; but if every elector should be 'presumed to be a member of the community to which he declared himself to belong', and if the Turks could obtain control of the police and the electoral machinery, a Turkish majority might be obtained. The Commission finally gave way to the Turkish demand for registration by declaration, apparently fair, but in reality opening the door wide to intimidation; the British representative on the Commission immediately resigned in protest. But since the Turks were still not assured of their majority, they brought pressure to bear on the French, who were anxious to preserve Turkey's friendship as an offset to Fascist Italy's threatening behaviour in the Mediterranean. A Franco-Turkish Treaty of Friendship in June 1938 permitted Turkish troops to enter the Sanjaq 'to assist the French in maintaining order'. The electoral Commission abandoned its work, accusing the French of systematic efforts, by means of arrests and other forms of intimidation, to deprive the non-Turkish majority of its freedom of voting. The Turkish troops marched in, and the final electoral lists only showed the Turks as constituting 63 per cent. of the total. A cabinet consisting entirely of Turks was formed. Finally, in June 1939, with France's need of Turkish support becoming greater as the shadow of impending war grew larger, she made a Declaration of Mutual Assistance with Turkey, in which Turkey was allowed to annex the Sanjaq.[1]

Meanwhile there was unrest in the Jebel Druze, the Latakia district, and the Jazira, where there were strong separatist movements among the minorities. Undoubtedly some of the inexperienced Syrian officials appointed by the Damascus government had acted hastily and irresponsibly in their efforts to bring about the political assimilation of these minorities, but on the other hand the separatists were encouraged by some French officials on the spot, anxious to create difficulties for the Syrian government.

[1] It was renamed Hatay ('Hittite-land').

But worst of all for the Syrian government, the Draft Treaty of 1936 had to face a formidable and growing weight of opposition in France. Besides those who were genuinely concerned over the future of the Christian minorities under a predominantly Muslim administration, there were others whose opposition to the tendency towards Syrian independence was less disinterested; and their influence on French policy was greater after the fall of the Front Populaire government. Moreover, the growing tenseness of the international situation made the French increasingly reluctant to weaken their strategic position in the Levant. Towards the end of 1938 the French Foreign Minister assured the Syrian Prime Minister, in return for new guarantees of French and minority interests, that the Treaty would be ratified before 31 January 1939; but a month later he yielded to the opposition of the Foreign Affairs Commission, and announced that the government did not intend for the present to ask parliament to ratify. Six months of deadlock between the nationalists and the French followed; and in July 1939 the High Commissioner once more suspended the Syrian constitution and appointed a council of directors to rule under his own orders. Separate administrations were re-established in the Jebel Druze, the territory of Latakia, and the Jazira.

★   ★   ★

Thus, while the twenty-one years that elapsed between the two Wars raised the Middle East as a whole out of the stagnation in which it had lain under the Ottoman Empire, and appreciably improved its economic and social conditions under European tutelage, the progress made towards political self-determination had by no means come up to the aspirations of the nationalist forces. Egypt and Iraq had achieved national sovereignty, though with important limitations in the field of foreign affairs, and subject to the presence of British garrisons on their soil; the Syrian nationalists had continually been frustrated of their hopes, most sharply in the last year when sovereignty seemed within their grasp; and whatever economic and social progress the Arabs of Palestine had made under the Mandate, their political status had been markedly worsened by the rapid increase in the Jewish immigrant community, for whose sake Palestine was subjected to crown-colony government with no direct authority for Arab politicians and no opportunity for men of talent and ambition to rise higher than very secondary positions in the administration. The states which had achieved full political independence were those on the outer edge of the Middle East: Turkey, Persia, Sa'udi Arabia, Yemen, under their autocratic rulers Mustafa Kemal Ataturk, Riza Shah, Ibn Sa'ud, and the Imam Yahya;[1] and even these, in ascending order, were hampered in their dealings with greater Powers by their economic weakness and the social backwardness of their peoples.

[1] Imam Yahya of the Yemen was murdered in a rising of 'progressive' elements in February, 1948; but the Crown Prince Ahmed succeeded in re-asserting his authority in the following month (cf. *Times* editorial, 16 March, 1948).

CHAPTER VII

The Second World War and After [1]

THE DENIAL of independence to the Arab populations of Palestine and Syria had created intense feeling against Britain and France, not only in these countries but among the politically-conscious younger generation in Egypt and Iraq also. In all these countries the rapid extension of a superficial education along Western lines had greatly widened the cleavage of opinion which naturally exists between middle-aged parents and their adolescent offspring. The young men resented the fact that political power in their own countries remained in the hands of the elderly, who were slow to admit the claims of the young to participate. The nationalists of the older generation had organized the young students and secondary-schoolboys for political agitation against the inhibiting Western imperialisms in such movements as the Wafdist Blueshirts in Egypt; and now the young men were themselves forming new extremist organizations which exalted the principle of devotion to a Leader on distinctly Fascist lines. Among such extremist organizations were the Misr al-Fatat or Young Egypt, also known as the Greenshirts, founded by the lawyer-demagogue Ahmed Husain; the Syrian National Party, founded by Antun Sa'adi, which drew its membership mainly from Lebanese who desired reunion with Syria; the Syrian League of National Action; and the Arab Club of Damascus, founded by a young dentist educated in Germany. In Iraq especially the great influence of the Army in public affairs, which reached a peak under the dictatorship of Bakir Sidqi but remained important down to the outbreak of war, stimulated the youth to the formation of extreme nationalist organizations run on militarist lines.

The Axis Powers were not slow to exploit this favourable situation. It appears that they had reached an agreement that the Levant and Egypt fell within the Italian sphere of interest, while

[1] The writer is now engaged in a detailed study of the Middle East in this period.

Iraq and Persia should come under the influence of Germany. From 1935 Radio Bari devoted itself through its broadcasts to inciting the Arab world against Britain, especially over the raging question of Palestine. The Italians had built up a powerful propaganda organization in Egypt, working under the auspices of the Italian Legation and through the medium of the 60,000 Italian inhabitants of the cities of Lower Egypt, who were brought under the aegis of the Fascist organizations; there can be no doubt that they were also used to spy on British activities. Having completed the conquest of Abyssinia in 1936, Italy proceeded to build up her strategic position against Britain in the Southern Red Sea. She fortified the port of Assab in southern Eritrea and, by playing on the suspicions of British policy in Aden in the mind of the Imam of the Yemen, persuaded that conservative monarch to admit into his country an Italian medical mission which was a convenient cover for anti-British propaganda and espionage. During the Palestine Rebellion both the German Protestant (Templar) colonies and some Italian Catholic orders extended their protection and material help to the Arab rebels, and some arms and money were smuggled in to them from the Axis Powers.[1] In 1938 the German radio took over from the Italians the broadcasting of anti-British propaganda in Arabic. In Iraq the German Minister, Dr. Grobba, was assiduous and open-handed in cultivating the young nationalists. Germans played cleverly on the Persians' hatred of both Britain and Russia and flattered their boundless vanity by emphasizing their Aryan origins. German propaganda films were provided free, and were believed to have amounted to 40 per cent. of all films shown in Persia. The Lufthansa obtained permission to land at Tehran on their Berlin–Tokyo route. Persian students, like those of the Arabic-speaking countries, were tempted by low fees to finish their studies in German universities; and in 1939–40 a number of German university lecturers and directors of technical institutes were imported into Persia. Leading Nazi personalities, such as Goebbels, Schacht, General von Blomberg, and Baldur von Schirach, paid official visits to Middle Eastern capitals.

In spite of this propaganda campaign the immediate reaction of the Middle Eastern countries to the outbreak of war was not unsatisfactory to Britain and France. Egypt and Iraq immediately

---

[1] Though the extent of this aid has probably been exaggerated by Zionist propaganda. (Barbour, op. cit., 192; *Great Britain and Palestine*, 1915–45, 119).

broke off diplomatic relations with Germany; the Arab Rebellion
in Palestine, already in its dying struggles, ceased with the arrival
of a cavalry division and other troops in the autumn of 1939; and
the Syrian nationalists were firmly repressed. The months of the
'Sitzkrieg', however, confirmed the idea, already prevalent in
Middle Eastern political circles, that this war between European
powers was none of their business.   The German invasion
of France, the entry of Italy into the war, and the capitulation
of France, leaving the small British forces in the Middle East
denuded of the support of the 100,000 French troops in the
Levant States, brought the war to the threshold of the Middle
East in one bound.   By this time the Allied disasters of that
dreadful summer and the isolation of Britain had not surpris-
ingly shaken the confidence of the Middle Eastern politicians
in her ability to survive. In Iraq the weak-willed Prime Minister
Rashid Ali al Qilani was merely the catspaw of four ambitious
colonels nicknamed the 'Golden Square', while a shadow-
cabinet of Palestinian extremists was directed by the hostile
Hajj Amin.   Freya Stark vividly describes how she encountered the Mufti in his hotel and saw 'little good, and certainly
nothing disinterested in that face. . . . He sat there all in white,
spotless and voluminous, wearing his turban like a halo; his eyes
light, blue, and shining, with a sort of radiance, like a just-fallen
Lucifer'.[1]   In these circumstances the Iraqi government refused to
break off diplomatic relations with Italy; and as the Battle of Britain
raged, 'the highest military authorities were openly broadcasting
to the Iraqi people that their army and air-force had the glorious
mission of renewing the heroic days of the Arab conquests and the
Crusades, and of liberating the oppressed brethren of Syria and
Palestine from the servitude imposed on them by Europe and the
Jews'.[2]

    In Egypt the British Embassy and military authorities had
reason to suspect the Prime Minister Ali Mahir, son of that
Mahir Pasha whom Cromer had caused to be removed from
office as Under-Secretary for War as 'a bad adviser, a cause of strife,
and an obstacle to harmonious co-operation' between Britain and
the young Khedive Abbas II.[3] Following in his father's footsteps,

[1] *East is West*, 143.
[2] *Round Table*, 1941, 705.
[3] Lord Cromer, *Abbas II*, 50–59.

Ali Mahir had acquired great influence over the young King Faruq, who since his accession in 1936 had taken growing offence at the authority and the personal attitude to him of the British Ambassador Sir Miles Lampson (now Lord Killearn).[1] It now appeared that the Prime Minister was actively encouraging the King to adopt a policy of reinsurance with the Axis Powers in view of the impending defeat of Britain, and he resisted British requests for the breaking-off of diplomatic relations with Italy. Such conduct in a country so vital for her imperial strategy could not be tolerated in this crisis of British fortunes; and in June 1940 pressure was exerted to obtain the dismissal of Ali Mahir's cabinet and its replacement by one more ready to co-operate. That the British suspicions were not without grounds was demonstrated some months later, when the columns advancing into Cyrenaica in Wavell's push captured on an Italian general a highly secret letter addressed by the G.O.C. British Troops in Egypt to the Egyptian Minister of Defence and discussing the defence of the Siwa Oasis, which had been entrusted to an Egyptian unit. The British authorities concluded that the Italians had obtained the letter before the departure of the Italian Legation staff, and accordingly suspected Ali Mahir and his 'inner cabinet'— Salih Harb, the Minister of Defence, and Aziz Ali al-Misri, the Chief of Staff—of being responsible for the leakage. The Egyptian authorities subsequently held an enquiry which purported to vindicate these persons, claiming that it was not established whether the leakage had occurred on the British or the Egyptian side.

Although Egypt did not declare war against the Axis, her army did assist in the defence of the Western Desert and in the anti-aircraft defence of the Canal Zone and the cities of Egypt; and in April 1941, stimulated by General Wavell's winter success in routing the Italian armies in Cyrenaica with a force only a fraction of their size, the Egyptian government accepted British representa-

[1] The remarks of Lord Lloyd on the relations between Lord Cromer and Abbas II apply with curious exactness to those between Lord Killearn and King Faruq fifty years later: 'There was a considerable school of thought which held, and not without some justification, that the Khedive was what he was largely because of the method which Cromer had used towards him. It was argued that at his accession Abbas's position vis-à-vis the overshadowing position of the great Consul-General had been one of great difficulty for a young and sensitive ruler, and that by no means enough had been done to help and encourage him.' (*Egypt since Cromer*, I, 71 f.)

tions that the consulates of such neutral, but unfriendly Powers as Japan, Hungary, Roumania and Bulgaria in such strategic centres as Alexandria, Port Said, and Suez were nests of espionage, and closed them down.

But the easy optimism engendered by Britain's swift liquidation of the grandiose Italian African empire in 1940/1 was soon to be rudely awakened. In April 1941 Germany struck at the Balkans and in one month overran Jugoslavia and Greece; at the same time Rommel and his Afrika Korps came to the help of the routed Italians in Libya and drove the British forces, depleted for the Greek campaign, back from the Gulf of Sirte to the Egyptian frontier. In Iraq, where the Golden Square and Rashid Ali had suffered a temporary reverse in an attempted coup d'etat in January, the incitement of the Mufti and his followers to a breach with Britain had been supported by the propaganda of the German Armistice Commission sent to the Levant States after the French collapse. Directed by Baron von Hentig, who had been a member of the German mission to Afghanistan in the First World War, it disposed of large sums of money and won the support of some of the Arab extremists in Syria. It apparently sent emissaries to the Mufti, who was in receipt of subsidies from the Axis through the Italian Minister in Baghdad. Early in April the invasion of Greece seemed to the conspirators in Baghdad to be the signal for their rising. How could Britain, represented in Iraq only by a small air-force and by a 'gentle, pleasant, and optimistic' ambassador with no previous experience of the Middle East, resist them? They overthrew the flabby existing government, reinstated Rashid Ali as Prime Minister, and sought to secure the person of the Regent for the boy-King Faisal II; he was however safely smuggled away by the American Minister. After this coup the Golden Square hesitated, since German help was not yet forthcoming. The newly-appointed British Ambassador, Sir Kinahan Cornwallis, with twenty years' experience of the Iraqis, seized this opportunity to secure the landing in Basra, under the terms of the Anglo-Iraqi Treaty, of Indian troops to reinforce the Middle East. When a second contingent arrived, the Iraqi government, encouraged by the German successes in Greece and Libya, demanded that the first contingent should leave Iraqi territory before the second disembarked. The British authorities refused to comply. On 1 May the Iraqi army invested the British air-base at Habbaniya with some fifty field-guns, while detachments seized the pumping-stations on the oil-pipeline to Haifa. By all normal rules Habbaniya should have fallen; but after four days' fighting the R.A.F. assisted by their Assyrian and Kurdish Levies succeeded in driving back the Iraqis, and were reinforced by a small motorized column, including the Arab Legion of Transjordan, hastily got together in Palestine and rushed across the desert. The Iraqis now appealed to Germany for help; but Hitler had decided that major operations to expel Britain from the Middle East must wait till after the launching of the invasion of Russia, now in an advanced state of preparation. The Germans were held up in Crete, whose conquest took them eighteen days instead of the two on which they had counted; and they could spare their Iraqi allies only some fifty aircraft. This was insufficient, and the Golden Square had failed to win the support of the apathetic Iraqi people. On 29 May, the British forces, still far inferior in numbers to the Iraqis, had reached the outskirts of Baghdad. Rashid Ali and his ministers, the Golden Square, the Mufti and his shadow-cabinet all decamped in haste, some to Persia, and some to Aleppo and eventually through Turkey to Axis Europe. An armistice was concluded on 31 May. Britain, pressed back on Egypt and Palestine by this premature pincer-movement of the Axis and its sympathizers, had fought back and won in the first great testing-time of the Middle East campaign. Beyond ensuring the establishment of a friendly government, she imposed no punitive terms on Iraq; but proceeded to attack the Vichy French in Syria, who had in their impotence harboured for many months the spies and propagandists of the Axis Armistice Commission, and had recently allowed German aircraft to refuel on Syrian airfields on their way to Northern Iraq, and material supplies to travel to Iraq by the Syrian railways. The Vichy French fought back grimly against the British and Free French, but by mid-July they were forced to capitulate, and under the Lyttleton-De Gaulle Agreement a Free French government was installed in the Levant States, British forces being free to operate there for the duration of the war. Meanwhile Hitler had invaded Russia. One of the only two routes by which contact between Russia and Britain could be established was through Persia, where the Germans had been steadily building up their staffs of technicians and spies during the past six months. A joint Anglo-Russian demand that the Persian government should expel them

o

met with the insolent reply that Persia was anxious to get rid of all foreigners.[1] The response to this was the joint Anglo-Russian invasion of Persia in August. The greater part of the Persian army was kept back by Riza Shah to overawe the unruly tribes who hated his tyrannical rule, and what was available was no match for the invading forces. Before September was out the avaricious old Shah had been forced to abdicate in favour of his young son. Russian and British troops occupied the Northern and Southern parts of Persia respectively, and the Trans-Iranian Railway and road-systems were extensively used for the supply of American and British munitions and supplies to Russia. The political situation was regulated by the Anglo-Soviet-Persian Treaty of 1942, whereby Persia gave the Allies full wartime facilities, and they undertook in return to withdraw their troops within six months of the end of hostilities. Nevertheless the sympathies of most politically-minded Persians remained with the Axis, and some officials continued during 1942 to intrigue with the German agent Franz Mayr, who had escaped when the Germans in Persia were rounded up for internment.

The Middle East political barometer continued to fluctuate with the changing strategic situation. By January 1942 the disasters of Pearl Harbour and Singapore, and the second British retreat in Cyrenaica before Rommel's forces, gave new encouragement to her enemies. In Egypt the government of Husain Sirri had since 1940 co-operated loyally; but having no majority backing in parliament its life was precarious and its policy correspondingly irresolute. Faced in the autumn of 1941 with a growing tide of pro-Axis and anti-British propaganda, in which the powerful and extremist Ikhwan al-Muslimin or Muslim Brotherhood organization played a prominent part, it acceded to British representations by arresting its leader Hasan al-Banna, only to release him a few days later, apparently under pressure from the Palace, which was believed to have been generously subsidizing him. A month later the breaking-off of diplomatic relations with Vichy France at Britain's request caused the resignation of the Foreign Minister, again apparently the victim of royal displeasure. In January 1942 the failure of the Egyptian authorities to break the black market and ensure a proper distribution of bread in Cairo coincided with the military disasters referred to above, and promoted a wave of

[1] Elwell-Sutton, op. cit., 186.

anti-British feeling, with students marching down main streets shouting, 'We are Rommel's soldiers'. For some time the British Embassy and military authorities had been coming to the conclusion that a stronger government in Egypt was necessary to secure the military position, and that this could only be secured by bringing back the Wafd, which had recently been growing restive in opposition. King Faruq, however, who had dismissed Nahhas from office in 1937 and was reported to be on the worst of personal terms with the Wafd leader, refused to accept him as Prime Minister and insisted on an all-party coalition under Ali Mahir, whom the British authorities obviously could not accept as Prime Minister. The young King was obstinate, and eventually on the evening of 4 February the British Ambassador and the G.O.C. British troops in Egypt found it necessary to present the King with an ultimatum: accept Nahhas or leave the country. The King yielded, the Wafd returned to office and easily secured its position in a general election. Though within a month the party's secretary, the capable but difficult Copt Makram Ubaid, and several of his supporters had seceded, apparently as the result of a personal difference with Nahhas, the Wafd government loyally co-operated with Britain in the anxious days of June–July 1942, when the Eighth Army was forced back from beyond Tobruk to the prepared position of al-'Alamein, only seventy miles west of Alexandria. In this second great military crisis of the Middle East campaign, faced clearly with choosing for Britain or the despised Italians, the Egyptian government and people stood firmly behind Britain. There was none of the prophesied sabotage and little anti-British propaganda; the only incidents were that two or three Egyptian Air Force pilots absconded to the enemy lines, and that the veteran Aziz al-Misri,[1] was detected in intrigue with two ineffectual German spies who had been introduced into Cairo via the Western Desert, and was interned for his pains. Arab Asia likewise, though apathetic towards the outcome of the war, did not choose or dare to stab Britain in the back in the perilous days of al-'Alamein and Stalingrad; and in Persia the intriguing Franz Mayr could only dream of the day when he would raise Persia against the British, and meanwhile scribble in his diary of 'those three great strategists—Rommel, Von Bock, and myself'.

[1] He had attempted to join the Iraqis in the putsch of May, 1941, but his aircraft was forced down ignominiously when only ten miles from Cairo.

As the year of trial and danger 1942 drew towards its close the picture changed. Montgomery was advancing from al-'Alamein and the Russians from Stalingrad. The movement had begun which did not stop till the remnant of the Afrika Korps surrendered at Cape Bon in May 1943. The German spies, saboteurs, and propagandists who continued to operate against the Middle East from their embassy and consulates in Turkey achieved nothing. In Tehran the British security authorities brilliantly captured two parties of German parachutists who had been sent to reinforce Franz Mayr, and eventually secured the surrender of Mayr himself and the remnants of his little band by the tribesmen among whom he had taken refuge. Apart from British plans for invading the Greek islands, the Middle East campaign was at an end; and the region could revert to its normal condition of political inflammation, exacerbated by its suppression during the war.

★   ★   ★

In Palestine the Arab Rebellion was already petering out during 1939, and in October of that year the Mufti and his entourage of extremists, no longer tolerated by the French in the Levant States, took refuge in Baghdad, from where his influence over the rebellion-weary Arabs of Palestine declined. It was hardly to be expected that the Arabs would take an active part in the war against the Axis, since many of them felt that Axis conquest would at least free them from the Zionist incubus, and few had much reason to feel any loyalty to Britain. On the other hand, they gave little trouble, their attitude remaining essentially neutral. The Jewish authorities pressed for permission to raise forces on a Jewish-national basis, but the government resisted this as it was unwilling to concede the principle of Jewish, as opposed to Palestinian nationality. Separate Jewish sub-units were, however, permitted from the start; the urgent need for man-power prompted further concessions; and the process culminated in 1944 in the creation of the Jewish Brigade with its distinctive Zionist colours. But while the Zionists co-operated whole-heartedly in the struggle against the Nazis, they continued to oppose the hated White Paper. In February 1940 the issue of the Land Transfer Regulations, denying Jews the right to acquire land in the greater part of Palestine, came as a severe blow to them, since they had hoped that the White

Paper policy might, owing to the war, never be put into effect.[1] They organized country-wide demonstrations with arson and some bomb incidents, but their co-operation in the war-effort nevertheless continued. Even the Revisionists concurred in this policy, and only a small fanatical dissident group of the latter, led by one Abraham Stern, and alleged to have contacts with the Italian Fascist government, continued their implacable terrorist antagonism to the Mandatory.

What continued to excite the whole Jewish community to still more furious protest, even with Palestine threatened with enemy invasion, was the insoluble question of immigration. The Mandatory had been compelled to limit this severely, having regard to the extreme sensitivity to this vital question of the Arabs, whose neutrality, both in Palestine and the neighbouring countries, it was essential to maintain during the war. All that the Jews saw was that thousands of their kin were thus denied a refuge in Palestine from the appalling Nazi terror in Europe; and in their horror and despair they were blind to the difficulties of the British government. The first strain came in 1940 with a succession of illegal immigrant ships from Europe, well organized on the Zionist side and encouraged by the Nazis, who saw in them a means of embroiling the British with the Arabs. The *Patria*, chartered to remove nearly 2,000 illegal immigrants from Palestine to Mauritius, was actually blown up in Haifa harbour by Jewish terrorists, causing 268 deaths among its helpless Jewish passengers. Another ship, the *Struma*, was held up in 1942 off Istanbul while the British and Turkish governments negotiated over its disposal. Before this was concluded the Turks ordered the unseaworthy and grossly overloaded vessel to return to the Black Sea port whence it had sailed. In heavy weather she went to the bottom with over 750 Jewish refugees.

These events caused a hardening of Zionist feeling in Palestine and an increased resort to terrorism. Abraham Stern had been shot in a gun-fight with the police, but some of his followers escaped from prison and continued the terror. The Revisionist Irgun Zvai Leumi (National Military Organization), which had actually assisted the British forces during the Iraq campaign of 1941, once

[1] Since the publication of the White Paper they had acquired twenty-five square miles of land in the area which the new Regulations closed to them, and the Colonial Secretary stated that he feared further unrest among the Arabs if land-restriction were not enforced.

more resumed its terrorist activities. Moreover, the official Zionist organization, under the leadership of David Ben Gurion and encouraged by the Zionists of the U.S.A., pleasantly remote from the realities of the Middle East problem, became more exacting and unequivocal in its demands, and in 1942 adopted the Biltmore Programme (drawn up, significantly, in New York). It demanded:

(1) The establishment of Palestine as a Jewish commonwealth.

(2) A Jewish army.

(3) Unlimited immigration, placed under the control of the Jewish Agency, which should also have authority for the development of unoccupied and uncultivated lands.[1] The Zionist underground army, called Hagana (self-defence), became more active. This organization traced its beginning to the self-defence organization formed by young Jews in Russia at the time of the pogroms of 1903.[2] It was transplanted to Palestinian soil before the First World War in the form of an organization of armed watchmen to guard the agricultural settlements from Arab attack. The British military authorities gave it tacit recognition and some arms during the Arab Rebellion of 1936–9, when Wingate's 'Night-Fighters' were organized from its ranks. Again in the perilous days of 1941–2 the Army recognized it as a home-guard in case the Germans broke through to Palestine. It now numbered some 60,000 young men and women, drawn principally from the settlements, who clandestinely carried out periodical training and military exercises. Some of the young Jews called up since the outbreak of war by the National Council of Palestinian Jews (Vaad Leumi) for national service were directed into the Hagana, and the thousands of Jews who were directed by the Zionist authorities into service in the British Middle East Forces continued to be under the clandestine orders of the Hagana high command. Information was now received for the first time of the Palmach, a crack force selected from the Hagana, permanently mobilized for shock-troop action, and numbering some 2,000 strong. The exigencies of the war brought the Palmach also into association with British specialist organiza-

[1] One of the foremost leaders of the principal Jewish party in Palestine, the Mapai labour party, explained to the Arabs in a book of essays, 'We shall be ready not to be your foes, and even to support your aspirations for independence, provided you cease disturbing us and provided you recognize Palestine as a Jewish State.' (Quoted by J. L. Magnes, *Foreign Affairs*, 1943, 240).
[2] *Palestine Post*, 25 June 1946.

tions, and some of its members were given commando training for action against the Germans. Many of the Palestinian Jewish troops in the Middle East Forces were employed in supply and ordnance companies along lines of communication and in base areas,[1] an admirable situation for the smuggling of arms to Palestine, to which they resorted on a large scale under Hagana direction. The organization of this 'underground railway' was excellent; there was no lack of funds and transport; and corruptible Allied and British soldiers were drawn into the racket. The difficulty of supplying the Middle East Forces by the dangerous and slow long-sea-route round Africa had caused the British military authorities to give contracts to Palestinian Jewish concerns for the manufacture of small-arms, including mortars, which they produced with efficiency; but these arms also found their way to the armouries of the Hagana. These were well-constructed underground caches, mainly in the collective settlements, though the search of Tel Aviv in July 1946 revealed arms-caches in the basements of the Great Synagogue and of a school. Ostensibly the Hagana's purpose behind all this arming and drilling was the self-defence of the Jewish community against Arab attack, such as had occurred before. the war; but the Zionist leaders made it clear that the self-defence of the community included resistance to any limitations placed on immigration or land-purchase, i.e. resistance to the obnoxious 1939 White Paper on all points. The reports of the accumulation of illicit arms were so frequent that late in 1943 two settlements were raided by military and police in order to search them. At Ramat ha-Kovesh the police met with furious resistance from both men and women with missiles and boiling water; and the brigadier in charge of the military party, who had had wide experience of civil disturbances in various parts of the world, declared that he had never seen anything to compare with the ferocity of the villagers. It was not for nothing that Ben Gurion had exhorted the Jewish youth to prepare themselves for the fighting which would fall to their lot at the end of the war.

During 1944 Jewish terrorism increased, in spite of the indefinite extension of the now-expired five-year period in which the final

---

[1] Which does not prevent an American Revisionist from building up a myth that 'At one time 40 per cent. of Alexander's effectives were Jewish boys from Palestine. They formed the intrepid desert scouts on which Alexander relied for much of his intelligence. . . . It was a Jewish contingent which held Tobruk during the siege.' (W. B. Ziff, *The Rape of Palestine* (New York, 1946), 111.)

75,000 Jewish immigrants allowed by the White Paper might come
in. Now that the war had receded from the Middle East, the
Zionists were free to begin an all-out campaign against the White
Paper policy of strictly limited immigration and land-purchase,
and their demand was now for a Jewish State into which any Jew
who wished might enter freely. The Irgun Zvai Leumi made an
unsuccessful attempt to kidnap the High Commissioner; and the
Stern Group went one better by murdering in Cairo the British
Minister-Resident, Lord Moyne, who, they believed, had as
Colonial Secretary obstructed the admission into Palestine of
Jewish refugees from the Axis terror. This murder came as a great
shock to the Jewish Agency, who evidently feared drastic action
against the whole community; and they made an offer to the
British military authorities to co-operate in rounding up the
terrorists. This co-operation produced some results over a number
of months: a number of suspected terrorists were arrested and interned, and as late as June 1945 the Agency gave the authorities
information which assisted in the detection of a terrorist plot to
bombard with delayed-action mortars the King David Hotel, the
headquarters of the British forces and the government secretariat.
But this liaison between the Agency and the British was subsequently discontinued, perhaps because it was found that the
Agency was exploiting it as a means of furthering its own subversive purposes.

★　　★　　★

At the outbreak of war the French had suspended the Lebanese
constitution and, there and in Syria, dissolved a number of extreme
nationalist organizations believed to be in sympathy with the Axis,
sentencing some of their members to long terms of imprisonment.
The majority of politically-minded Syrians, like their brethren in
Palestine, decided that there was nothing to choose between oppression by a democracy and that exercised in the name of Fascism;
and consequently the general attitude towards the war was one of
apathy and scepticism towards both sides, though some flirted with
the Axis Armistice Commissions and a few committed themselves
more deeply.

On the first day of the Allied invasion of the Levant States in
1941, the Free French General Catroux proclaimed that he had

come to put an end to the mandatory régime and declare Syria and Lebanon free and independent. But the Free French reluctantly allowed nationalist exiles to return; they made no constitutional concessions beyond a formal declaration of independence; and the Syrian and Lebanese governments were filled with French puppets. There was no change in the methods, and little change in the personnel, of the French administration. In the spring of 1943, however, the French permitted the holding of elections, which resulted in Syria in an overwhelming victory for the National Bloc led by Shukri al Quwwatli, and in Lebanon for a complete defeat of the French-supported Lebanese separatists led by Émile Edde. The elections were thus a signal defeat for the French, and it was to be expected that the new governments would not be slow to attack the French limitations on their independence. The French Committee of National Liberation, the acting French government in Algiers, insisted, however, that no radical changes could be made without the approval of the League of Nations, which had authorized the original mandate, or its successor; and that any concessions by France depended on the conclusion of treaties recognizing her special position and interests. It was indeed difficult for the French Committee, which still had to justify to the forty million Frenchmen under German occupation its claim to speak in the name of France, to sign away at this stage any of the hard-won and jealously-guarded rights of France in the Levant; and it was equally hard for the two nationalist governments of Syria and Lebanon to admit any further limitation of the sovereignty for which they had struggled for a generation. The first challenge came from the Lebanese government led by Riyadh as-Sulh, which in November 1943 unanimously voted amendments to the constitution throwing off all French limitations upon its sovereignty. The French Délégué-Général responded by suspending the constitution, arresting the Lebanese president and the majority of the cabinet, and appointing the pro-French Emile Edde as head of the state. The townspeople proclaimed a general strike, there were bloody clashes with French troops in Beirut and elsewhere, and two ministers who had escaped arrest began to organize their retainers in the mountains into armed bands. The British government declared that it regarded the Lebanon as 'of vital importance to the war-effort both as an operational base and from the point of view of communications' and was therefore 'directly concerned in any threat of a breakdown of law and order'. It accordingly brought pressure[1] upon the French to release and reinstate the imprisoned president and ministers. Having reluctantly and sulkily accepted the inevitable, the French did transfer many services to the new governments, and by the end of 1944 the only important attribute still withheld was the control of the locally-recruited Troupes Speciales, which was, however, of particular importance for Syrian and Lebanese prestige. The French made these concessions with an ill grace, and they execrated the British Minister, Sir Edward Spears, and his staff for their unconcealed sympathy with the nationalists.

Sir Terence Shone, who succeeded Sir Edward Spears early in 1945, made every effort to improve relations between the French and the local governments and bring negotiations to a satisfactory conclusion. But the French demanded the right to maintain bases and troops in both countries, apparently imagining that time had stood still since 1936. On 17 May, nine days after VE-day, a French cruiser arrived at Beirut with Senegalese troops on board. The Syrian nationalists immediately assumed that military pressure was about to be exerted on them; the French declared that the troops were merely to replace others who were being repatriated; the British made every effort to dissuade the French from disembarking them at this delicate juncture, but De Gaulle, now installed in Paris as head of the provisional government, was characteristically obstinate.[2] The situation deteriorated rapidly, riots and fighting occurred in the principal Syrian cities, and on 29 May the French repeated their exploits of twenty years earlier by bombarding Damascus with aircraft and field-guns. Next day the British military authorities received instructions to intervene and restore order. As long as the war with Japan continued, Britain could not allow the security of her line-of-communications to be threatened by anti-European disorders which might spread to other Middle Eastern countries. The French commander sulkily complied with a British order to cease fire and confine his troops to barracks, and order was restored. Relations between Britain and France were very strained, the French again accusing the British of

[1] Mons. R. Montagne declares that the talks between General Catroux and the Nationalists were at that moment progressing favourably. (*International Affairs*, XXIII (1947), 120).
[2] The French were faced at this moment by a local rising in Algeria in which 110 French citizens were massacred, and 1,500 Muslims killed in the subsequent reprisals. (R. Montagne, *International Affairs*, XXIII (1947), 47.)

having deliberately and consistently abetted the nationalists against them in order to oust France from her position in the Levant. In December 1945 the two Powers agreed to consult on the re-grouping and evacuation of French and British troops. Since, however, it was envisaged that they should remain in Lebanon until U.N.O. had decided on the organization of collective security in this region, and since the agreement entailed British recognition of French 'interests and responsibilities' in the Levant, the Syrian and Lebanese governments appealed in February 1946 to the Security Council for the immediate withdrawal of the foreign troops from both countries. Britain and France accepted an American compromise-resolution expressing confidence that the troops would be withdrawn as soon as practicable and that negotiations to that end should be undertaken without delay. The evacuation of Syria was completed in April, and that of Lebanon by the end of the year. Because, however, the Syrian government has recruited a number of British among its foreign advisers, while refusing to employ Frenchmen or even admit them to the country unofficially, the French are still inclined to accuse Britain of break-ing the spirit of the agreement between them.

★   ★   ★

Throughout the war the Jewish Agency had kept up an intense and effective propaganda-drive among the British and Allied forces in Palestine, sparing neither effort nor expense in providing them with organized hospitality of every kind, encouraging them to spend their leave in the collective settlements, and demon-strating the high idealism and devotion and the material progress and efficiency of the National Home, to say nothing of its ability to get on with the ordinary Arabs 'if they were not incited against us by the effendis and British officials'. When visitors were in a settlement, its few 'tame' Arabs were paraded for inspection, of course with a Jew to interpret.[1] While this propaganda was variously directed to all interests, imperial, commercial, liberal, and socialist, the demonstration of the collective settlements and of the large part played in the life of the community by the Histadruth trades-union organization appealed particularly to Socialists,

---

[1] The stage-management of the fellahin has sometimes broken down, with revealing results; cf. R. H. S. Crossman, *Palestine Mission*, 157 f.

especially the serious-minded, rather naive young men with a secondary-school education who were numerous among the junior officers and N.C.O.s of the British wartime army. Consequently, the Zionists were greatly encouraged by the coming to power in July 1945 of the Labour party, whose executive had only six months before declared its support for unlimited Jewish immigration, the Arabs being 'encouraged to move out as the Jews move in'. But the new government, shocked by the plunge into the responsibilities of office, was not stampeded into a precipitate change of official policy. While three months passed without any statement from London, Dr. Moshe Sneh, the 'security member' of the Agency Executive, proposed in September to its London office 'that we cause one serious incident. We would then publish a declaration to the effect that it is only a warning and an indication of much more serious incidents that would threaten the safety of all British residents in the country, should the government decide against us.... The Stern Group have expressed their willingness to join us completely on the basis of our programme of activity. This time the intention seems serious. If there is such a union, we may assume that we can prevent independent action by the Irgun Zvai Leumi.'[1] This revealing document demonstrated collusion on a high level between the Agency Executive and the terrorist organizations whose activities they always officially deplored and declared themselves powerless to prevent. How long this collusion had been going on, it is at present impossible to say, but the phrase 'this time' implies that it was nothing new. The London office gave their approval to the proposed operation, Weizmann himself evidently being a party to what was afoot.[2] On the night of 31 October–1 November, the Palmach blew up the railways in 153 places, completely disrupting the system, and destroyed three police launches used for intercepting illegal immigrants. The Irgun Zvai Leumi attacked the railway-yards at Lydda, and the Stern Group attempted to blow up the Haifa oil-refinery. The Agency signalled to its London

[1] *Palestine, Statement on Information relating to Acts of Violence* (Cmd. 6873, July 1946). On the publication of this White Paper the Jewish Agency made a perfunctory denial of its authenticity; but there can be no doubt of the genuineness of the intercepted Jewish Agency telegrams which it publishes in extenso.
[2] Bernard Joseph, acting head of the Agency Political Dept., to London, 10 October 1945: 'If Hayyim meant us only to avoid a general conflict, not isolated cases, send greetings to Chill for the birth of his daughter.' Shertok, head of the Political Dept., duly replied with this code-phrase two days later.

office: 'The activities have made a great impression. The authorities are bewildered . . . and are waiting for instructions from London.' The British government had meanwhile come to the conclusion that in determining a post-war policy for Palestine the collaboration of the U.S.A. must be sought, since both political parties in that country had courted the Jewish vote in the presidential election of 1944 by pledges of support for the full Biltmore Programme, and President Truman had in October 1945 called upon the British government to open the gates of Palestine immediately to 100,000 displaced Jews in Europe. Britain, with her reduced power and authority in the world, could not afford to continue to have American opinion irresponsibly directed against her over Palestine. Accordingly on 13 November the Foreign Secretary announced that it had been agreed to set up a joint Anglo-American Committee of Enquiry, 'to examine the position of Jews in those countries in Europe where they have been the victims of Nazi persecution . . . and the political, economic and social conditions in Palestine as they bear upon the problem of Jewish immigration and settlement therein, and the well-being of the peoples now living therein'.

The Zionists immediately denounced the Foreign Secretary's statement, which had been accompanied by some blunt comments on their recent conduct. A protest strike throughout Palestine was ordered, and in Tel Aviv Jewish hooligans set fire to government buildings. On 12 December the Inner Zionist Council announced, 'The policy to which the British government pledged itself in the Balfour Declaration and the Mandate sprang from the recognition that the Jewish problem can be effectively solved only by the greatest possible concentration of Jews in Palestine and by the restoration of Jewish nationhood. . . . The Jewish Agency . . . upholds the right of every Jew impelled by material or spiritual urge to settle in Palestine. . . . The Jewish people . . . will spare no effort, or sacrifice until the restoration of the Jewish Commonwealth of Palestine has been achieved.' As if to add point to this challenge, the Irgun Zvai Leumi a fortnight later blew up the C.I.D. H.Q. in Jerusalem, killing seven police and soldiers, while two more were killed in simultaneous attacks in Jaffa and Tel Aviv. Summoned to Government House, Ben Gurion and Shertok declared that the Agency completely dissociated itself from these murderous attacks and expressed their profound sorrow at the loss of life.

'But,' they stated, 'any effort by the Agency to assist in preventing such acts would be rendered futile by the policy pursued in Palestine by H.M. Government, on which the primary responsibility rests for the tragic situation created in the country. It was difficult to appeal to the Yishuv (the Jewish community) to observe the law at a time when the mandatory government itself was consistently violating the fundamental law of the country embodied in the Mandate.'

The Anglo-American Committee of Enquiry began its hearings in Washington in January, proceeded to London and Europe, and held its hearings in Jerusalem in March. During this period there was a slackening of terrorism, though there was another combined operation in February, the Palmach blowing up the R.A.F. radar-station at Haifa and attacking camps of the Police Mobile Force, while the Irgun and the Stern Group attacked airfields and damaged aircraft to the value of a million pounds. The illicit periodical of the Hagana, now exalted to the title of 'Jewish Resistance Movement', boasted, 'The first warning of 1 November by the Jewish Resistance was disregarded, and the whole Yishuv has been compelled to carry out a second warning.'

With some difficulty in reconciling the British and American points of view, the Committee of Enquiry produced a unanimous report on 1 May. Its effect on British readers was one of disappointment at a series of platitudes and palliatives and evasions of a clear-cut decision.

It turned down proposals for partition in favour of a continuation of the mandate 'until the hostility between Jews and Arabs disappears' (Arts. 3 and 4). 100,000 immigration certificates were to be immediately granted for Jews who had been the victims of persecution, and their admission to Palestine pushed forward as rapidly as conditions permitted; Palestine alone could not meet the immigration needs of the Jewish victims; but immigration was to be promoted under suitable conditions, 'while ensuring that the rights and position of other sections of the population were not prejudiced'. (Arts. 2, 1, 6.) While the Land Transfer Regulations were to be replaced by the free purchase and lease of land, the Jewish National Fund ban on the employment of non-Jewish labour was to be prohibited. (Art. 7.) Art. 8 indirectly criticized the Zionist proposals for a 'Jordan Valley Authority' which would dispose of the waters of the Jordan and its tributaries without reference to the governments of Transjordan and Syria from whose territories an important part of this water is derived.[1] Finally Art. 10 recommended that it should be made clear to both sides that any attempts at violence would be resolutely suppressed: 'furthermore, we express the view that the Jewish Agency should at once resume active co-operation with the Mandatory in the suppression of terrorism and illegal immigration, and in the maintenance of law and order'.

The Arab reaction to the Report was a protest against the modification in favour of the Zionists of the 1939 White Paper which, though they had received it with coldness at the time, they had now come to regard as the palladium of their national aspirations. They demanded the abrogation of the Mandate, the withdrawal of British troops, and the establishment of an Arab democratic state, and threatened to appeal to Russia for support. The Zionists characteristically selected from the Report and publicized, as being the whole Report, those Recommendations which suited them, and were completely silent about those that they found inconvenient. They were in fact prepared to accept the Report as a first instalment, but no more, of progress towards their Jewish State.

The British Prime Minister told the House of Commons that the Report would be considered as a whole in all its implications. It was clear from the facts presented regarding the illegal armies maintained in Palestine that it would not be possible to admit 100,000 immigrants unless and until these formations had been disarmed and their arms surrendered. It was essential that the Agency should take an active part in the suppression of terrorism. The Government wished to ascertain to what extent the Government of the U.S.A. would be prepared to share the additional military and financial responsibilities.

The Zionist leaders were furious at the suggestion that they should agree to the 'liquidation of the Community's defences', and in spite of their recent collusion with the terrorists reverted to their constant pretension that terrorism was but 'the acts of an irresponsible few'.[2] The American President and people, who had clearly imagined that their responsibility for Palestine was

---

[1] cf. M. G. Ionides, 'Irrigation in Palestine', *The World To-day*, III (1947), 188 ff.

[2] *Palestine Post* leading article, 2 May 1946.

ended with the publication of the Committee's report, were embarrassed by the challenge that they should share the burden of imposing the proposed new policy on the country. In June the President was advised by his cabinet to accept an invitation from London to send representatives to discuss the new problems it raised.

On the night of 16–17 June the Palmach attacked the frontier communications of Palestine, destroying five road- and four rail-bridges, and doing damage estimated at £250,000. The illicit Zionist broadcasting-station accepted full responsibility on behalf of the 'Resistance Movement' for the renewal of its activity 'as a result of the delaying policy of the British government'.[1] It was clearly time to put an end to the campaign of 'vilification, incitement, and violence' pursued by the Zionist leaders. On 29 June the military occupied the Jewish Agency building and arrested prominent Zionist leaders, including Shertok and the Canadian-Jewish lawyer Bernard Joseph who was his political second-in-command; Ben Gurion was away in Europe. Many Palmach commanders were interned, and a whole series of well-furnished arms-caches discovered in the settlement of Yagur, a Palmach headquarters.

While conversations between the American cabinet mission and the British experts were in progress, shortly after mid-day on 22 July the Irgun blew up a corner of the King David Hotel, killing ninety-one persons, mainly Arab and Jewish civil-servants.[2] The horror of this outrage had not passed away when the British government announced on 31 July that the Anglo-American Experts had produced a Federal Plan for dividing Palestine into two main autonomous provinces, Arab and Jewish, broadly managing their own affairs, including the control of immigration 'so long as the economic absorptive capacity of a province was not exceeded'.

[1] Action had already been threatened a month previously in a broadcast 'delivered at the request of Shertok'. (The July 1946 White Paper, quoting a Jewish Agency telegram.)

[2] On 25 July 1947, the Irgun issued a statement declaring that the Hagana had been consulted and informed in the preparations to blow up the King David, and after several hesitations agreed to the attack after the arrest of the Jewish Agency leaders in the previous month. The Irgun had kept silence for a year but was now making this disclosure because the Hagana were now collaborating with the British. (*Times* Correspondent in Jerusalem, 27 July 1947; the Hagana at that time were helping the British to search for two British N.C.O's kidnapped as hostages by the Irgun.)

While the Arab States accepted the British government's invitation to a conference to discuss the details of this plan, the Palestine Arabs, encouraged by the well-timed escape of the Mufti from France to Egypt,[1] refused to attend the conference unless they were given a free choice of their representatives, including the Mufti. The Jewish Agency Executive decided that 'it could not participate in any discussions based on the Federal Plan, since it would deprive the Jewish people of its right under the Mandate in 85 per cent. of Western Palestine;[2] it did not provide genuine self-government; and it did not secure freedom of Jewish immigration and settlement'. It would, however, be prepared to participate 'if the establishment of a viable Jewish State in an adequate area of Palestine were the purpose of the discussion'. This 'viable Jewish State' was later defined as consisting of the whole of Galilee and the coastal plain (as proposed by the Royal Commission's Partition Plan of 1937), plus the Southern District with, if possible, a continuous boundary connecting them, the whole to comprise 65 per cent. of the total area of Palestine. Describing this as a 'supreme sacrifice', the Zionist official spokesman obligingly added that 'the Arabs would be allotted the central plateau', and suggested that the Christian Holy Places should be handed over to an international régime of the Churches.[3]

While these parleys with Zionists and Arabs were going on, the British authorities in Palestine had to deal with the rising flood of unauthorized Jewish immigration by sea from Central and Eastern Europe, where the desperate Jewish survivors of the Hitler terror had, since the collapse of Germany, been encouraged by a concerted barrage of Zionist propaganda to expect and demand immediate admission to Palestine, and were further impelled by pogroms in Poland and Hungary. Jewish troops in the Allied armies and other Zionist agents acting under the direction of the Jewish Agency had skilfully organized escape-routes to the Mediterranean coast, and purchased or chartered ships for their onward voyage to Palestine. Most of the liberal funds for these operations came from Zionist organizations in the U.S.A., which

---

[1] No doubt with the connivance of some French officials.

[2] The proposed extent of the Jewish province was unofficially understood to approximate to that of Plan B of the Palestine Partition Commission (1938), roughly restricting the Jewish area to the status quo but taking in some small Arab enclaves.

[3] *Palestine Post*, 25 October 1946.

P

conducted their appeals for subscriptions quite openly in the press.[1] The British government stated that 'food, clothing, medical supplies, and transport provided by U.N.R.R.A. and other agencies for the relief of suffering in Europe were diverted to this "underground railway to Palestine".'. The majority of the immigrants selected by the Zionist authorities were young men and women, to swell the population of the agricultural settlements and the ranks of the Hagana. By mid-August there were sufficient unauthorized immigrants in camps in Palestine awaiting legalization to fill the monthly quota of 1,500 for three months ahead, and thousands more were reported to be on the way. The government therefore resolved to transfer all unauthorized immigrants arriving after 11 August to Cyprus. This policy was received with angry demonstrations and invective by the Zionists. Within a fortnight two attempts were made to sabotage the ships used for the transportation to Cyprus. The Zionists decided to raise £100,000 for the furtherance of immigration 'regardless of the illegal White Paper restrictions which would doom the National Home to stagnation'; they had previously always pretended that the exodus from Europe was entirely a spontaneous, unorganized affair.[2]

The London Conference opened in the presence of representatives of the Arab States, but without either the Arabs or the Jews of Palestine. The Foreign Secretary was reported to have stated that the government was not prepared to consider any solution which disregarded the presence of an organized community of 600,000 Jews who insist upon their political rights as a group or the necessity for Palestine to contribute to a solution of the refugee-problem. The Arabs, on the other hand, would propose only the creation of an independent state offering equal rights for all citizens permanently resident since 1939 and those acquiring citizenship after that date; freedom of education for the Jews and the use of Hebrew as an official language; but complete stoppage of Jewish immigration and the retention of the existing Land Transfer Regulations, with no modification of these two provisions except with the

[1] Even subscriptions for the terrorist organizations were exempt from American income-tax as 'charitable' donations.
[2] The claim that the National Home would stagnate without a high level of immigration went to confirm the Arab fear that under the government's Federal Plan or under Partition the Zionists would pack their territory with settlers who, at a suitable occasion, would spontaneously invade the Arab territory. By the end of May 1947 the number of Jews in the Cyprus camps was nearly 15,000 or ten months' quota.

consent of the majority of the Arabs in the legislature. Meanwhile, the government carried on parallel negotiations with the Agency with a view to resolving the deadlock, and after the Inner Zionist Council had issued an appeal to the Yishuv to isolate the terrorists and deny them all support, the government on 5 November released the detained Jewish leaders. The effect of this clemency was only to increase the wave of terrorism; and during the entire year more British personnel, military and civil, were killed by the terrorists than in any single year of the Arab Rebellion, the total being seventy-three against the 1938 peak-figure of sixty-nine. The total casualties of all nationalities from political unrest were 212 killed and 428 injured.

The terrorist campaign ceased, however, as if by magic with the opening in December of the twenty-second World Zionist Congress, in the elections for which in Palestine the Revisionists had scored a remarkable success, being second only to the Mapai (Labour) party. However, the Yishuv had only 21 per cent. of all the seats at the Congress, while the American Zionists held first place with 32 per cent. The prevailing mood of the delegates was an extreme one, the great majority of the American Zionists being united with the Revisionists in demanding a Jewish State in the whole of Palestine. Weizmann appealed to the Congress to work for an understanding with Britain for a Jewish state in 'an adequate part' of Palestine. He warned them that they were faced with the alternatives of slow progress or the destruction through terrorism and counter-measures of all they had gained in twenty-nine years, and that he could not continue to remain their president if the Congress saddled the Executive with an unworkable policy. However, the Congress resolved by 171 votes to 154 that the Movement should not participate in the resumed London Conference unless they received immediate concessions in the all-important matter of immigration; and on 7 January 1947 Shertok told a press-conference that since the Agency's compromise-offer of the previous autumn had met with no response from the British, it now stood for an independent Jewish state in the whole of Palestine, guaranteeing equal rights to the Arabs, but aiming at attaining a numerical majority as soon as possible by the introduction of 700,000 immigrants.

Terrorist activity was resumed in the New Year. On 12 January the Stern Group attempted a bomb-outrage comparable with the

King David disaster against the Haifa police compound, killing five persons and injuring thirty-four. The Vaad Leumi passed a resolution repudiating murder as a means of political resistance. It condemned the intimidation of the Jewish community by the terrorists, their impairing of 'national discipline' and their claim 'to decide when or where the struggle of the Jewish people should be waged'. Asked, however, at a press-conference whether the community was called on to intervene if the terrorists attacked the British, an Agency spokesman admitted that 'from the text of the resolution that would not appear to be the case',[1] and subsequently Mrs. Meyerson, head of the Agency Political Dept., and others explained that the Yishuv could not be expected to act as 'informers' against their kin.[2] On 26 and 27 January the terrorists kidnapped two British civilians, one a judge actually taken from his court, as hostages for a terrorist under sentence of death for his part in an outrage in which five persons were killed. They were set free after the High Commissioner had given an ultimatum to the Agency; but on 31 January, in consequence of a terrorist threat to 'turn Palestine into a bloodbath' if the death-sentence were carried out, the government issued an order for the evacuation of all British women and children and other non-essential civilians, and the concentration in guarded cantonments of those who remained. On 3 February the Government called on the Agency and the Vaad Leumi, in view of their 'open and continued refusals' to co-operate against terrorism, 'to state categorically and at once whether they were prepared publicly to call upon the Jewish community to lend their aid to the Government by co-operating with the police and armed forces in locating and bringing to justice the members of the terrorist groups'. They replied that 'the Yishuv cannot be called upon to place itself at the disposal of the Government for fighting the evil consequences of a policy which is of that government's own making, and which the Yishuv regards as a menace to its existence. . . .'

On 14 February the British Foreign Secretary announced that the government would submit the question to U.N.O., as both parties had rejected a new federal plan which would have admitted 96,000 Jewish immigrants in the next two years, subsequent immigration being controlled by the High Commissioner after

[1] *Palestine Post*, 22 January 1947.
[2] ibid. 3 February 1947.

consulting both Jews and Arabs. The Arabs had rejected any further immigration, and the Zionists refused to admit the principle that the Arabs should have any say in determining Jewish immigration.

On 1 March, after the detention of an illegal immigrant ship, terrorist outrages caused the deaths of twenty persons and the injury of twenty-five others. The government then imposed statutory martial law on Tel Aviv and neighbouring Jewish towns and on part of Jerusalem, affecting more than 40 per cent. of the whole Jewish population. After eleven days it was officially announced that 'in spite of the refusal of the Jewish official bodies to assist the security forces in combating and rooting out the gangsters, help has been received from members of the Jewish community.... The total number of arrests effected during the past fortnight is seventy-eight, of which fifteen are members of the Stern Group, twelve I.Z.L., and fifty-one others connected with terrorism.' Martial law was subsequently withdrawn, it not being desired to extend indefinitely the loss, unemployment, and dislocation of the economic situation, which was reported to have cost the Jewish community £500,000.

At the end of April a special session of the General Assembly of U.N.O. met to consider the Palestine problem, to the accompaniment in Palestine itself of a continuous terrorist campaign. After a fortnight's debate which reflected the many international cross-currents affecting the issue, the Assembly set up a special committee of representatives of small and medium Powers with no direct interests or commitments in Palestine 'to investigate all questions and issues relevant to the problem' and make a report for the next session of the Assembly in September, with proposals for a solution. The Committee conducted its inquiries in the Middle East from 16 June to 24 July, being boycotted throughout by the Arabs of Palestine, but hearing statements from representatives of the Arab states. Jewish terrorist activity, which had ceased while the Anglo-American Committee of 1946 was in the Middle East, went on during the presence of the U.N. Committee, doubtless because three terrorists were under sentence of death for their part in a raid on Akka Prison. Nor did the Hagana allow the Committee to leave without witnessing the arrival of the largest single contingent of illegal immigrants ever to reach Palestine, numbering 4,500 in all; when intercepted, the American-Jewish crew and the passengers fiercely resisted and broadcast a commentary for the benefit of the Committee. On 31 August, while a minority of three made proposals approximating to the Anglo-American Federal Plan of July 1946, a majority of seven of the eleven members recommended to the General Assembly a sharper partition on the lines of the Royal Commission Report of 1937, though the two states so formed would remain in economic union. They proposed to award to the Jewish state, in addition to rounding off its present holdings, the whole of the Beersheba sub-district of Southern Palestine and Eastern Galilee, though the Arabs were to keep Western Galilee. In the transitional period of two years 150,000 Jews were to be admitted, as against the 100,000 proposed for the same period by Britain in January, and the Land Transfer Regulations were to cease in the area of the Jewish state. The scheme contemplated that Britain would continue to administer the country during the transitional period under the auspices of the U.N., and if so desired with the assistance of members of the U.N. The difficulties inherent in the scheme were obvious: while the Zionists' immediate aims were largely met, half-a-million Arabs were to be included in the area of the Jewish state, and by the loss of Jaffa the Arabs were to be left without a port of their own; they were to accept in the interim period an even higher rate of immigration than in the peak years 1934–35 before the Arab Rebellion, with no guarantee that the subsequently unrestricted population of the Jewish state might not at some suitable opportunity erupt in their direction; all this without any compensation except their independence, recognition of which was to be conditional on their guaranteeing fundamental liberties, non-discrimination, and signing the treaty of economic union with the Jewish state; this treaty of economic union would presumably take precedence over any desires the Arabs might have for closer union with other Arab states. Finally, although the six weeks before the publishing of the Report had been marked by the worst riots between the two communities in the Tel Aviv-Jaffa area since the Arab Rebellion the two states were to be presented with an immense problem of policing, since their modest areas would each consist of three separate sectors, touching only by means of two specially-created 'points of intersection'.

On 26 September the Colonial Secretary made it clear that Britain would not feel able to implement a policy not acceptable

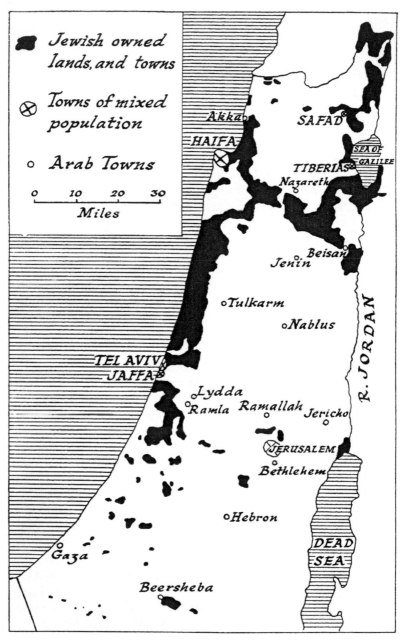

Jewish owned lands, and towns

⊗ **Towns of mixed population**

○ **Arab Towns**

0   10   20   30
Miles

Akka
SAFAD
HAIFA
SEA OF GALILEE
TIBERIAS
Nazareth
Beisan
Jenin
Tulkarm
Nablus
R. JORDAN
TEL AVIV
JAFFA
Lydda
Ramla
Ramallah
Jericho
JERUSALEM
Bethlehem
Hebron
DEAD SEA
Gaza
Beersheba

12. 'UNPARTITIONABLE' PALESTINE

Unshaded areas are in Arab possession, though considerable areas are used only for rough grazing and would require a great outlay to improve them.

to Jews and Arabs, and in the absence of a settlement must plan for the early withdrawal of the British forces and administration from Palestine. On 2 October the chairman of the American section of the Jewish Agency told the U.N. General Assembly, 'Should British forces not be available, the Jewish people of Palestine would provide without delay the necessary effectives to maintain public security'. On 29 November the Assembly approved the partition plan with minor amendments, though the necessary two-thirds majority was obtained only by some remarkable lobbying, which at the last moment swung eight doubtful votes into the partition lobby. *The Times* correspondent commented: 'The general feeling among the delegates was that, regardless of its merits and demerits and the joint support given by the U.S.S.R. and the U.S.A., the partition scheme would have been carried in no other city than New York. . . . The strength of the Jewish influence in Washington has been a revelation.'[1] Immediately guerilla warfare broke out in Palestine: 'The Arabs were determined to show that they would not submit tamely to the U.N. plan of partition, while the Jews tried to consolidate the advantages gained at the General Assembly by a succession of drastic operations designed to intimidate and cure the Arabs of any desire for further conflict.'[2] In January 1948 the British Government resisted Zionist claims for recognition of their armed forces and the right to import arms before the ending of the Mandate on 15 May. After the problem of executing the partition scheme had been referred to the Security Council, the United States on 19 March admitted that it could not be carried out peacefully, and proposed instead that Palestine should be placed under temporary United Nations trusteeship. The Security Council's appeal for a truce between Arabs and Jews served once again to protract the discussion without reaching any decision. Meanwhile, as the British troops were withdrawn the Zionists, by a vigorous counter-offensive, had by the end of April achieved complete military superiority over the Palestine Arab 'Liberation Army' in the plains. On the afternoon of 14 May the Jewish state of Israel was proclaimed,[3] and was immediately recognized by the United

---

[1] 1 December 1947.
[2] Sir Alexander Cadogan to the U.N. Palestine Commission, 21 January 1948.
[3] The termination of the mandate at midnight was anticipated because the Sabbath began at sunset on 14 May.

States, where an outspoken Zionist supporter had on 28 April been appointed special assistant for Palestine affairs to the Secretary of State. Recognition by Russia and her satellites followed, and the armies of the neighbouring Arab states crossed the frontiers into Palestine.

* * *

The Zionists are intensely and justly proud of what they have achieved in material and social development in the last thirty years, and desperate as a result of the decimation of their kin in Europe. They do not, however, base their demands to settle in Palestine only on recent persecution, but on what they claim to be the bitter experience of many centuries. 'The soul of the Jewish people is being destroyed by exile. This started long before Hitler. The exile has continued for nearly 2,000 years and we are all suffering from its effects; the poisoning effects of soul-destroying minority existence.... As relentlessly as wind and rain carry away the good earth when it is not protected by vegetation, so does minority life carry away from the soul of man those qualities that are essential for the harmonious development of a healthy human being. Kindness, cheerfulness, brotherliness, all these tender qualities are washed away, eroded by the flood of cruelty and hatred raging around the minority; and what remains in the soul is as hard as rock. And as barren. Only bitterness and dull frustration. Since the advent of Hitler the flood of hatred has risen higher. The erosion of the Hebrew soul goes on at a terrifying rate. What the world sees is only a pitiful collection of miserable human beings called D.P.s. . . . What the world does not see is the accumulating bleakness in the soul of this people: the devilish transmutation of good into evil that goes on, not only in the D.P. camps, but wherever there are Jews.'[1]

This being so, the present-day Zionist claim is not merely an appeal for asylum, but a demand for statehood falling into line with the constant endeavour to establish a new Jewish state in the centuries which followed the destruction of their kingdom by Nebuchadnezzar.[2] As they then sought Persian favour to right the wrongs done them by Nebuchadnezzar, and the favour of the Roman Republic to right the wrongs done them by the Seleucids, so in the First World War they sought the favour of Britain and

[1] S. Rosoff, 'Soul-Erosion', *Palestine Post*, 2 August 1946.
[2] Toynbee, *A Study of History*, one-vol. abridgement, 521 f.

the U.S.A. to right the wrongs done them in Eastern Europe by establishing them in Palestine. Protecting Powers have, however, always failed to satisfy Jewish political ambitions to the full: and so they rose against Artaxerxes III in the last years of the Persian Empire, against the Roman Empire, and against the British mandate. The terrorists (drawn from the younger generation, indoctrinated in nationalism in the Jewish educational system of Palestine or in the grim school of the Hitler Terror) are the modern counterparts of the militant Zealots who carried on terrorism against the Romans. The attempt to break Arab resistance to Jewish predominance is paralleled by the Maccabean coercion of the semi-Hellenized communities who resisted the new Jewish state. At present the United States is the protecting Power; but should her support be withheld or prove inadequate, there is a group within the Zionist movement which would try to enlist active Russian support.

On the other hand the 'Arabs'[1] of Palestine, supported by the politically-minded of the Arab States, are defending what they conceive to be their rights as a people against this 'invasion' of more energetic, more skilful, and far better equipped aliens. That they had lived for centuries under a foreign government does not weaken their case, as they see it. They had preserved, even in decay, the essentials of their culture, their language and their religion; and they had begun early in this century to stir themselves against the foreign ruler, who, after all, was of their own religion and culture, and to demand the right of national self-determination. The politically-conscious among them detest the idea of ceding any part of what they have for 1,300 years regarded as *their* land, especially now that their cousins in Syria, Iraq, and Egypt have achieved their independence. Unwisely, however, the 'Liberation Army' attacked prepared Zionist positions instead of following the guerilla tactics for which they were better fitted, and were heavily defeated. Dissensions broke out among their commanders, and the wealthier town-Arabs ignominiously hurried across the frontiers to safety as the Zionists began their counter-offensive. The massacre by Jewish extremists of 200 Arab villagers, including 100 women and

---

[1] It must be emphasized that the seventh-century Arab conquerors constituted only a minority of the existing population, and that consequently the present-day Arabic-speaking population is an amalgam of all the racial strains that have entered the country from the earliest historical times.

children, at Deir Yasin on 9 April, hastened the stampede. The towns of Haifa, Jaffa, Akka, Tiberias, and Safad were quickly lost, and the leadership of the Mufti and his Higher Executive discredited; but the intervention of the Arab states' armies brought about a revival of the mercurial Arabs' confidence.

True, there have been Arabs who would admit in private the material and cultural advantage to themselves of Jewish settlement in Palestine; but they have always added that it must be restricted to a limit that would not become an obstacle to their own political independence. There are Jews, such as the small Ihud group led by the wise and tolerant Dr. J. L. Magnes of the Hebrew University, who have seen the desirability of reaching an understanding with the Arab population and who were willing to this end to give up the idea of Jewish statehood; but even they spoke of numerical equality, which would inevitably mean Jewish economic and technical superiority. The forces in either community that have actively sought an understanding with the other do not amount to more than 10 per cent.; there is a larger proportion that would like a quiet life; but these submit, from fear of the consequences, to the uncompromising nationalism of the Jewish Agency and the Arab Higher Executive respectively. There is in particular the political influence exerted by the Jewish trades-union organization Histadruth, which is closely linked to the Jewish Agency and embraces at least 40 per cent. of the entire Jewish community.[1]

At the third corner of this infernal triangle stood the British government, which all-too-lightly entered into conflicting undertakings thirty years ago in the quest for imperial security. The Balfour Declaration and the Mandate were 'never conceived to cover the contingency of a mass exodus from Europe by millions of despairing refugees, and contemplated only the creation of a Jewish Home where Jewish culture and institutions could live secure in a land whose people had been for hundreds of years Arab by speech, race, and tradition.'[2] Such a Home of over 600,000 Jews now exists in Palestine; in no other country between the two wars did an alien community increase by immigration so rapidly in proportion to the indigenous population; the Yishuv enjoyed a large measure of self-government, which would have been increased if agreement had been reached between the two

[1] *Palestine Post*, 27 August 1946.
[2] *Times* leading article, 11 December, 1946.

communities. But it was never part of the British pledge to force the Arabs to submit to a Jewish majority, still less to accept a Jewish State.

★   ★   ★

Had the British Embassy and military authorities in Egypt not supported the return to power of the Wafd early in 1942, it would have made trouble throughout Egypt which might seriously have embarrassed the British at a time when they were fully engaged with the Axis forces in Libya. The British authorities must have been aware, as a result of previous experience, that the advent of the Wafd government would mean a decline in administrative efficiency and, in condition of wartime scarcity, an increase in corrupt practices even beyond the Egyptian norm. But the supreme necessity of prosecuting the war presumably made these disadvantages appear a lesser evil than the alternative of nation-wide anti-British agitation organized by the Wafd; and the British authorities probably did not appreciate the extent to which the ageing Nahhas in indifferent health was becoming the tool of his enterprising wife and her family and friends. After Makram Ubaid's breach with Nahhas, the keen-witted and spiteful Copt devoted himself to the compilation and eventual publication in a 'Black Book' of charges of corruption against those near to Nahhas.

King Faruq was naturally anxious to avenge his humiliation of 4 February by ridding himself at the first opportunity of the contumacious Nahhas, and the Black Book charges provided him with admirable justification for such an act. The first royal attempt to dismiss the government was prevented by the British Embassy in the spring of 1943, shortly before the final expulsion of the Axis from North Africa. In the following year the failure of the Wafd to deal adequately with the severe and acute malaria epidemic of Upper Egypt, which was aggravated by a wartime decline in nutrition below even the miserable peace-time standards and caused the deaths of scores of thousands of wretched villagers, and the growing volume of rumour about the prevalance and scale of corrupt practices very near to the Prime Minister himself, greatly impaired the prestige of the Wafd, even among its customary supporters. The recession of the war from the Middle East made the military necessity of keeping the Wafd in power no longer so compelling in 1944 as it had been previously; and though it was said that in the first half of that year Lord Killearn fought a rear-guard-action for Nahhas, for whom he evidently had a personal regard, by the late summer the situation was becoming untenable. Had Britain persisted in supporting the Wafd regardless of the hostility of the influential upper-class and the wider circle of the King's supporters, she might have had to face widespread agitation in Egypt and the resignations of many key officials. This in turn might have paralysed the complex Egyptian administrative machine at a time when the country was still intended as an important link in communications for the war against Japan; for the Wafd is notoriously lacking in trained and efficient administrators, and there were no British personnel available for an emergency. The suggestion that a continuation of the Killearn-Nahhas combination would have prevented or moderated the subsequent Egyptian demand for radical revision of the 1936 Treaty argues a fundamental ignorance of the Egyptian political character, since the Wafd would have demanded a handsome reward for its collaboration during the war. The Foreign Office wisely decided that its support of Nahhas should cease, and that internal Egyptian politics must be allowed to take their course. Nahhas was dismissed from office in terms of ignominy by a royal rescript of October 1944, and succeeded by an anti-Wafdist coalition which secured a majority in an election which the Wafd boycotted.

When the Allied victory in the war had become clearly only a matter of months, it became evident that as soon as it was over Egypt would ask for a revision in her favour of the 1936 Treaty. Revision after ten years was provided for, on the understanding that the alliance should be preserved. Nationalist feeling in Egypt was rising, particularly after the fall of the Wafd. The Prime Minister who succeeded Nahhas was murdered by an extremist because he was believed to be too pro-British. With the close of the war the Wafdist press began to clamour for treaty revision. The Prime Minister Nuqrashi Pasha tried to temporize, but nationalist pressure forced him to present a Note in December 1945 requesting the evacuation of all British troops and the establishment of effective Egyptian sovereignty over the Sudan—the so-called 'unity of the Nile Valley'. Britain announced her willingness to open conversations; but before these could begin, violent demonstrations of students and workers occurred in Cairo and Alexandria, organized by the Wafd to embarrass the government by demanding the immediate evacuation of British troops; serious damage was done to the Anglican Cathedral and the Bishop's house in Cairo. These riots, and British doubts about Nuqrashi's ability to pilot the proposed negotiations through against the weight of Wafdist opposition, led to his resignation in mid-February. Sidqi Pasha, still at seventy-one years of age regarded as the 'strong man of Egypt' and the inveterate enemy of the Wafd, succeeded him. When he began to form the delegation for the negotiations with Britain, the Wafd, with little appreciation of the extent to which it had been discredited by its corrupt and inefficient last term of office, demanded the right as in 1936 to appoint the chairman and the majority of the delegates. Sidqi offered them two out of twelve places, which they refused; and the old man then proceeded to form his delegation without them. The talks began in Cairo on 23 April 1946; and on 7 May the Foreign Secretary announced Britain's intention to withdraw all her forces from Egypt, provided that Egypt made satisfactory arrangements for affording Britain the necessary assistance in time of war or the imminent threat of war, in accordance with the Alliance. The gesture did not, however, evoke a cordial response in Egypt: the Egyptians hoped for the complete abolition of the Alliance, claiming that it was inconsistent with the Charter of U.N.O. Regardless of the fact that their geographical position makes them, like Belgium, a cockpit of the nations whenever the peace of the Middle East is disturbed, they hoped to keep out of the struggle with Russia which they saw looming up, and which they feared might be less profitable and more uncomfortable for Egypt than the two German wars had been. *The Times* commented: 'Some leaders of Egyptian opinion are still remote from the outside world, and do not understand the gravity of its problems, its general bad temper, and the speed and power of modern methods of aggression. They seem to believe . . . that the United Nations is a tap which, when turned, pours out security.'[1] They thus consistently sought to evade the British proposal (Art. 2) for a joint Anglo-Egyptian Defence Council to organize the defence of Egypt. In October Sidqi travelled to London for personal talks with the Foreign Secretary

[1] 28 August 1946.

in the hope of clearing the deadlock. When the majority of the delegation declared their objection to Art. 2 even in its watered-down form[1] and accused him of giving the Sudan a chance of separating from Egypt, he persuaded King Faruq to dissolve the delegation and empower himself and the Foreign Minister to continue the negotiations.

At this stage, however, the question of the Sudan suddenly assumed an acute form. The text of the Bevin-Sidqi Sudan Protocol read: 'The policy which the High Contracting Parties undertake to follow in the Sudan within the framework of unity between Egypt and the Sudan under the common crown of Egypt shall have the objective of ensuring the well-being of the Sudanese, the development of their interests, and active preparation for self-government and the consequent exercise of the right to choose the future status of the Sudan. Until the High Contracting Parties are in full agreement as regards this latter objective after consultation with the Sudanese, the Agreement of 1899 will continue' and the appropriate articles of the 1936 Treaty would remain in force. At the opening of the Egyptian parliament after Sidqi's return the Royal Address had declared that 'One of Egypt's first aims would' be to assure the well-being of the Sudanese, develop their interests, and prepare them for self-government'; but Sidqi and other Egyptian statesmen continued in their public speeches to emphasize the approaching assumption of Egyptian sovereignty over the Sudan and say little or nothing about self-government for the Sudanese. This roused to vigorous action the Sudanese Umma party, consisting of men of substance who desire to exercise their authority in a self-governing Sudan independent of Egypt.[2] Saiyid Sir Abd ur-Rahman, son of the Mahdi who led the revolt against the Egyptians in 1881, went to London to present the Umma case; and on 7 December, the Governor-General of the Sudan was authorized to announce that 'while the British government were proposing to acknowledge the Egyptian Crown as the titular sovereign over the Sudan, the government were determined that nothing should be permitted to deflect the Sudan government . . . from the task of preparing the Sudanese for self-

[1] 'In case of a threat of war to an adjacent country the two parties agree to discuss the situation in order to take the necessary measures until the Security Council takes steps to secure peace.'

[2] The less wealthy and influential 'intelligentsia', on the other hand, look to Egypt to put them in high office, and are organized in the Ashiqa party.

government[1] and for choosing freely what their future status should be. The Sudan Protocol in fact provides that the Sudanese people shall, when they are ripe for self-government, be free to choose the future status of the Sudan. Nothing in the proposed treaty can prejudice the right of the Sudanese to achieve their independence.' Sidqi promptly resigned. Nuqrashi, who succeeded him, made the uncompromising statement to the Chamber of Deputies, 'In affirming the *permanent* unity of Egypt and the Sudan under the Egyptian Crown we are but expressing the *unanimous* will and wishes of the inhabitants of this valley', though he added the customary saving clause about 'leading the Sudan towards self-government'. The Arab League was committed, presumably by its Egyptian secretary-general Azzam Pasha, to support the Egyptian demand for permanent unity with the Sudan. The British government suggested the establishment of an Anglo-Egyptian-Sudanese commission to prepare the Sudanese for self-government in a period not exceeding twenty years, and the Cairo Embassy stated that the government would do nothing to encourage the Sudanese to separate themselves from Egypt. But on 25 January 1947 the Egyptian government announced its intention of submitting to the Security Council its two grievances, the continued presence of British troops in Egypt and the status of the Sudan; and after nearly six months delay its complaint was finally presented on 11 July.

When the case came before the Security Council in August, Nuqrashi asked it to direct the British to withdraw their troops from Egypt by 1 September, to withdraw from the Sudan and end the present administration there. He rejected the suggestion that the 1936 Treaty was still binding on Egypt, since she had signed it under the pressure of British occupation; in any case it was a 'temporary expedient' in face of the days of war, and the principle of an Anglo-Egyptian alliance was incompatible with the Charter of U.N.O. All attempts by the Security Council to bring about a compromise failed, since Nuqrashi insisted that the withdrawal of British troops from the Canal Area should be completed before negotiations were renewed. At the end of 1947 the British mission to the Egyptian army was dissolved, and the Egyptian currency

[1] The proportion of Sudanese in the senior division of the civil service has risen from under 1 per cent. to about 15 per cent. in the last twelve years; cf. *The Sudan, A Record of Progress*, 1898-1947 (Sudan Govt.).

had already been detached from its link with sterling. Early in 1948, however, moderate Egyptian opinion was reported to be coming round to the reopening of negotiations, largely on account of the increasingly menacing international attitude of the U.S.S.R.[1] but this could hardly be realized at the moment, in view of what had just happened in Iraq.

There, while there had been a succession of moderate governments since the suppression of Rashid Ali's putsch, extremist forces on both the right and the left wings had been gathering strength since the end of the war and were acting together in opposition.[2] It was largely in order to spike the extremists' guns that Prime Minister Salih Jabr asked in 1947 for a revision of the Anglo-Iraqi Treaty of 1930. He arrived in London on 6 January 1948, armed with a vote of confidence by 70 per cent. of the Chamber.[3] But when the terms of the new Treaty which he signed at Portsmouth were announced on 16 January (giving the R.A.F. continued access to the two air-bases 'until such time as peace-treaties have entered into force with all enemy countries . . . it being understood that the peace-treaties are to be deemed to be fully in force when the allied forces are withdrawn from the territories of all ex-enemy states'), a violent revulsion occurred in Baghdad, and on 21 January the Regent broadcast a promise that the Treaty would not be ratified. On 27 January the Regent announced the resignation of the Prime Minister, and a right-wing government came into power two days later. In March the Sudanese Advisory Council unanimously approved constitutional proposals, after the Egyptian Government had refused to discuss them with the Sudan Government.

To sum up, it is probable that none of the Arab states, except Transjordan and perhaps Sa'udi Arabia, will be prepared to enter into security pacts with Britain or the U.S.A., unless they feel themselves much more imminently threatened either by the U.S.S.R. from without or by Communism from within.[4] The present struggle with Zionism is calculated only to increase their xenophobia.

[1] *Times* Cairo correspondent, 5 February.
[2] *The World To-day*, February 1948, 50 f.
[3] Eliz. Monroe, in *Observer*, 25 January.
[4] cf. *Times* editorial, 30 March 1948.

Q

CHAPTER VIII

Present-Day Economic and Social Conditions

'The social scene grows out of economic conditions, to much the same extent that political events in their turn grow out of social conditions.' (G. M. Trevelyan, *English Social History*, p. vii).

THE NATURAL economic assets of the Middle East are not numerous. The cultivation of high-grade cotton in Egypt from early in the last century has brought prosperity to a small number of landowners and middle-men, and has added greatly to the aggregate national wealth of Egypt; but most of this added wealth has been taken up by the extraordinary increase of the population, so that the individual real income has risen little. There are such locally important exports as Palestinian citrus and Dead Sea chemicals, Turkish chromium, and Iraqi dates; but the commodity which now bulks largest in the economy of the Middle East as a whole is the oil-deposits, located principally in the Persian Gulf region, but with outliers on the shores of the Red Sea and possible deposits elsewhere.[1] The existing Middle East oilfields, which began to be exploited only at the beginning of this century, are estimated to contain 30 per cent. of the total world reserves of crude oil,[2] and furnish the governments of the countries in which they lie with royalties as large or larger than their revenues from all other sources. Other mineral resources are scanty, and are unlikely

[1] cf. G. M. Lees, in *Royal Central Asian Journal*, XXXIII (1946), 47 ff.

[2] The part played by oil in modern politics is notorious. In the Middle East the British were first in the field with the Anglo-Persian Oil Co. before the First World War; but after the close of that war the Americans became aggressive competitors for concessions, demanding in Iraq an Open Door which they had conspicuously failed to grant to other nations in the Philippines and other parts of their economic empire. One American historian has admitted that the U.S.A. had in its oil offensive at the Middle East 'misused the lofty principles of the open door and the equality of economic opportunity'. American oil-interests were alleged to have encouraged nationalist Turkey in its claim in the early 'twenties to the vilayet of Mosul with its oil-deposits. Eventually the British oil-interests were constrained in 1925 to buy off the Americans by yielding to them a quarter-share in the Iraq Petroleum Co. (H. A. Foster, *The Making of Modern Iraq*, chs. VII and VIII.) Since that time British oil-interests have acquiesced, as an alternative to aggressive competition in which they were likely to be worsted, in a progressively increasing American participation in exploiting the oil of the Middle East. American interests now have exclusive rights in Bahrain

to make a large contribution to the region's economic future. Its main asset lies then in the primary products of agriculture and stockbreeding. Here the adverse effects of a limited and seasonal rainfall are reinforced by the persistence of antiquated farming methods and systems of land-tenure, comparable with those of Western Europe in the Middle Ages. As a result, production falls far below the standards of more advanced agricultural countries. It was estimated before the war that, except for the Jews of Palestine, the average male agricultural worker produced only about one-fifth of the goods produced by his counterpart in Britain, and that the individual's share in the national income of these countries (again excluding Jewish Palestine) was also only about one-fifth of that of Britain, though still in excess of over-populated India and China.[1]

An important cause of the poverty of the rural masses is the inequitable distribution of land in most of the Middle Eastern countries, where a small number of wealthy landowners own a large proportion of the land, and there are thousands or millions of dwarf-holders, tenants, and landless labourers. 'In Egypt in 1933 39 per cent. of the land was held in large estates by 0.6 per cent. of the total number of owners, while no less than two-thirds of the owners held an average of only two-fifths of an acre each. Such minute holdings could hardly be economically sound, even if devoted to intensive vegetable and fruit production and aided by co-operative societies for marketing the produce, which is not the case. . . . With few exceptions, those who have absolute or hereditary titles to any considerable area of land are, to all intents, absentee landlords. . . . The landlord is a receiver of rent in cash or kind; he may even sell the right of collecting the rent to the highest bidder, with obvious consequences to his unfortunate tenants; consciously or unconsciously, he is in effect an exploiter of the land and

and the whole of Sa'udi Arabia, and a half-share with British interests in the rich Kuwait oilfield, as well as their share in the Iraq Petroleum Co. In December 1946 the Anglo-Iranian Oil Co., hitherto under exclusive British control, conceded to two American companies 'substantial quantities of crude oil over a period of years'. It is proposed that to this end a new pipeline should be built to the Mediterranean, in addition to the existing Iraq Petroleum Co. line and the projected line of the Arabian-American Oil Co. Russia twenty years ago had a concession in North Persia which was never developed and lapsed; her demand for a concession covering most of North Persia was rejected by the Persian parliament in 1947. France has a quarter-share in the Iraq Petroleum Co.

[1] See tables in Bonne, op. cit.

his tenants. It is hardly necessary to point out that the blame for this disastrous state of affairs rests not with the individual landlord but with an age-old social system in which a sense of responsibility for the well-being of the land and its workers did not develop. . . . There can be no question whatever of the urgent necessity of attempting to graft on to the system this sense of responsibility, for history shows that if the problem of the absentee landlord is allowed to drift, it is liable to be solved by an agrarian revolution. . . . Throughout the Middle East the peasant-proprietor is in the grip of the money-lender. Although they own their land, they have not the means to improve it and are no better off than the small tenants of the large landlord who hold only an annual lease.'[1]

Owing to the resultant lack of enterprise of the fellahin and the primitiveness of their equipment, in some countries a considerable proportion of the land which is capable of cultivation by the most modern methods is left uncultivated. It is estimated that in Egypt, Palestine, and Transjordan over 70 per cent. of the cultivable land is already utilized, while in the mountainous Lebanon the rate of utilization is so high that the only outlet for an increasing population has for some decades been emigration. On the other hand, in Syria and Iraq there are vast areas cultivated centuries ago which might once more be brought under crops by modern methods of irrigation. It is estimated that in Iraq irrigated cultivation could be extended to three and a half times its present area.[2] While Egypt and Lebanon are already seriously over-populated, and the rapid natural increase in Palestine threatens over-population in another generation, Syria and Iraq have only three and four million inhabitants respectively, or considerably fewer than they supported in antiquity; and an extension of irrigation would undoubtedly permit a corresponding increase in their population.

'The whole area, with the exception of the Jews in Palestine, is included in the groups of population which derive at least 70 per cent. of the energy of their diet from cereals and roots. A considerable part of the population probably belongs to the group so deriving 80 per cent. of its calories. That is to say, the area is included among the worst-nourished parts of the world. It is possible to make certain broad statements which are true of populations in general which fall into this category. Malnutrition is wide-

[1] Keen, op. cit., 13 f.
[2] *Times*, 25 June 1947.

spread, and starvation threatens the poorest. Deficiency-diseases are frequent . . . and the picture is complicated and often obscured by infectious disease.'[1] In spite of improved public health services in the past thirty years, malaria remains a great scourge in many rural areas, notably in Syria. It is not a killing disease; but where it exists, 'the people, owing to general debilitation . . . are physically and morally incapable of taking advantage of such social services and opportunities for advancement as are provided. Without a much higher degree of control than at present exists, progress in education, agriculture, and social welfare generally would be impossible in the areas affected.'[2] In Egypt the well-being of the very dense rural population is at a very low level and may even be declining, partly as a result of the very rapid increase in its numbers, which have again doubled themselves since 1900.[3] Despite the spread of health-services infant mortality has actually shown an upward trend since 1919,[4] and in spite of the great increase of population the total consumption of such necessaries as meat and cereals, and such simple luxuries as coffee and tobacco, actually declined between 1924–5 and 1937–8, both average years.[5] Concentration on the production of cotton as a cash-crop, replacing the former self-sufficiency of the country in staple foods, has placed the Egyptian economy at the mercy of fluctuating world prices for cotton over which she has no control; and it is stated that 'the giving-over of a good part of the cotton-acreage to food crops, as in the war, is required as a permanent feature and would greatly benefit the health, fitness, and productive capacity of the population'.[6] Malaria is less of a scourge in Egypt

---

[1] Worthington, op. cit., 159.
[2] Worthington, op. cit., 142.
[3] The total population of Egypt in 1936 is computed at nineteen and a quarter millions (*Times*, 14 April 1947). 'If allowance is made for the fact that only 3½ per cent. of the area of Egypt is fit for cultivation, the density becomes more than double that of the U.K. If further allowance be made for industrial development as against agricultural, it is probably not inaccurate to state that the population-density of Egypt is eight times greater than that of the U.K., in relation to total resources.' (K. A. H. Murray, in *International Affairs*, XXIII 1947, 13.)
[4] Worthington, op. cit., 187.
[5] Issawi, op. cit., 55.
[6] Worthington, op. cit., 163. Failure to find markets during 1946 for more than about one-third of the crop of high-grade long-staple cotton, to say nothing of the accumulated surplus of the war-years, has caused the Egyptian government to limit the acreage for this grade of cotton during the 1947–8 season to under 40 per cent. of that of the previous year. (Annual Report of the National Bank of Egypt; *Times*, 14 April 1947.)

than in the Levant, though an acute epidemic in Upper Egypt in 1942–3 caused scores of thousands of deaths among the under-nourished villagers. Its place as a major debilitating disease is taken by the endemic worm-diseases contracted as a result of insanitary habits of excreta-disposal. Three-quarters of the whole population are estimated to be chronically infected, with a greatly lowering effect on its vitality. The incidence of these diseases is believed to have been considerably increased by the great extension of peren-nial irrigation with its thousands of channels, from which the fellah, working bare-foot, is reinfected as often as he is cured.[1] Another major scourge is the eye-disease of trachoma, estimated to affect 90 per cent. of the population of Egypt and a large proportion of those of the neighbouring countries, with consequences ranging from impaired vision to total blindness.

The public-health services of the Middle Eastern countries, especially those least subject to European direction or advice, naturally reflect the wide social gap that separates the professional class from the masses, and the small extent to which the former have as yet acquired a sense of service to the community as a whole. One is left with the impression that the health-services of the inde-pendent countries are designed for the benefit of the medical pro-fession rather than for the healing of the sick. In the capital cities there are government hospitals with imposing buildings and well-equipped laboratories. The provincial capitals are equipped on a more modest but similar scale; but even in the largest hospitals the standard of nursing tends to be unsatisfactory, sometimes even de-plorable, because the sense of service and duty is wanting; and the great majority of medical men and women produced by the training-schools, 'including nearly all the best, are inevitably at-tracted to careers in the towns, so that the towns tend to be over-doctored and the rural areas left with few or no medical men. . . . The spirit of service and public responsibility, which is usually associated with the medical profession, is wanted in the Middle East even more than technical advance.'[2]

Since 1939 increased consideration has been given to the raising of the economic standards of the Middle East. There was first of all

---

[1] Worthington, op. cit., 150 f.
[2] Worthington, op. cit., 174 ff. Some 60 per cent. of the doctors in Persia are stated to practise in Tehran (E. M. Hubback, in *Spectator*, 20 June 1947.)

the question of attaining regional self-sufficiency during the war. It has also been belatedly realized that a region, placed so strategically for world-communications and subsisting at so low a level, is a centre of social unhealth for other nations; and more specifically, that the urban and rural proletariat of such a region is potentially ripe to be attracted to Communism. The British Prime Minister told the Arab League delegates in London in September 1946: 'I believe that the Arab states now have the opportunity of inaugurating important economic developments, from which the common people of their countries would greatly benefit and which would increase their strength and stability. I am happy to see that co-operation in such developments is one of the purposes of the Arab League. I can assure you that H.M. Government will, in so far as you ask for their help, do everything in their power to help you in promoting economic expansion and social progress.' A fortnight later the Director of the Office of Near Eastern and African Affairs of the U.S. State Department similarly declared, 'Our primary policy . . . is to take whatever measures may be possible and proper to promote directly and indirectly the political and economic advancement of the Near and Middle Eastern peoples. . . . We should give appropriate assistance to developing the economics of the countries of the Near and Middle East and to creating a higher standard of living for their people.'

The prospects for greatly expanding industrialization are hampered by the lack of raw materials for manufacture, except for such local assets as the oilfields, the Egyptian cotton, and the Dead Sea salts. In Palestine the Zionists claim that there is a sufficient reservoir of relatively skilled Jewish labour to make practicable manufacture from raw materials largely imported. Nevertheless, the Anglo-American Inquiry Committee expressed considerable reserve about the future of Zionist industry: 'There is boundless optimism and energy, great administrative capacity, but a shortage of skilled labour and, as a result, more quantity than quality of output. . . . There is the question, how far the consolidation and further growth of Jewish industry and trade are dependent upon maintenance of the momentum provided by continuing immigration. . . . There is the question whether the high costs of production and inferior quality of some products in Jewish industry will permit the establishment of a firm position in the home market without inordinate protection. There is the related question how

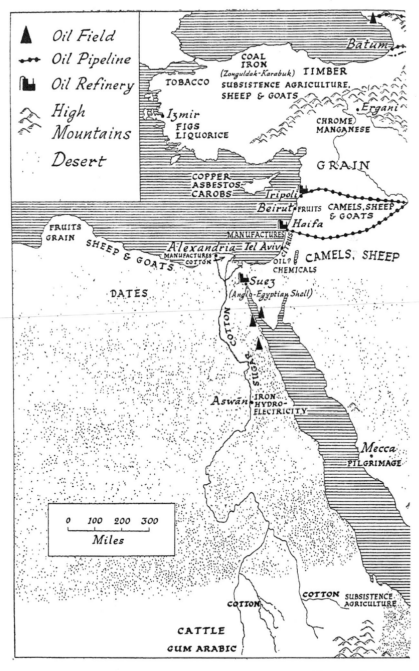

Oil Field ▲

Oil Pipeline ▬●▬

Oil Refinery 🏭

High Mountains ⛰

Desert

Batum ▲

COAL
IRON
(Zonguldak-Karabuk) TIMBER
TOBACCO SUBSISTENCE AGRICULTURE,
SHEEP & GOATS

Izmir
FIGS
LIQUORICE

.*Ergani*

CHROME
MANGANESE

G R A I N

COPPER
ASBESTOS
CAROBS

Tripoli 🏭

Beirut FRUITS CAMELS, SHEEP
& GOATS

🏭 *Haifa*

FRUITS
GRAIN

SHEEP & GOATS

Alexandria = *Tel Aviv*
MANUFACTURES
COTTON

MANUFACTURES

OIL? 🏭

CAMELS, SHEEP

CHEMICALS

🏭 *Suez*
(Anglo-Egyptian Shell)

DATES

COTTON

SUGAR

Aswan IRON
HYDRO-
ELECTRICITY

Mecca
●
PILGRIMAGE

0   100 200 300
|—|—|—|—|
Miles

COTTON SUBSISTENCE
AGRICULTURE

COTTON

CATTLE

GUM ARABIC

13.   MIDDLE EAST

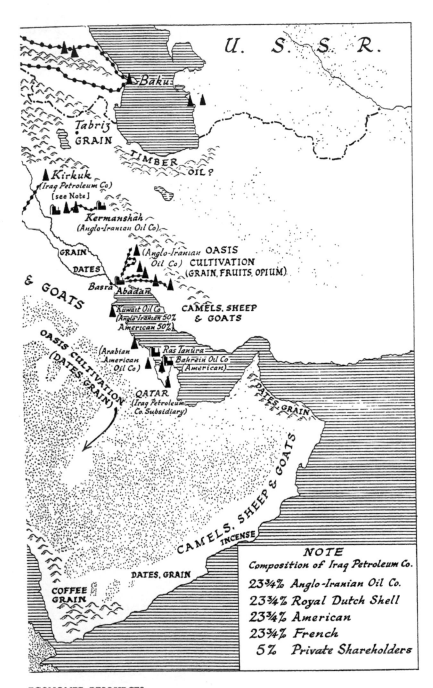

ECONOMIC RESOURCES

far external markets can be retained . . . in the face of competition from advanced industrial countries and possible continuation of the boycott of Jewish products in neighbouring Arab states.'[1] In the other Middle Eastern countries industrial skill is so wanting that the advantage of cheap labour is more than outweighed, and it becomes more than ever difficult to compete against the mass-production of the highly industrialized countries without recourse to heavy tariffs.[2] The advantages of industrial development are not yet fully apparent to the majority of conservative politicians who rule these countries, since they derive their wealth mainly from agriculture. While grandiose plans of economic development are drawn up from time to time, they are apt to be sacrificed to political considerations. For example, the award of the contract for the construction of a hydro-electric plant at the Aswan Dam, which has important industrial potentialities for Egypt, was delayed for a year by the Egyptian government's pre-occupation with treaty-revision.

In view of these limitations that must for some time to come restrict any large-scale industrialization of the Middle East, the possibilities of improving its agriculture and stock-rearing must be examined. The Middle East Supply Centre's expert concluded that new agricultural systems and techniques are best tried out 'in areas that are relatively undeveloped and unoccupied or where, after the existing structure has disintegrated into chaos, a stable and authoritative administration takes over, as happened in the Sudan. . . . But the greater part of the population is concerned in, and a very considerable area of the land is occupied by, the practice of firmly entrenched systems of agriculture . . . and here the methods needed

---

[1] Chs. VIII 7, IV 19. Figures quoted by a Jewish business-man (*Palestine Post*, 27 December 1946) afford striking evidence of the combination of high wages and low output in Jewish industry, since the writer admits that 'in this respect the local textile industry is not exceptional'. The following indices, referring to the textile industry in July 1945, are based on the figure of 100 for the U.K. rate in each case:

	Average wage	Average output per operative.	Manufacturer's costs (Wages/output).
U.S.A.	163	193	84
Jewish Palestine	147	71	203

[2] In the relatively advanced Turkish coalfields of Zonguldak, for example, the output per man is only about half the by-no-means adequate British figure, and the mines are run at a loss made up by a subsidy from other nationalized industries. (M. Philips Price, in *Manchester Guardian*, 5 and 7 December, 1946.)

to foster the process of evolutionary change are all, in essence, educational. Among the problems are (a) to develop among the larger landowners the sense of their responsibilities to the land and its workers: (b) to cultivate among the tenants and peasant-proprietors a desire to improve the lot of themselves and their families; (c) to evolve a type of education for rural children that will fit them to live in and profit by a rural environment; (d) to train teachers for rural schools, and members for the Agricultural Department, who will be able to evoke and guide the move towards rural development.'[1] In Iraq the British Middle East Office is associated with the Iraq government in a scheme for greatly extending irrigation, with accompanying progress in education and other services; and the Foreign Secretary has hinted at 'great schemes of irrigation and other things on the way' in the Middle East as a whole.[2] The United States has commercial agreements with Sa'udi Arabia and the Yemen which may greatly develop those countries.

Zionism also has its concrete plans for the economic future of a much wider area than Palestine. Dr. A. Bonne, director of the Economic Research Institute of the Jewish Agency, published in 1943 a book *The Economic Development of the Middle East*, with the sub-title: An Outline of Planned Reconstruction after the War. He summed up his thesis in the concluding paragraphs of the book: 'It is possibly no mere coincidence that the Jews . . . now find themselves in Western Asia at the precise moment when this sub-continent enters upon a new phase in its history. . . . The transformation of the Orient and the securing of better social and economic conditions calls first and foremost for the presence and co-operation of a human element in fairly large numbers who are willing and competent to act as pioneers of this process. . . . Obviously the world has not yet realized the full extent of these immense possibilities. But it should now recognize that these neglected spaces can be brought to new life by utilizing the creative capacities of those who were once a, if not the, spiritual driving force of the Orient.'[3] Underlying this self-regarding reasoning lay the assumption that within twenty years of the end of the war the Jewish population of Palestine would have increased to

[1] Keen, op. cit., Ch. III.
[2] *Times*, 25 June 1947; 30 May 1947.
[3] op. cit., 132 f.

2,100,000, constituting 58 per cent. of the resultant population.[1] The Arabs of Palestine and the neighbouring countries are, however less inclined now than ever to purchase the promise of material progress at the price of surrendering Palestine to the Jews. Jewish offers of material improvement, and President Truman's offer of generous subsidies to the Arabs if they would accept Jewish large-scale immigration, overlook the fact that, while many Arabs are venal, they are accustomed to drive a hard bargain. To many of them, and those the most influential, the mirage of self-government is far more attractive than all the prospects of the economic improvement of their countries; the masses are accustomed to poverty and will listen to their own political leaders rather than to foreigners who offer them opulence with a political 'string' attached. It will probably be at least two generations before the spread of education corrects the present over-emphasis on politics and neglect of economic considerations, unless the process is accelerated by a social revolution induced from outside the Arab world.

★　　★　　★

The partial conversion of the Fertile Crescent and Egypt from a pre-capitalist to a capitalist economy, which has gathered impetus in the past thirty years, has tended to increase the disparity of wealth between the very rich and the very poor and to segregate classes; but it has also called into being a middle-class following various skilled or semi-skilled professions and occupations, and enjoying varying levels of wealth and comfort.[2] The upper-class consists of the wealthy landowners and merchants, with no such sharp division between the two occupations as formerly existed in some European countries: while some members of a well-to-do family are concerned with their estates, others engage in commerce. The long exposure of Egypt to foreign commercial and cultural

---

[1] p. 65. No less a Zionist authority than Dr. Weizmann has repeated to the U.N. Committee on Palestine this figure of one and a half millions for the potential increase of the Jewish population of Palestine (8 July 1947).

[2] cf. the effect of the Industrial Revolution in Britain; Trevelyan, op. cit., 546. In peninsular Arabia the traditional form of society, that of the Bedouin tribe and the sedentary oasis, is still uncontaminated by outside influences; but the presence of enormous quantities of oil and the granting of concessions in return for much-needed royalties must inevitably mean the extension of Western influences, which will eventually cause conditions in those parts of Arabia most affected to resemble those in the Fertile Crescent to-day.

influences and her advanced state of political emancipation from foreign control have caused the upper-class there to begin to lose its predominant political position to the middle-class. The wealthy Pashas are still individually very powerful, but relatively unorganized as a class, since while some have belonged for the past generation to the small Liberal-Constitutional party, many have preferred to remain independent of party ties. Sidqi Pasha is perhaps one of the last of this class to wield political power in Egypt; but as long as the King can turn to it for support against the republican-minded Wafd intent on a party-dictatorship, the upper-class will continue to have an influence far beyond its restricted numbers. It is interesting to observe how, as in nineteenth-century Britain, this ruling-class is transferring its interest from land to finance-capitalism as a means of preserving its wealth and the privilege that goes with it. Sidqi himself is president of the Federation of Egyptian Industrialists and director of nineteen different companies.

The Wafd, while claiming to represent the masses, is in its personnel essentially composed of middle-class politicians. Its successive leaders, Zaghlul and Nahhas, were men of the people who had risen into the professional class through the administrative or legal career. Though the Wafd has the advantage of being the only party well-organized throughout Egypt and has a much richer political war-chest than any other party, it has under Nahhas been greatly weakened by 'maladministration when in office, dissension, expulsions, and resignations' to form the new Sa'dist and Kutla parties, formed respectively in 1938 and 1943 and now headed respectively by Nuqrashi and Makram Ubaid. 'Nahhas is the only surviving lieutenant of Zaghlul now left in the Wafd and its one outstanding figure, and many observers believe that it is only his strong and engaging personality that saves it from disintegration. The party is completely dominated by the masterful Pasha. Acceptance of his will rather than agreement with any programme is the chief condition of membership. As a result the calibre of Wafdist candidates for parliament is declining. . . . Following the average party-leader is like going on an expedition under sealed orders. Nobody but the captain has any idea of the objective, and it is often doubtful if that objective is anything more than the immediate interests of the leader and his intimates and the enjoyment of the sweets and fruits of office.'[1]

[1] *Times* Cairo correspondent, 23 December 1946.

In Turkey the Kemalist national revolution introduced a large measure of state-control in industry[1] and created a privileged class of senior civil-servants with an interest in the maintenance of the new régime. But since the death of Ataturk and particularly during the Second World War the state machinery has not worked too well. There has been a good deal of waste and inefficiency and some of the old corruption, which Ataturk tried ruthlessly to suppress, has crept back again. This helps to account for the emergence in 1946 of the so-called Democratic party in opposition to the People's party founded by Ataturk which, unlike many totalitarian parties elsewhere, has always admitted in principle and has recently permitted in fact the existence of legal opposition parties, unwilling as it may be to see them attain power. The Democratic party consists in the main of well-to-do merchants and traders who desire greater economic freedom and the abolition of the state monopolies which restrict their trading activities.

While Egypt and Turkey have advanced some distance towards middle-class rule, in the countries of the Fertile Crescent the landowning and mercantile class is still predominant politically, and a distinct middle-class is only in an early stage of emergence. The governments of these countries are formed almost exclusively from the upper-class. A striking feature of political life in Syria (and to a lesser degree in Lebanon) is the manner in which the great landowners exert their influence and pursue their rivalries by means of armed retainers, for all the world like medieval barons, except that automatic weapons are now the vogue and that the ballot-box plays a curious and unreal role on this Montagu-and-Capulet scene. In 1943, for example, the Lebanese cabinet-minister Majid Arlan raised his Druze henchmen in the mountains against the French; early in 1946 Bedouin deputies drew revolvers and fired several shots in the Syrian Chamber to intimidate a critic; in March 1947 the most recent of many clashes between two rival factions in Tripoli was reported to have caused the deaths of fifteen to twenty persons. During the Mandatory period the French were probably

[1] This was not a matter of political ideology. 'Kemalist Turkey, intent on liberating the country from foreign economic control, made one of its main concerns the transfer to Turkish hands of the principal national sources of wealth and industries. As private capital was scarce the State had to take a hand in the process. . . . Thus the State found itself quite inadvertently committed to a policy of a State-Socialism owning or controlling the principal industries, communications, mines, and banks.' (*Times* Correspondent in Turkey, 13 May 1947.)

not averse to these phenomena, which tended to divide and weaken the nationalist opposition to themselves.[1] In Palestine the vendetta carried on in the second phase of the Arab Rebellion, especially in 1938, by the dominant Husaini faction against its rivals the Nashashibis and others is an example of the same phenomenon, normally repressed by the Mandatory. In Transjordan, Sa'udi Arabia, and the Yemen personal autocratic government of the traditional type still persists, and the king's ministers are in very truth no more than the servants of their master. As a consequence of all this the Arab League, which came into being in the spring of 1945 as a federation of the governments of the Arabic-speaking states, 'to draw closer the relations between them, to co-ordinate their political action with a view to close collaboration, to safeguard their independence and sovereignty . . . and to achieve a close co-operation in economic, cultural, juridical, social, and health matters,'[2] can hardly be said to have manifested a progressive social outlook. Its active secretary-general, Abd ur-Rahman Azzam, has indeed stated that 'The Prophet was the first socialist, and it is the duty of all his present-day followers to do all in their power to encourage the growth of socialism'.[3] But on the whole the remark of a *Times* correspondent[4] remains true that 'The main, if not the only, cohesive force within the League is an ingrained and traditional xenophobia, directed according to circumstances against the French, the British, or the Jews'.

The internal rifts latent within the Arab League are consistently exaggerated by those who wish to destroy such Arab unity as exists; but they cannot be ignored. The rivalry between King Ibn Sa'ud on the one hand and the Hashimite rulers of Iraq and Transjordan on the other was a serious obstacle to the very inception of the League.[5] King Abdullah of Transjordan has never renounced his father's claim to be King of the Arabs. He plans to cement the sovereignty of his Hashimite family over the whole Fertile Crescent. He has intrigued with all the forces in Syria, communal, social or personal, opposed to the existing government there, in the hope

---

[1] The hanging in 1946 of the Alawi chief Sulaiman Murshid was due to his intrigues with the French; and it remains to be seen whether similar strong measures will be taken in the future against other headstrong 'barons'.
[2] Edward Atiyah, in *Spectator*, 12 October 1945.
[3] *Palestine Post*, 15 July 1946.
[4] September, 1945.
[5] J. Lugol, *Le Panarabisme*, 252 f.

of restoring the Greater Syria over which his brother Faisal ruled from 1918 to 1920;[1] and he regards Ibn Sa'ud as a barbarous intruder from Najd into his own ancestral Hijaz. Egyptian politicians desire that the pre-eminence of Egypt in population and wealth should continue to be reflected by her predominant influence in the Arab League; Syrians, on the other hand, regard the Egyptians as intellectually and culturally inferior to themselves, as speaking an uncouth kind of Arabic, as Arabized Africans rather than true Arabs. In Lebanon the majority of the Maronites, or about one-third of the whole population, reject the notion that Lebanon has any place in the Arab League, and wish to maintain and strengthen their links with France as a bulwark against Muslim encroachment; and though the governments of the last four years are opposed to this pro-French element, they have to defer to local Christian fears and suspicions by emphasizing the distinctness and independence of Lebanon, while Arab League personalities are constantly assuring Lebanon that her peculiar status will be respected. The activities of King Abdullah and the Iraqi politicians who support him have ranged the rest of the Arab League against the Hashimite dynasty, and the two blocs so formed are constantly manoeuvring for position; but the anti-Hashimite block of Egypt, Sa'udi Arabia, Syria and Lebanon has in itself no cohesive force other than the common opposition to King Abdullah.

The budgets of the independent Arab countries are marked by a characteristic desire to build up armies and air-forces out of their slender financial resources as a matter of national prestige, however unserviceable these forces may be in practice. Other disproportionately large sums are expended by the states of Arab Asia, none of which numbers more than 4,000,000 inhabitants and those poverty-stricken, on diplomatic representation abroad and official ostentation at home. During the War, faced with the difficulties arising from the stoppage of supplies from overseas, not only did these independent administrations fail to prevent a manifold increase in the cost-of-living, caused in part by maldistribution and widespread hoarding and black-marketing on the part of producers and merchants, but in some cases highly-placed members of the administrations themselves were involved in these malpractices; and widespread famine in areas that were not self-sufficient in grain

[1] *The World To-Day*, January 1948, 15 ff.

was averted only by the organizing ability and authority of the Anglo-American Middle East Supply Centre.[1]

Attempts are being made to develop the social side of the Arab League by such projects as the simplifying of passport regulations, the development of international communications, the co-ordinating of law, public health, and education; but as long as any part of the Arab world remains subject to foreign encroachments on its independence, and as long as the governments of the Arab world remain dominated by the ageing personalities of the Arab Awakening and the Revolt, so long will the Arab League continue to be obsessed with politics, propaganda, and boycotts; and so long will accusations of widespread nepotism and the inefficiency that goes with it be levelled with much justice at the Arab administrations.

*   *   *

The younger generation of the growing middle-class is the product of the school-system modelled on more-or-less European lines and expanded with perilous rapidity in the period between the two wars. The very considerable increase in the educational budgets of Egypt and Iraq since these countries achieved self-government over twenty years ago has not yet produced a commensurate raising of educational standards, and could not indeed be expected to do so. It has first been necessary to educate a corps of teachers along the new lines appropriate to the awakening of the Middle East. There has been some wastefulness inevitable in the administrative machinery of these countries at their present stage, and due in part to inexperience and in part to graft. One is sometimes tempted to suspect that the zeal to expand the school-system so rapidly derives, not only from a laudable desire to educate the masses, but also to render them more receptive of nationalist propaganda and to find white-collar employment as teachers for large numbers of young effendis.[2] The younger men have suffered somewhat from the quality of the education imparted to them, in

---

[1] K. A. H. Murray, in *Royal Central Asian Journal*, XXXII (1945), 233 ff.

[2] A good example of the tendency to spend disproportionately on the middle-class teacher is provided by a statement of the Egyptian Minister of Education. After referring to an appropriation for the education of 250,000 children at an initial cost of £1 2s. 6d. per head, he spoke of the opening of two schools for training 180 students as 'lady social visitors' at an initial cost of £111 per head, or just one hundred times the other *per capita* allocation. (*Middle East Opinion* (Cairo), 23 September 1946.)

R

which the forming of character and a broad understanding of the world about them has been neglected in favour of a superficial instruction administered mechanically by teachers whose own educational attainments are still often inadequate. Education is directed far too much merely to the passing of examinations calling for text-book knowledge learned by rote, rather than to the cultivation of original thinking and the exercise of the critical faculty; and the ultimate goal of such education being safe employment in a government office,[1] not the moulding of an intelligent citizen of sound character and ability to perform a useful function in the community, what has been learnt tends to be discarded thankfully as soon as the final examination has been left behind. Cairo University students have in recent years gone on strike, and even overturned and set fire to trams, in protest against the raising of the examination pass-standard; and attempts by parents to bribe examiners in order to get a backward candidate passed are not uncommon. Even in the most advanced countries, of course, education tends to lose sight of its true function on account of the inhibiting effect of the examination-system; but this defeat is felt with particular acuteness in the Middle East, where the quality of education is further impaired by the crude and excessive nationalist content of much historical and cultural instruction.

The present younger generation, having imbibed more formal instruction than its parents, and being drawn from a wider and more comprehensive social background than the wealthy elder-statesmen, resents the fact that the latter have thus far enjoyed the fruits of political power, an exclusiveness for which foreign imperialism can no longer, as formerly, be everywhere blamed. They accuse their rulers, with much justice, of corruption and family-partiality; but it is questionable how far their indignation is genuinely moral, and how far they are moved by the fact that they themselves are not the beneficiaries of these malpractices. Forced by their education into a bottle-neck in which there are far fewer desirable administrative or professional posts than candidates for them, and unfitted for commercial careers in competition with Europeans, they are driven to seek the patronage of the political leaders; and those who fail in this rigorous competition tend to

[1] Although Iraq has already rather more lawyers than it can hope to employ, 1,000 youths entered the Law School in 1946. (*Times* Baghdad Correspondent, 25 June 1947.)

seek compensation for their frustration and inadequacy in some form of political extremism. If they belong to a racial or religious minority, as for example the Armenians in Aleppo and Beirut, the Kurds and Orthodox Christians in Damascus, or the various alien communities in Egypt, they often turn to Communism; if Muslim, they resort more readily to the innumerable extreme nationalist parties which spring up ephemerally in every Middle Eastern country. This is the type of dissatisfied young man that supported the military Golden Square in Iraq, that flirted with the Nazis during the Vichy period in Syria, that supports the Young Egypt party (Misr al-Fatat) or forms the rank-and-file of the Muslim Brotherhood (Ikhwan al-Muslimin). This last powerful movement was the creation of an Egyptian schoolmaster Hasan al-Banna about 1930, and has won some hundreds of thousands of followers in Egypt, and more recently some thousands in neighbouring countries, by its appeal for a rejection of European civilization with its alleged materialism and corruption, and a return to the simple brotherhood of primitive Islam. Violently anti-foreign, anti-Communist, and anti-Zionist, the movement has been called Fascist by those who find it convenient to attach this label to everything they dislike; but it has more evident affinities with Gandhi's *swaraj* in its desire to throw off foreign forms and rebuild upon the essentials of its native culture, though being Muslim it conspicuously lacks the Mahatma's ideal of non-violence. Like Gandhi too, its leader, while apparently of personal integrity, is sufficient of a realist to understand that a political movement must have material backing if it is to be effective; and just as Gandhi, for all his contempt for wealth, tacitly accepted the dependence of *swaraj* on the Hindu plutocracy, so al-Banna has accommodated himself from time to time to what seemed the strongest force in Egyptian politics. In the early years of the war the Ikhwan were subsidized by, and made propaganda for, the Palace; after the return to power of the Wafd al-Banna yielded to the menaces of Nahhas and transferred the allegiance of the Ikhwan to him; but it deserted the Wafd when that party fell in 1944; and recently, no doubt with the tacit approval of the government coalition, it was denouncing the Wafd as permeated with Communists, taking orders from Moscow and being 'unethical, unpatriotic, and un-Muslim'.[1] All the time it has gained adherents among the uncritical thousands of the semi-

[1] *Times* Cairo correspondent, 13 May 1947.

educated, disillusioned by the ineptitude, corruption, or indifference of the professional politicians; it has held out before them the elimination of the foreigner and the Copt as competitors for the limited number of desirable jobs, and a paper-programme of social justice based on the Qur'an and the Sunna; but there have been some indications in the past year that it may be passing the peak of its influence.

To sum up, the younger generation of the educated class present a rather pathetic picture of 'wanderers between two worlds'. They have not yet had time to acquire more than the bare externals of Western culture without usually grasping its inner quality. Many of them, however, having grown up in an atmosphere of materialism, have turned from their own Arab and Muslim culture, feeling shamefacedly that it has been weighed against that of Europe in the only test they recognize as valid, that of material success, and found wanting; and when they do claim merit for their own civilization, it is too often without apparently being able to express wherein that civilization has in the past excelled. Professor H. A. R. Gibb, whom no one could accuse of lack of sympathy for Arab cultural aspirations, has stated, 'I have not seen any book written in Arabic for Arabs themselves which has clearly analysed what Arabic culture means for Arabs.'[1] Their superficiality and instability of thought is not, however, the inherent fault of this generation so much as its misfortune in being a generation of transition, neither fully Muslim nor fully European, neither fully traditional nor fully emancipated. Albert Hourani has analysed the phenomenon in a penetrating passage: 'The change is not from one static position to another, but from a static community ruled by custom to a dynamic society, moulded and governed by positive laws and by a conception of individual, social, or national welfare. It may be that the difficulties will so press on the Arabs that they will accept self-division as inevitable and give up the attempt to reconcile the new and the old. If that happens they will become Levantines. To be a Levantine . . . is to belong to no community and to possess nothing of one's own. . . . The special mark of the present age is the spread of the Levant inland. . . . In a sense every . . . educated Arab of the towns is forced to live in two worlds. Not only his way of thought but his social life is becoming daily more deeply affected by Europe and America; but at heart he is still an Arab and usually a Muslim.

[1] *The Near East, Problems and Prospects*, ed. P. W. Ireland (1942), 60.

A few may be strong enough to face the problem and create a new unity out of discordant elements; but the majority are likely to take the line of least resistance, and passively acquiesce in their division of soul.'[1]

In the melancholy which pervades this passage Mr. Hourani is characteristic of the Arab intellectual of his generation—over-formal, self-conscious, frustrated, politics-ridden. But there are some signs that the teen-age adolescents of to-day, starting their stage in the upward climb out of stagnation on the shoulders of Messrs. Atiyah and Hourani, as it were, may find it easier to laugh at life. The increased interest in sport of the schoolboys of the present-day Levant should give them a healthier outlook on life, and they may grow up more physically self-reliant and extroverted, provided that the eventual achievement of self-government in their countries is not followed by a reaction against Western habits of body and mind. At all events the only hope of the Middle East for the next generation lies in those educated young men (and to a lesser degree young women also) who are for the first time in the history of the region studying the conditions of the masses and considering how they may be improved. The Village Welfare Service in Syria indicates the beginnings of such a movement.[2] In Egypt also 'there is evidence that the younger and more thoughtful men—and there are plenty of them—are tiring of the personality system' which at present dominates Middle Eastern politics. 'Their goal is a better Egypt. . . . Many Egyptians who hold aloof from party affiliations would eagerly support a programme designed to rid Egypt of poverty, ignorance, and disease. . . . But first the net of narrow parochialism, meaningless slogans, mendacious propaganda, and distorted history in which the older leaders have enmeshed them must be cut away.'[3] This can hardly be achieved as long as foreign imperialism can be blamed for every defect in the body politic; and even when these countries have achieved full independence, habit and the self-interest of the political bosses will be slow to allow the social conscience free scope and development. In Egypt and the countries of the Fertile Crescent it is doubtful whether, owing to the self-regarding conservatism of

[1] *Syria and Lebanon*, 69 ff.
[2] Dr. Bayard Dodge, in *Middle East Agricultural Development Conference* (Cairo, 1944), 215.
[3] *Times* Cairo correspondent, 23 December 1946.

those in power, effective social reform can be achieved by evolutionary and constitutional means. Palliative five-year-plans and the like will be drafted and duly pass into law, but how many of them will be translated into action?

★ ★ ★

While the masses still hold as unquestioningly as ever to their traditional Islam, there has been a marked trend towards materialism, agnosticism, and atheism among the upper and middle-classes, especially among their younger members, as a result of contact with Western ideas. Many of the young nationalists are conscious of being Muslims only as a political bond with the masses, and of Islam only as a political rallying-cry against the foreigner. Between these sceptics and the mass of the population come the 'ulama, the preachers, the graduates of the Muslim seminaries, whose indurated conservatism of centuries has barely been touched by more modern ideas. Some beginnings of reform in Al Azhar, the ancient and well-frequented Muslim university of Cairo, have been effected in the last fifteen years, but the process is bound to be very slow. Islam has fallen into such a state of moral, intellectual, and spiritual catalepsy that it will take many decades, if not centuries, to reanimate the inert hulk; and it is doubtful if outside forces, whether the impact of the Anglo-American world or that of Soviet Russia, will give traditional Islam so long a respite.

Nor can it be said that Christianity in the Middle East is in much better case. It makes virtually no converts from Islam, and is in fact losing in Egypt hundreds of Copts annually to Islam for political reasons. Except in Lebanon it is the religion of a minority, suspected by the Muslim majority, with some justification, of intrigue with one or other European Power, and driven by this very circumstance to regard its religion as a political instrument rather than as a way of life.[1] While some Christian Arabs are trying to fuse their religious differences with the Muslims in the crucible of Arab nationalism, the Muslims, conscious of their own intellectual inferiority, are slow to give them full confidence. Some Christians accordingly entertain the idea of concentrating their numbers by

[1] A vivid picture of the mingled physical fear and intellectual contempt with which the Lebanese Christians regarded their Muslim rulers before the First World War is given in Edward Atiyah's *An Arab Tells his Story*.

migration into the Lebanon, which they think might thereby be made strong and homogeneous enough to remain permanently independent of Muslim Syria. Christian unity is, however, greatly impaired by its division into sects—Orthodox, Catholic, Monophysite, and Protestant—no fewer than ten of which exist in Syria and Lebanon; and their mutual repulsion is hardly less than the antipathy with which all regard the Muslim majority. The growth of nationalism and the struggle for independence has everywhere subordinated religion to politics, and it cannot be said that a genuine sense of religion, as opposed to the externals of religious sectarianism, is an important social force in any wide circle in the Middle East to-day.

$$\star \qquad \star \qquad \star$$

In spite of attempts made to improve the economic standards of the rural masses by a few benevolent landowners or by government action such as the not-very-successful efforts in Egypt and Palestine to reduce individual self-interest and mutual suspicion by promoting a rural co-operative movement, the country-people of the Middle East are for the most part bound by their age-old traditions of agricultural technique and social organization. The urban workers on the other hand have been much more affected by the process of modernization, mechanization, industrialization in the last thirty years; and with these Western methods of economic organization has come the associated Western social grouping, the trades-union. This arose first in Egypt, as being the country which was exposed to Western industrialization much earlier and more deeply than the countries which remained till 1918 integral parts of the Ottoman Empire. The first Egyptian trade-union was the League of Cairo Cigarette-Factory Workers founded in 1903; but a more important union was the Syndicate of Manual Workers, mainly those in the State Railways, which was formed in 1908. It is significant that this syndicate was from its early days courted by the Nationalist party, which opened night-schools for the general education and political indoctrination of the workers. Soon after the First World War workers in some industries, encouraged by the Wafd, obtained the guarantee of sick-pay and a retiring bonus; but the growth of trades unions made little progress, possibly because of the workers' mistrust, instinctive in the Middle East, for the effendis who were trying to organize them into this unaccustomed social pattern. In 1931 Sidqi Pasha, who had come into office as the result of a Palace-organized reaction against the Wafd's bid for dictatorship, dissolved the existing trades-unions as a centre of Wafdist political activity, and instead set up an official Labour Office in the Ministry of the Interior, closely connected with the Department of Public Security. On the return to power of the Wafd in 1936 the trades unions were once more allowed to function, and at the outbreak of the Second World War they had some 20,000 members, chiefly concentrated in the larger towns. The movement still had no political ideology of its own, however, but continued to be the catspaw of the existing political parties. In the early part of the war the Cairo unions were manipulated by a member of the Royal Family, the Nabil Abbas Halim, as an instrument of pro-Palace and anti-British propaganda, which finally resulted in his internment at the request of the British authorities. The number of trades-unionists in Egypt has now risen to some 150,000, and the movement has passed distinctly under the control of Communists or 'fellow-travellers', as a result of the heightened prestige of the U.S.S.R. during the war and the greater facilities for Communist propaganda since the opening of the Russian Legation in Cairo in 1943. The decline in real wages during the war on account of the greatly increased cost-of-living has stimulated labour unrest and political extremism. A group of trades-union leaders has formed a 'Workers' Committee for National Liberation' with a very radical anti-capitalist policy. Once again genuine labour unrest has been exploited for political ends by the Wafd in order to embarrass the government in power. It was the Wafd-organized 'students' and workers' committees' which staged the anti-British demonstrations and murderous riots early in 1946; and eventually in July Sidqi Pasha struck at these subversive forces by extensive arrests and the suppression of eleven organizations, both intellectual and trades-unionist.

Thus in Egypt the acute need for an improvement of the workers' conditions of life has continually been exploited and diverted by political manipulators, who have shown no sign of genuine sympathy for the workers, to factious purposes which offer no guarantee that they would serve the workers' interests. In Palestine, in spite of the prevailing conflict of the Zionist and Arab nationalisms, trades-unionism has had a less chequered and more constructive history than in Egypt. Immediately after the First World War the Histadruth trades-union organization, which already played an important part in the life of the Jewish community, sought to foster trades-unionism among the Arabs, partly in a genuine attempt to organize the Arab workers in a way which they themselves found good, partly to eliminate the competition of cheap unorganized Arab labour, and partly perhaps in the hope of stimulating among the Arabs a class-struggle which would cut across and weaken the Arab anti-Zionist national movement. Whatever the motives, the Zionist attempt to create a parallel Arab trades-union movement had little success, and in 1925 the independent and anti-Zionist Palestine Arab Workers' Society was formed. By the outbreak of the Second World War it had some 17,000 members in twenty branches, representing thirty-six craft unions; under its aegis were operated a sick fund, a saving-bank, six co-operative stores, and a co-operative tailoring-shop. Under the leadership of Sami Taha, a 'decent steady trades-unionist',[1] its policy was generally moderate, in view of the still modest role of industrial labour in the economic life of Arab Palestine, and it was usually willing to negotiate with employers or with the government Department of Labour for the welfare of its members. The increased demand for Arab labour in wartime activities greatly strengthened its bargaining powers; its demands became more exacting, and it was more ready to enforce them through strikes. Meanwhile in 1941 a group of young Arabs with Communist leanings, disliking the influence in the Arab Workers Society of its legal adviser, the wealthy lawyer Hanna Asfur, had formed a rival organization, the Federation of Arab Trades Unions, with some 1,500 members in Haifa and supporters in other towns. This group, profiting from the more lenient attitude of the police towards left-wing activities following the Russian entry into the war, began a weekly newspaper *Al-Ittihad*, edited by its secretary Emil Tuma. In August 1945 a major secession from the Arab Workers Society occurred, the majority revolting against the influence of Hanna Asfur and joining the Federation of Arab Trades Unions in a new left-wing organization, the Palestine Arab Workers' Congress, electing Bulos Farah, a product of the Comintern Training School in Moscow, as one of their delegates to the International Trades Unions Congress in Paris. In January 1947 the Arab Workers' Con-

---

[1] He was murdered by an extreme nationalist, September 1947.

gress claimed to comprise 60 per cent. of organized Arab labour in Palestine.

In Lebanon there was a great increase in industrial activity during the war, and a corresponding increase in the scope of organized labour. Most unions there are united in a Federation of Trades Unions organized by the active left-winger Mustafa al Aris. The wealthy minority that rules the Lebanon is trying to combat the growth of this Federation by encouraging a rival 'company-union'. Trades-unionism is less developed in Syria, which is economically and socially far less advanced than the countries already mentioned; it is strongest among the Armenian colony in Aleppo. In economically undeveloped Iraq also trades-unionism is weak, except in the Iraq Petroleum Co. and in the State Railways; it was until recently officially discouraged by the governments that succeeded the military Putsch of 1941. In Persia the growth of the Tudeh (Workers') Party and trades-unionism was so intimately bound up with the Russian occupation that it is more appropriately treated in the chapter 'Russia and the Middle East'.

★   ★   ★

For centuries one-half of the population of all classes—the women—have been kept in ignorance, and those of the upper classes in seclusion. In the last forty years the veil has been lifted somewhat, and in the more modernized parts of the Middle East the education of girls is now an accepted thing. In Egypt, for example, the proportion of girls to the total number of children actually on the registers of schools has since 1935 risen from about one-fifth to two-fifths. The first women students were admitted to the Fuad I University in 1929, one year after it opened, and there are now a few women, including one professor, on its teaching staff. Some 3 per cent. of the doctors in Egypt are women, a total of about 150, though they are not yet accepted on the staff of the Cairo University Hospital. There are some Egyptian women lawyers. A bill was submitted to the Egyptian parliament in January 1947 to extend the suffrage to women, though with a literacy qualification which is not applied to male voters. Women play some part in the Egyptian trades-union and left-wing movements.[1] One of the feminists' aims which most deserves sympathy

[1] Andrew Roth, *Palestine Post*, 27 December 1946, 7 February 1947.

is that of reforming the Muslim divorce-laws, which completely subject the wife to her husband's caprice. The other Middle Eastern countries are less 'advanced' than Egypt,[1] and everywhere the forces of reaction against the education and emancipation of women are still strong. Even in Egypt a bill was recently introduced into parliament to ban women lawyers, but was defeated. There is some reason to fear that the achievement of complete independence and the decline of direct European influence may, temporarily at least, affect adversely the course of their emancipation.[2]

★　　★　　★

To sum up, the present economic and social situation of the Middle Eastern countries presents many disquieting features. They are ruled by ageing men of the upper-class whose political charter has been the achievement of national independence from foreign imperialisms, and who are insufficiently sensitive to economic and social change. The impact of Western liberalism and industrialization has in the last hundred years shaken the Middle East out of its post-medieval trance; but its ability to adjust itself to the changed conditions is still being tested, it has not yet been conclusively demonstrated. Before it has successfully emerged from this test, it is already being subjected to the still more formidable impact of the Russian Communist theory and practice of materialist determinism. To this new challenge the elder statesmen can reply only with the repression of 'subversive elements', with schemes of economic and social improvement which will convince those familiar with the history of Middle East paper-reforms only when they have been realized in fact, and with lip-service to the idea of social welfare which is rarely confirmed by their conduct. The younger generation has the advantage of having grown up in a more mechanized environment running at a faster tempo than their fathers, and thus finds it less difficult to adjust itself to extraneous influences; but on the other hand, it lacks the comparative stability and what passed for a philosophy of life enjoyed by the older men who passed their formative years amid the traditionalism of the Ottoman Empire; and it is therefore almost completely at a loss for

---

[1] For progress in Iraq, cf. Freya Stark, *East is West*, 178 ff.
[2] After the expulsion of the French, Damascus became for a time the scene of a 'puritan reaction' (Prof. H. S. Deighton, in *International Affairs*, XXII (1946), 520).

any principles, other than the lowest one of material self-interest, to guide it in its personal and social conduct. Muslim traditionalism has been tried in the fire of history and found wanting; Anglo-American liberalism is associated with an insensitive and socially-exclusive imperialism in its British aspect, or with a somewhat blatant display of wealth and an uninformed or perverse support of Zionism in the U.S.A. The Nazi *Fuhrerprinzip*, which in the specious glitter of its chromium-plate and ersatz-leather appealed to not a few, has been bombed out of existence. The Russian system, with prestige enhanced by its much publicized successes in the war, holds out hopes of improved material circumstances and greater consequence to the 'under-privileged', while younger men of the middle-classes who are instinctively anti-British and were formerly pro-Nazi have tended since the war to look to Russia for support, with reckless disregard of the heavier hand that might replace the influence of Britain. Organized urban labour has natural ideological affinities with the Russian system. While Communism has recently made considerable progress in gaining control of the trades-union movement, it has not yet had much effect on the fellahin. But the slogans of 'distribution of land' and 'cancellation of debts' could be as attractive in the Middle East to-day as they were in the Athens of Solon: In Azerbaijan the Russian-inspired 'Democrats' proclaimed peasant-proprietorship as one of the principles of the constitution, and were reported to have begun dividing up the estates of absentee landlords among the fellahin before they were expelled. Such a reform, however dishonestly proclaimed and imperfectly executed, would win the support of large numbers of landless fellahin throughout the Middle East. With the alternatives of nationalist isolationism, Western liberalism, and Communism before it, it remains to be seen whether the Middle East will succeed in making for itself a synthesis or a selection of these variant policies or whether, as seems at present more likely, it will passively have its future dictated for it by stronger external forces. Nationalism is in itself a means, not an end, and a mere attempt to perpetuate present privilege cannot make the Middle East strong and independent. However much it decides to retain its own culture as the basic stock, it must still choose between Anglo-American liberalism and Russian Communism as a suitable rejuvenating strain to graft on to that stock.

CHAPTER IX

Russia and the Middle East, 1907–47

THE SUBJECT falls into six clearly-distinguished chronological phases:
  (1) The Tsarist Régime, down to 1917.
  (2) The Revolutionary Wars, 1917–21.
  (3) The Inter-War Period, 1921–39.
  (4) The period of 'Friendship' with Germany, 1939–41.
  (5) The War, 1941–45.
  (6) The Post-War Period.

★   ★   ★

(1) The Tsarist Period

With the signing of the Anglo-Russian Agreement over Persia in 1907 the Russian government set to work to absorb completely the northern zone of Persia. Its policy was made easier by the fact that the British government was anxious to avoid friction with Russia, in view of the overriding need to maintain the Triple Entente as a bulwark against Germany, and had instructed its Minister in Tehran in this sense. The Persian constitutional revolution, which had begun in 1905, was now in mid-career, and had inevitably upset what little stability there was in the internal régime of Persia. In 1909 the Russians sent a military force to support the reactionary Mohammed Ali Shah. The Persian constitutionalists succeeded, however, in deposing him, and power passed into the hands of the extremist so-called 'Democrats', whose attitude was exasperatingly hostile to the Russians. In 1911 the ex-Shah, with the connivance of minor Russian officials if not of the government, passed through Russia in disguise with a consignment of arms and ammunition and made a landing on the Caspian coast of Persia, but was defeated and forced to withdraw. The Russians frustrated attempts by the Persian government to meet its great financial difficulties and made impossible the efforts of the American financial adviser. They constantly found or created pretexts for further intervention, protecting rich landowners and merchants in Khurasan, collecting Persian revenues in Azerbaijan, importing Russian subjects into Asterabad to till lands they had bought at a nominal price as a result of pressure. In 1911 Russia went behind her allies' backs to conclude the Potsdam Agreement with Germany, recognizing the German interest in the Baghdad Railway in return for German recognition of her own interest in North Persia, arranging to link the projected Persian railway-system with the Baghdad Railway via Khaniqin, and promising Germany an open door for her trade with Persia.

During the First World War the operation of pro-German armed bands in Central and South Persia, and of the Turks in Western Persia, gave the Russians good reasons for occupying a broad belt of North Persia, including the towns of Kermanshah, Isfahan, and Meshed. By a secret agreement of March 1915 the Allied promised Russia Istanbul and the Straits and full liberty of action in the northern zone of Persia, in return for which Britain was to be free to annex both the southern and the neutral zones laid down by the Agreement of 1907.

★   ★   ★

(2) *The Revolutionary Wars, 1917–21.*

The outbreak of the Revolution in March 1917 was followed by the headlong demoralization of the Russian army and its withdrawal from Persia, which gave the Turks an opportunity to invade Western Persia again. In March 1918 the Bolsheviks, who had seized power four months before, were compelled to conclude with Germany the Treaty of Brest-Litovsk, which allowed the Germans to conduct military operations on Russian territory and obtain essential supplies, such as the Caucasian oil. It was this treaty, made at a time when the Allies were fighting for life against Germany, at least as much as any dislike for the Bolshevik régime as such, that caused the Allies to support the local anti-Bolshevik forces and to undertake military operations against the Reds.[1] A small British force operating in North-West Persia temporarily occupied Baku in support of an anti-Bolshevik 'Central Caspian Force' consisting mainly of Armenians, but had to withdraw before a Turkish attack. An Indian force occupied Meshed, and a British naval flotilla operated on the Caspian from the summer of 1918 to that of 1919, re-occupying Baku from the retreating Turks and defeating a Red flotilla.

The great German spring offensive of 1918 on the Western Front had convinced most politically-minded Persians of the certainty of a German victory, and as late as September 1918, when Sir Percy Cox went to Tehran as Minister to bring the Persian government round to a more pro-British way of thinking, he found that it was on the point of throwing in its lot with Germany.[2] When Germany collapsed the extreme 'Democrats', who in their hatred of Russia had backed the Germans and Turks during the war, now turned to support the Turkish nationalists and the Bolsheviks. Cox felt that the country was ripe for Bolshevik revolution on account of the hopeless misgovernment by the Persian ruling-class, and recommended to the Foreign Office that Britain should guarantee the integrity of Persia in return for a new Anglo-Persian agreement. This fell in with the views of Lord Curzon, who had said, 'The integrity of Persia must be registered as a cardinal precept of our imperial creed.' By August 1919 accordingly[3] Cox had negotiated a draft Agreement: the hated Anglo-Russian Agreement of 1907 was considered cancelled; Britain offered to supply advisers, officers, and equipment for the establishment of internal order; there was to be joint Anglo-Persian enterprise in building railways and improving communications generally; and Persia was to receive a loan of £2,000,000. The draft was generally well received in Persia except by the extreme 'Democrats', the most conservative mujtahids (Shi'i divines), and the Russian-officered Cossack Brigade. The Persian Prime Minister could probably have got the draft Agreement ratified by the Majlis (parliament) had he presented it immediately, but he procrasti-

---

[1] Sir Bernard Pares pertinently compared Britain's reaction to the French armistice in 1940 (*Russia* (1941), 109).
[2] Cox, in *Gertrude Bell's Letters*, II, 521.
[3] The Persian delegation to the Peace Conference had unsuccessfully demanded the cession to Persia of Transcaucasia including the Baku oil-region, Turkish Kurdistan, part of Iraq, and Turkestan as far as the Oxus, in spite of the fact that she had no army capable of defending even her existing territories.

nated and allowed the opposition, which now regarded victorious Britain as a greater menace than defeated Russia, to gather strength.

By the end of 1919 Trotsky had organized the Red armies and broken the threat of the counter-revolutionary Whites. Under trades-union pressure Britain had ceased her active intervention against the Bolsheviks, and in the spring of 1920 the British forces were withdrawn from Transcaucasia. In April the anti-Bolshevik republic of Azerbaijan collapsed, and Soviet troops entered Persian territory. With their support a group of Persian communists set up a Soviet government in the Caspian province of Gilan. Persian politicians, impressed by the proximity and the strength of the Russians, became more and more non-committal about the draft agreement with Britain. There was an inspired press-campaign in favour of Bolshevism, the semi-official *Iran* declaring that its doctrines closely resembled the pure gospel of Islam. The Cossack Brigade, the only organized troops in North Persia, was defeated by the Reds, and the whole country seemed at their mercy; but at this stage an outstanding and determined officer Riza Khan, assumed command of the Cossack Brigade. In February 1921 he marched on Tehran and arrested the cabinet. The new government promptly denounced the draft agreement with Britain, and instead accepted the generous terms offered by the Russians. In the Soviet-Persian Agreement signed in Moscow the Russian government renounced all concessions made to the Tsarist government, on condition that they should not be transferred to any other Power. All debts to the Tsarist government or to Russian capitalists were cancelled, and Russian capitulatory rights abolished. Each party undertook to prohibit organizations conspiring against the other party. Russia undertook to observe Persian sovereignty and territorial integrity, and in return Russian troops were to be allowed to enter Persian territory, if Persia were unable to prevent a third party from preparing an invasion of Russia on Persian soil. The Russians followed up this success by making treaties of mutual assistance against 'an imperialist state which follows a policy of invading and exploiting the East' with the nationalist Turkey of Mustafa Kemal and the nationalist Afghanistan of King Amanullah, both of whom had recently been in conflict with Britain. As a token of goodwill the Russians handed back to Turkey the frontier-provinces of Kars and Ardahan which the Tsars had annexed.

(3) *The Inter-War Period*, 1921–39

In the Treaty of Lausanne of 1923 which established the independence of nationalist Turkey and regulated her relations with the Western Powers, she had to concede the demilitarization of the Zone of the Straits: the warships of all nations, with slight restrictions, were free to enter the Black Sea. This was obnoxious not only to Turkey, as limiting her sovereignty, but also to Russia, as exposing her Black Sea coast to the threat of an enemy navy; and in 1925, while Turkey was involved in the acute dispute with Britain and Iraq over the possession of the villayet of Mosul, Russia concluded with her a new Treaty of Friendship and Neutrality. Though official relations between Russia and Turkey remained cordial and the Russians gave some technical help with the industrialization of Turkey, there was little contact or cultural interchange between the two peoples. The Turkish dictatorship permitted the works of Marx and Lenin to be read, but imprisoned active Communists under laws which forbade associations with the purpose of propagating ideas of class distinction or of class conflict, or with internationalist intentions.[1]   In 1936, when Italy had emerged as the aggressive naval power which threatened the *status quo* in the Mediterranean, Turkey proposed to the signatories of the Treaty of Lausanne that the régime of the Straits needed revision, and obtained important concessions in the Montreux Convention. She was now allowed to fortify the Straits, and in time of war to close them to the warships of all Powers, unless acting under the Covenant of the League of Nations. A compromise was thus reached between the Russian claim for wide discrimination in favour of Black Sea Powers, and the British argument that the Straits should be equally open or equally closed to the warships of all Powers.[2]   In the early summer of 1939, when Turkey entered into pacts with Britain and France directed primarily against Fascist Italy, *Izvestia* welcomed them as 'links in the chain which is the only sure means of preventing the extension of aggression to new parts of Europe'.

In Persia Riza Shah, like Ataturk, followed a strongly nationalist and anti-foreign policy, and his commercial relations with Russia

---

[1] Arts. 66 and 69 of the People's Party Programme.
[2] *Survey of International Affairs*, 1936, Part IV (i).

S

were darkened from time to time by embargoes and boycotts. However, Russia supported him in his dispute with the Anglo-Iranian Oil Co. in 1932, and by 1936 she was taking 28 per cent. of Persia's exports and supplying 30 per cent. of her imports. 'Russian engineers and technicians began to pour into the country. Russian contracts were obtained for flour-mills and bakeries, granaries and workshops. Russian surveyors were employed on new road-projects, and Russian pilots and tank-experts began to appear in unusually large numbers.'[1]

During this period the Soviet government was not in diplomatic relations with any of the other Middle Eastern countries, and her connexion with them was virtually confined to the encouragement given by the Comintern to the embryonic Communist parties in those countries. The conservative governments of the Middle East, whether mandatory or nominally independent, were strongly opposed to Communism, and Egypt went so far as to deprive of his nationality any Egyptian who visited the U.S.S.R.

★   ★   ★

(4) The period of 'Friendship' with Germany, 1939–41

In August 1939 the Soviet government, having reached the conclusion that Britain and France could not be brought to an alliance on its somewhat exacting terms, preferred to do a deal with Germany, and Molotov concluded with Ribbentrop the opportunist and cynical Treaty of Friendship and Non-Aggression. In furtherance of its new friendship with Hitler, the Soviet government concluded a new commercial treaty with Persia in March 1940, which allowed Persian goods in transit to Germany to cross Russia duty-free, and so assisted the greatly increased German trade with Persia. The Turkish Foreign Minister had been in Moscow at the time of the signing of the Treaty with Germany, but failed to reach an understanding with Molotov, who required as the price of a Black Sea mutual-assistance pact that the Turks should in all circumstances keep the Straits closed to the warships of any nation hostile to the U.S.S.R.; and this the Turkish government held to be inconsistent with their agreements with Britain and

---

[1] Elwell-Sutton, op. cit., 162. Germany, Persia's second-largest customer, took in 1936 13 per cent. of her exports and supplied 15 per cent. of her imports.

France. The Soviet press thereupon linked together Italy and Turkey as attempting to disturb the peace of the Balkans. Anti-Soviet feeling in Turkey was stimulated by the Soviet invasion of Finland, since Turkish theorists were aware of the distant connexion between the Finnish and Turkish languages. Following the German publication of captured French documents in July 1940, the Soviet accused the Turkish government of conniving at Anglo-French plans, now revealed, for bombing the Caucasian oilfields and the pipeline to Batum, as a potential source of supply to Germany. At the Hitler-Molotov meeting in November 1940 the Russians, according to the captured German minutes, asked for the control of the Straits, as well as for the right to expand 'south of Batum and Baku'.[1] In March 1941, when Hitler was on the point of invading Jugoslavia and Greece, Russia assured the Turks of her neutrality. Her establishment in May of diplomatic relations with Rashid Ali's government in Iraq, when it was already in armed conflict with the British, who for their part had warned the Russians of Hitler's preparations to invade them, is an incident whose significance has not yet been clarified.

★   ★   ★

(5) The War, 1941-5

After the Anglo-Russian invasion of Persia in August 1941, the northern zone which came under Russian military occupation was withdrawn behind the now familiar 'iron curtain': the Persian government's authority ceased to be effective there, and British and American officers found great difficulty in entering the Russian zone even on official business. The American Dr. A. C. Mills-paugh, then Administrator-General of the Finances of Persia, has accused the Soviet government of seeking a 'thorough-going and exclusive domination over the entire country. . . . They intended that Persia should be a puppet-state, and until that end was attained, the Soviet government would not be interested in stability or good government in Persia. Chaos served their purpose better than order. They wanted the kind of government that could be purchased, hoodwinked, or intimidated.'[2] In Tehran the Tudeh or

---

[1] *Nazi-Soviet Relations*, 1939–1941. (U.S. State Department, 1948), 217 ff.
[2] *Americans in Persia* (Washington, D.C., 1946).

Workers' Party came to life, with an ostensibly moderate socialist programme. It did not originally have obvious connexions with the Russians, but unsuccessfully sought the support of the British Embassy; some of its leaders were, however, men who had taken part in the shortlived Soviet Republic of Gilan twenty years before, and had since lived in exile in the U.S.S.R. It formed trades-unions in the principal industrial cities of Tehran, Tabriz, and Isfahan, and obtained for the workers some concessions from their employers; but from 1943 onwards it became openly the pro-Russian party.[1] In March 1944 the Persian government rejected applications by representatives of British and American oil-companies for concessions in south-east Persia, and on 2 September the cabinet resolved that it would make no concessions to any foreign oil company until the foreign armies had been withdrawn from Persian soil. Only four days afterwards the Persian Ambassador in Moscow informed his government that the Assistant Commissar for Foreign Affairs, Kavtaradze, wished to discuss with the Persian government an old oil-concession in Khurasan, which had been registered in 1925 as a Persian company financed by the Soviet government; the Majlis had, however, never ratified this concession, and no oil had in fact been found. M. Kavtaradze arrived in Tehran a week later and asked for a five-years' exploratory concession for almost the whole of North Persia. When the Persian government demurred, it became the object of a violent propaganda attack from the Tudeh party, and M. Kavtaradze issued thinly-veiled threats at his press-conferences. Weeks passed without the negotiations reaching any conclusion; and on 2 December the Majlis finally screwed up its courage, and rushed through a bill prescribing a penalty of eight years imprisonment for any minister or official who approved an oil-concession to any foreign company before the end of the foreign occupation of Persia. M. Kavtaradze had to return to Moscow without achieving his object. During 1945 the attitude of the Soviet military to the Persian authorities in the northern provinces became increasingly unco-operative.[2]

Following the Anglo-Russian Alliance of June 1941, the two Powers sought to reassure Turkey in August by guaranteeing their loyalty to the Montreux Convention, declaring that they had no

[1] On the combination of 'half-baked' ideologues and genuine would-be reformers in the Tudeh membership, see A. C. Edwards, in *International Affairs*, XXIII (1947), 54 f.
[2] For details, see A. K. S. Lambton, *International Affairs*, XXII (1946). 265 ff.

aggressive designs nor any demands to formulate in regard to the Straits, and pledging themselves to respect the territorial integrity of Turkey. As long as the Russians were on the defensive against the Germans, Russian leaders hinted at rewarding Turkey with territorial acquisitions at the expense of Bulgaria, Greece, and Syria.[1] Public opinion in Turkey, however, had not been sorry to see the Germans invade the U.S.S.R. It had come to regard both the German and, after the invasion of Finland, the Russian armies as potential threats to the integrity of Turkey, and was gratified to see them destroying each other; as a popular slogan put it, 'The Germans in the hospital and the Russians in the grave'. The Pan-Turanian irredentists, who dreamed of forming a confederation under the leadership of the Turkish Republic of all the Turkish peoples of Russian and Chinese Turkestan, 'regarded as inevitable the defeat and disintegration of the U.S.S.R. and were confident that the liberation of Russian Turkestan was at hand. When, however, it was the Germans, and not the Russians, who suffered defeat, the Turkish authorities appear to have decided that it would be politic to suppress the pan-Turanians, thinking no doubt that the denunciation of the movement and the arrest and trial of its leaders would gain them good marks in Moscow. The proceedings in 1944 received the greatest possible publicity. Moscow, however, was far from being impressed. In fact the Russians regarded the whole affair as so much eyewash, and did not hesitate to say so in their press and radio.'[2] They began to assail the Turks for the economic aid they had given to the Germans—concessions which, in fact, the Turkish government had felt constrained to make in order to maintain its precarious neutrality, with the German troops occupying the line of the Maritza only 130 miles from Istanbul. In March 1945 the Soviet government denounced the twenty-year-old Turco-Soviet Treaty of Friendship and Neutrality.

★   ★   ★

(6) The Post-War Period

It appears that when in June 1945, one month after the close of the war in Europe, the Turks approached the Soviet government

---

[1] *Times* correspondent in Turkey, 3 April 1947.
[2] A. C. Edwards in *International Affairs*, July 1946, 398.

for a new treaty of alliance, they were informed that this was conditional on the establishment of a new régime for the Straits, and also on the return to Russia of the provinces of Kars and Ardahan, which she had voluntarily restored to Turkey in 1921; apparently she now hoped to find oil there. At his speech at Fulton (Missouri) in March 1946 Mr. Churchill disclosed that at the Potsdam Conference the U.S.A. and Britain offered Russia a joint guarantee of the complete freedom of the Straits in peace and war; 'but we were told that this was not enough. Russia must have a fortress inside the Straits from which she could dominate Istanbul'. In the months that followed, Armenians, both within the Soviet Republic of Armenia and in other parts of the world, were encouraged to make propaganda for the return to Russia of Kars and Ardahan. In December 1945 the Soviet press and radio gave wide publicity to the claim put forward by Georgian professors to a coastal belt of north-eastern Turkey some 180 miles in length, on the grounds that this had been Georgian territory 2,000 years ago. The Soviet propaganda contained sinister hints that she desired to see in Turkey a 'government inspiring greater confidence' than the existing one; and any signs of a rapprochement between Turkey and the Arab League were strongly denounced. In August 1946 the Soviet government made positive proposals for the revision of the Montreux Convention, the essential point being that 'The Soviet Union and Turkey, as the Powers most interested in and capable of ensuring the freedom of merchant shipping in the Straits, should organize by joint means the defence of the Straits in order to prevent their use by other states for purposes hostile to Black Sea Powers.' Next month, to the accompaniment of propaganda charges that the Turks had allowed Britain to establish military bases in the neighbourhood of the Straits, the Russians delivered a second Note, rejecting the Turkish proposal of an international conference of the signatories of the Montreux Convention and the U.S.A., and warning them that any attempt to bring in the U.S.A. or Britain, would, of course, run directly contrary to the security interests of the Black Sea Powers. Towards the end of November the Communist bands which had for some months been harassing Northern Greece, with the connivance of the Russian satellite-states in the Balkans, began to operate close to the Turkish frontier. Turkish garrisons were accordingly strengthened, and a home-guard organized in every village in the frontier district. In mid-

December the Istanbul police arrested over seventy persons belonging to two 'Socialist' parties, suppressing the parties and six
newspapers and periodicals published by them. The American
offer of financial aid to Greece and Turkey in March 1947 greatly
changed the strategic situation on this important sector of the
Russian war-of-nerves. While *Pravda* denounced the American
action as 'the liquidation of Greek and Turkish sovereignty and the
brutal establishment of American hegemony', the Turks were at
once relieved of the 'crushing sense of insecurity and isolation'[1]
which had subjected them during the past two years to the economic and psychological strain of keeping under arms one million
men who had already been kept mobilized throughout the war.
When the steady consolidation of Russian power in the Balkans
caused a member of the Democratic party on 22 December to
inquire about Turkey's attitude to the two great ideological blocs,
Foreign Minister Hasan Saka replied that Turkey remained loyal
to the United Nations and refused to be drawn into ideological
quarrels; her policy was to rely on her own forces, to grasp hands
extended in a spirit of friendship, and to resist with all her strength
aggression from any quarter. This unexpectedly non-committal
statement gave rise to some concern in Ankara;[2] and it produced,
as it was perhaps designed to do, an announcement from the U.S.
Navy Department on 9 January 1948 that fifteen warships,
including four modern submarines, would be handed over to
Turkey in April.

In October 1945 a new 'Democratic Party' was formed in
Azerbaijan, the richest province of Persia, which produces the
bulk of its grain and contains about one-third the total population
of the country. The province had been under Soviet occupation
since 1941, and it appeared that a considerable number of Communists had been introduced from Soviet Azerbaijan, divided
from Persian Azerbaijan only by an arbitrary frontier and not by
any linguistic or cultural differences. The new party was led by
Ja'far Pishevari, who had taken part in the formation of the Soviet
Republic of Gilan in 1920 and had returned to Persia with the
Soviet army in 1941. All the local members of the Tudeh joined
the new party and there followed an armed revolt of a peculiar
kind. 'A few Russians in a town or village would let it be known

---

[1] *Reuter's* Correspondent, Istanbul, 19 March 1947.
[2] *Observer* special correspondent, 4 January 1948.

that the Democrats were taking over the administration, and that they would not tolerate intervention from the government gendarmes or anyone else. Then at night the armed Democrats would enter the few key-buildings and take over. Sometimes there would be a little shooting, and a few gendarmes or other opponents killed. In the morning the mass of Democrats would arrive, singing and with banners, and would take over. Throughout, the Russians remained discreetly in the background.'[1] The active Democrats, who with their supporters numbered only about 10 per cent. of the population, advanced southwards on the provincial capital of Tabriz. Its Persian garrison of 400 men was confined to barracks by the Russian military authorities and capitulated to the Democrats on 15 December. An autonomous State of Azerbaijan was proclaimed under the leadership of Pishevari. According to Moscow radio, it had been 'elected by a free vote'. While it recognized private property as legitimate, it undertook to confiscate and share out among the peasants the estates of 'reactionary landlords who have fled the province'. Credits would be made available to peasants to buy land from landlords 'willing to sell at reasonable prices'. The Persian government, receiving no reply to its proposal to the Soviet government to negotiate over Azerbaijan, appealed to the Security Council. When the case came up on 28 January 1946 M. Vyshinsky stated that the Persian government had broken off previous negotiations early in December, and that Russia was now ready to continue them. The Council accordingly resolved that the two parties should inform it of the results of their negotiations. In the meantime, however, the seventy-two-year-old Persian Prime Minister, who had been subject to increasing left-wing pressure to dismiss a number of cabinet ministers and other officials who were alleged to be under British influence, had resigned. The Majlis elected as his successor, by the narrow margin of fifty-three votes to fifty-one, Qavam as-Sultani, a wealthy owner of lands in Azerbaijan. When he was previously Prime Minister early in 1942 there was reason to believe that he took some steps towards 'reinsurance' with the Germans; and now it was generally expected that, while taking a strong line with any internal opposition, the 'ancient equivocator'[2] would seek a reasonable compromise with the Russians. The

[1] Jon Kimche, in *Tribune*, 18 January 1946.
[2] Robert Stephens, *Observer*, 24 November 1946.

14. PERSIANS, KURDS AND THE U.S.S.R.

Soviet Embassy in Tehran, which had for several weeks avoided contact with the previous Prime Minister, promptly paid courtesy visits to Qavam; and on their invitation he set off for Moscow on 19 February at the head of a carefully-picked mission. While American and British troops were withdrawn before 2 March, the day appointed for the withdrawal of all foreign troops from Persia, the Soviet radio announced on 1 March, while Qavam was still negotiating in Moscow, that Russian troops would be withdrawn 'from those parts of Persia which are undisturbed; those in other areas would remain pending a clarification of the situation'. Qavam returned to Persia without reaching any agreement; but on 3 April the Persian delegate informed the Security Council that ten days previously the Soviet Ambassador had informed the Persian government that the Red Army would begin its evacuation immediately and complete it in five to six weeks; he had also proposed a joint Soviet-Persian oil corporation and an autonomous government for Azerbaijan. On 5 April an agreement was signed setting up a joint oil-company in North Persia for a period of fifty years. For the first twenty-five years Russia was to own 51 per cent. of the shares, to pay the costs of prospecting and provide the machinery, and in return receive half the oil. Persia was to be free to dispose of the other half, but for geographical reasons Russia would be the most likely buyer. Concessions to other Powers in North Persia were barred.[1] The evacuation of British troops duly began, and an Azerbaijani mission led by Pishevari arrived in Tehran for talks with the Persian government. Qavam had meanwhile been suppressing the most actively anti-Russian elements in Persian political life, threatening in a radio speech to 'destroy them like harmful insects'. His negotiations with the Azerbaijanis were none the less difficult, since at the first obstacle that presented itself Tabriz radio announced a treaty of mutual assistance with the 'national government' of Persian Kurdistan, where unruly tribes had with Russian support been in revolt against the central government for some years. When a second deadlock was reached, the Persian spokesman having informed the Security Council that his government was unable to confirm the Russian evacuation of Azerbaijan as it did not exercise effective authority there, pressure was again exerted on it through a Tabriz radio allegation of a Persian armed attack and the proclamation of a military government in Azer-

[1] *Times* Tehran correspondent, 11 July 1947.

baijan. Agreement was, however, finally reached in June: Azerbaijan was to have an autonomous provincial council, with a
governor-general appointed by the central government; it was to
retain three-quarters of the provincial revenues; its 'national army'
was to come under the command of the Persian army, details being
worked out by a joint commission. While, therefore, the central
government received acknowledgment of its *de jure* authority in
Azerbaijan, the 'Democrats' remained in actual control; and for
five months the name of the province disappeared from the news-
paper-headlines. The Soviet propaganda-machine had, however,
been carrying on a campaign against the Anglo-Iranian Oil Co. in
South Persia for some time. It was accused of encouraging opium-
smoking among its Persian workers in order to render them insensible of their poverty, and *Pravda* righteously remarked that
'the brazen and imperious behaviour of the British oil company is
an example of disrespect for the sovereignty of a small country'.
In July the local Tudeh party organized a political strike of 100,000
of the oil-company's workers, and seventeen people were killed in a
clash between Tudeh adherents and Arab workers. Simultaneously
the Iraq Petroleum Co. had to deal with a strike at Kirkuk, in which
five people were killed in a clash between strikers and police. Evidently this was the beginning of a typical 'softening-up' process,
but the despatch of a brigade group of troops from India to Basra
prevented further developments. In September the Persian Propaganda Minister, Prince Muza'far Firuz, who had shown himself
outspokenly pro-Russian in recent months, announced that while
visiting Isfahan he had unearthed a separatist plot among the chiefs
of the powerful Bakhtiari tribe to set up with foreign help a 'reactionary feudal tribal government'. Moscow radio named two
British consular officials whom it accused of inciting the Bakhtiari
to revolt, and the Persian Ambassador in London asked the Foreign
Office to inquire into their conduct; but evidence in support of
these allegations was not forthcoming from the Persian government. Later in September the great Qashqai tribe revolted in Fars
province, seizing the provincial capital of Shiraz and the port of
Bushire; simultaneously the Arab tribal chiefs of Khuzistan
province appealed to the Arab League for protection against Persian oppression. The Qashqai chiefs demanded the creation of an
autonomous provincial council with the right to retain two thirds
of the provincial revenues, and to approve or veto the appointment

of officials; they also called for the resignation of the Persian cabinet, except for Qavam himself, and the release of the arrested Bakhtiari chiefs. It was evident that the southern tribal chiefs, seeing the apparent drift of the Persian government towards subservience on Russia, had decided to strike in defence of their own traditional authority against the Tudeh, which had been strong enough in Tehran to muster some 50,000 adherents for the May Day labour demonstration and had been given three seats in the cabinet early in August. Warned by these ominous signs of provincial disintegration, and by appeals from merchants and mujtahids to protect the country from foreign ideologies and end the coalition with the Tudeh and the Azerbaijani Democrats, the Prime Minister decided that it was time to 'hedge'. In mid-October he pacified the Qashqai rebels by dropping from his cabinet the three Tudeh representatives and Prince Firuz, whom he appropriately appointed Ambassador to Moscow. He then turned to the question of general elections for a new Majlis, having dissolved the previous one in March. The Tudeh wanted them at once, in order that the new Majlis might ratify the all-important Soviet-Persian oil agreement. The Prime Minister at length announced that they would begin on 7 December, under the supervision of government forces throughout the country in order to ensure freedom of voting and suppress possible disturbances. The Governor-General of Azerbaijan was informed that government forces would enter his province also for that purpose. Despite the protests of the Azerbaijani provincial council and a call to arms, the government troops crossed the provincial border on 10 December. They met with only slight opposition, since the 'Democrat' forces were found to be ill-equipped and undisciplined, and there were many desertions. Tabriz was occupied, evidently to the hearty satisfaction of the overwhelming majority of the population. Some of the 'Democrat' leaders, including Pishevari himself, fled over the border into Soviet territory. The Soviet propaganda treated the collapse of their puppet with remarkably little concern, waiting evidently for Persian ratification of the proposed oil-concession. Persian elections, are, however, a leisurely process, and the new Majlis was not ready for official duties till 26 August 1947. By that time the Soviet propaganda had lost patience, strongly attacking 'Persian reactionaries', 'stranglers of the working class', and the 'intriguers of the Anglo-Iranian Oil Co.' On

12 August the Soviet Ambassador handed to the Persian Prime Minister for signature a draft oil-treaty on the lines agreed at Moscow in the previous year.[1] When the Persian Government pointed out that it was necessary first to obtain the consent of the Majlis, a second Soviet Note was presented on 15 September demanding swift action without 'delaying tactics'. On 22 October the Majlis, against the advice of the Prime Minister, adopted by 102 votes to 2 a bill rejecting the oil-agreement of 1947 and proposing new negotiations. A third Soviet Note on 20 November accused the Persian Government of 'treacherously violating' its undertakings. By this time Qavam as-Sultani was hopelessly isolated in the Majlis, partly as a scapegoat for the rejected agreement and partly on account of the corruptness of his administration (though by Persian standards it was probably not outstanding in this respect); and though he made a desperate bid for popularity in an anti-foreign broadcast, he fell to a vote of no-confidence on 10 December. On 31 January 1948 a fourth Soviet Note accused the Persian government of lending itself to American plans for converting Persia into a 'military-strategic' base, and darkly reminded it of the Soviet-Persian Treaty of 1921 (which gave Russia the right to send troops into Persia 'if a third party should desire to use Persian territory as a base for operations against Russia').[2] The Persian Government in reply accused the Russians of harbouring the Azerbaijani and Kurdish rebels against Persian authority.

As a result of her wartime alliance with Britain, Russia was able for the first time to open legations in the Middle Eastern capitals— Cairo, Beirut and Damascus, Baghdad. In this new international relationship it was no longer possible for Middle Eastern governments to repress left-wing movements as indiscriminately as hitherto; the prestige won by the Red Armies in the war caused a considerable increase in the membership of left-wing parties in the Middle East; and in Egypt Nahhas welcomed the establishment of a Russian Legation, which might enable him to drive a harder bargain with Britain in the future. The tone of Soviet propaganda has been critical of the Arab League, as a British creation representing in the main conservative interests; but it is always ready to abet the

---

[1] *Times* diplomatic correspondent, 18 August 1947.
[2] do., 3 and 4 February 1948.

nationalists in their efforts to throw off British influence, and the
left-wing parties have been quick to adopt such catchwords as
'national,' 'liberation', and 'democratic' in their titles. There is a
'National Liberation' committee, party, and league, in Egypt, Iraq,
and Palestine respectively, and a 'National Co-operation Front' in
Cyprus, the counterparts of the 'National Liberation Front' which
is seeking to seize power in Greece. Some of the 'intellectuals' who
form the leadership of these movements join them out of genuine
disgust at the inefficiency and corruption of the present ruling-
class; others despair of ever finding what they consider, none too
modestly, a fair return for their abilities under their present conservative rulers; and some are chronic malcontents who, in their
envy of the established order and hatred of the British influence they see behind it, have sold themselves to Communism
now as they sold themselves to Nazi propagandists nine years
ago.

In the cities of Egypt bookshops dealing in Soviet and Communist propaganda were opened in the latter part of the war, and
Communist opinions gained some adherents among members of
the foreign communities and Egyptian students and organized
labour. In a number of strikes in 1945–6 the strikers appeared to be
well supplied with funds from some undisclosed source. The
Egyptian authorities, always on the alert for any revolutionary
movement, for which Egypt with its glaring contrasts of wealth
and poverty provides a favourable field, arrested seventeen alleged
Communists in December 1945; and in July 1946 nearly 300
suspects, apparently 'intellectuals' for the most part, were arrested,
and eleven social or cultural organizations suppressed. They were
alleged to be working in league with the radical wing of the Wafd
to organize opposition to Sidqi's negotiations for a revision of the
Anglo-Egyptian Treaty. No positive charge was made that the
movement was Russian-inspired, though the paper *Akhbar al-Yom*
declared that it was doubtful whether the full facts would be disclosed 'owing to international considerations'; and it is significant
that about this time Soviet press and radio propaganda had been
applauding the Wafd for its opposition to compromise with
Britain. In October a royal decree was signed, prescribing severe
penalties for persons who sought 'to spread propaganda to change
the basic constitutional principles of the country' or to form without official permission societies with an 'international colour-

ing', or who received funds from abroad for subversive purposes.

Before the First World War the Russian Church had assiduously cultivated the Orthodox Christian communities in the Levant, attracting them by a richly-endowed educational mission which established in Syria and Palestine 100 schools with 360 teachers and some 10,000 pupils. After the Revolution the Soviet government claimed the properties of the Russian ecclesiastical mission and the schools, but the mandatory governments of the Levant States and Palestine held that in view of its open persecution of religion in Russia the claim was unreasonable. The properties were accordingly administered by the mandatories, and most of the schools lapsed for lack of subsidies from Russia. In March 1945 the Russian Patriarch, recently set up in Moscow by the Soviet government, visited the Holy Land in state, and celebrated a solemn liturgy at the Church of the Holy Sepulchre which was attended by representatives of all the oriental churches. It was reported in August 1947 that agreement had been reached on the recognition of the Soviet title to property in Syria and Lebanon which had belonged before 1917 to the Tsarist government or the Russian Church.[1]

At the beginning of 1946 the Soviet Minister in Beirut offered Russian support to the Syrian and Lebanese governments in their efforts to get rid of the British and French occupying forces, and the Soviet veto was exercised in the Security Council to quash an American compromise-resolution, because it did not state that the presence of these forces was a threat to international peace.[2] Here again no indication of collusion between the Soviet diplomatic missions and the local left-wing movement has been published, though it was unofficially stated in the summer of 1946 that Soviet agents were spending large sums on propaganda. The conservative Syrian Muslim population has been little affected by Communism, and those attracted to it belong in the main to minorities: the large Armenian communities in Aleppo and Beirut, urbanised Kurds and Orthodox Christians in Damascus. In Beirut and other parts of Lebanon the large class of semi-educated Levantines employed at poor wages as teachers, clerks, mechanics etc. constitute, next to the Persian Tudeh, the most vigorous Communist party in the

[1] *Bourse Egyptienne*, 12 August 1947.
[2] *The World To-day*, III (1947), 84.

Middle East, and have a powerful influence over the Lebanese trades-union movement. The Syrian and Lebanese governments were reported to have detained some 500 suspected Communists in the summer of 1946; but during 1947 the propaganda made by the agents of King Abdullah of Transjordan for his Greater Syria project, in which no Arab can believe that he does not have at least the tacit approval of the British government, caused the ruling clique in Syria to seek the support of the Communists, who are naturally hostile to Abdullah as an ally of Britain. [1]

In Iraq there are two Communist parties which appear to differ over personalities rather than policy. Some fifty members were arrested in January 1947 and seven leaders were sentenced to long terms of imprisonment for 'conspiracy to overthrow the government by force, and inciting members of the armed forces and the police to bear arms against the government'. The left-wing press appealed to Arab nationalist sentiment in strongly attacking the Turco-Iraqi Treaty. The main instrument of Russian policy in Iraq has, however, been not the class-struggle, but the discontent of the Kurdish minority in Northern Iraq, which is nearly one-fifth of the total population of the country and has been neglected by the Arab politicians of Baghdad. This discontent has periodically found expression in tribal revolts, duly countered more or less effectively by Iraqi military expeditions. This normal routine was given a new direction when in 1945 the leaders of the rebellious Barzani Kurds escaped into Persian Kurdistan and joined forces with Kurdish rebels against the Persian central government who were receiving strong Soviet encouragement from Azerbaijan. [2] Iraqi fears of a Soviet-inspired Kurdish irruption from Persia into Iraq in the spring of 1946 did not, however, materialize; and the collapse of the 'national government' of Persian Kurdistan in December, following the Persian government's assertion of its authority in Azerbaijan, eased the tension in Iraq. In April 1947 the Persian authorities executed three of the Persian Kurdish rebel leaders, and drove the Barzanis back to the Iraqi frontier, where their deputy-leader Sheikh Ahmed surrendered to the Iraqi authorities. Some 1,500, however, escaped back into Persia, and a thousand with their leader Mullah Mustafa crossed into Russian territory.

[1] *The World To-Day*, January 1948, 25.
[2] On this movement, see Archie Roosevelt Jr., in *Middle East Journal*, I (Washington, 1947), 247 ff.

In Palestine the former united Communist party split during the war into Jewish and Arab sections, since they could not reconcile their attitudes towards Zionism. The Jewish Communists are still an insignificant fraction of their community, completely over-shadowed by the Zionist movement. The Arab left-wing move-ment has made considerable headway among the semi-educated and the ranks of organized labour, and is strongly opposed to the conservative leaders of the Arab nationalist movement. *Ittihad,* the left-wing organ of the Palestine Arab Workers' Congress and the 'intellectual' League of National Liberation, has constantly de-manded that the unrepresentative Arab Higher Executive should give place to a new organization in which the workers would be represented. On the Zionist question both the Jewish and the Arab Communists repeated the party-line, as stated by M. Gromyko to the U.N.O. Assembly in May 1947, that the solution of the Palestine problem lay in the ending of British control, after which Arabs and Jews could be left to settle their differences in a bi-national 'democratic' state. On 13 October, however, the Soviet representative at U.N.O. came out in support of the partition plan, and on 31 December M. Gromyko spoke at a Jewish dinner in New York of the new Jewish State as an instrument of the 'liberation of the peoples of the Arab East from the last shackles of colonial dependence'. In response the two parties on the left wing of the Zionist movement, which between them polled nearly a quarter of all the Palestine votes for the last Zionist Congress, merged on 24 January 1948 in a new group which had on its central committee the former Hagana leader Dr. Moshe Sneh. On 31 January the British government protested to the Communist government of Bulgaria against its allowing 19,000 illegal Jewish immigrants to sail from Bulgarian ports in the latter part of 1947.[1]

The Soviet demand early in 1946 that she should be given the trusteeship of the former Italian colonies of Tripolitania and Eritrea was withdrawn in favour of the compromise-agreement to maintain the *status quo* for one year after the Italian peace-treaty came into force. Russia was duly represented at the meetings to consider the future of the Italian colonies which began on 3 October 1947. At the end of January 1948 she protested against the American decision, announced a fortnight before, to reopen the Mallaha airfield near Tripoli; it was, however, explained that

[1] *Times* diplomatic correspondent, 7 February.

T

this arrangement would continue only so long as Britain remained responsible for the territory.[1]

Before the First World War the Russian Church sent repeated missions to Ethiopia to induce union between the two churches.[2] Since the recent war Russia has established diplomatic relations with Ethiopia. The Russian propaganda-machine denounced the British proposal in 1946 for a united Somaliland, and in January 1948 the Italian Communist paper *Unita* accused the British government of responsibility for the deaths which had recently occurred at Mogadishu in a clash between Italian colonists and the Young Somali League, provoked by the former.[3]

The governments of the Arab states have shown concern at Russian post-war policy in the Middle East in proportions varying with their proximity to the U.S.S.R., their antipathy to Communism, and their personal ambitions and standing in the complex internal politics of the Arab League. Iraq has been the Arab country most exposed to the Russian activities of the past three years, and it was therefore natural that the names of Nuri as-Sa'id, Iraq's elder statesman and the ablest judge of foreign politics in the Arab world, and of King Abdullah of Transjordan should have been connected with a plan to bring Turkey and the Arab League into a defensive alliance, which would also include Persia, and Afghanistan, who with Turkey and Iraq were signatories of the 1937 Saadabad Pact of mutual assistance.[4] The visits of Nuri and Abdullah to Turkey have established in treaty-form an entente between Turkey and Iraq and Transjordan, significantly the most pro-British of the Arab states; but the factors militating against the Arab League as a whole entering into closer association with Turkey are numerous. Syrian politicians still hope to recover the lost sanjaq of Alexandretta (the Hatay), while the Turks insist that they should acknowledge its cession to Turkey as final; Ibn Sa'ud and Faruq are both jealous and suspicious of the Hashimite dynasty, while King Abdullah's open effort to succeed his brother Faisal as king of a Greater Syria has been supported by a body of malcontents in Syria, but is actively opposed by the rulers of Syria,

---

[1] *Times* diplomatic correspondent, 31 January 1948.
[2] J. Richter, *History of Protestant Missions in the Near East*, 57.
[3] *Times* diplomatic correspondent, 28 January.
[4] This Pact was occasioned by the challenge to the *status quo* in the Levant and Middle East presented by the rise of Italy as an aggressive naval and military power. (*Survey of International Affairs*, 1936, 201 ff.) Subsequent attempts to read into it an anti-British or anti-Russian orientation are gratuitous.

Lebanon, and Sa'udi Arabia. Azzam Pasha, the secretary of the Arab League, is reported to be jealous of Nuri Pasha. Though King Faruq visited Turkey in September 1946, Egyptian nationalist opinion resented Turkish suggestions that Egypt should renew her alliance with Britain so as to strengthen the front against any Russian aggression. Now that the Turks have secured guarantees of American support, they are probably less inclined to embroil themselves in the fickle politics of the Arab League, close association with which would probably be a hindrance rather than a help to Turkish interests.

The Russian statesmen to-day regard the Middle East as a 2,000-mile-long breach in the deep defensive glacis which they have been busily constructing since the war from the Baltic to the Pacific, and as a base from which some of their most precious assets, the cornlands of the Ukraine and the oilfields of the Caucasus, appear exposed to aerial invasion at short range by the 'capitalist' Powers. They have, therefore, sought to convert Turkey, the Fertile Crescent, Persia, and Afghanistan into a series of friendly satellite-states. The most suitable time for attempting this consolidation of their position was immediately after the War, when public opinion in Britain was war-weary and in large measure averse from opposing an ally whose superior social and political virtues had been extolled in four years of propaganda; when the Russians 'thought they could see the British Empire crumbling, and that expansion to fill Britain's place in Europe and the Middle East would be easy and inexpensive';[1] and when 'there was a serious chance that the United States might refuse to help Britain hold the line'.[2]

Secondly, Stalin stated in February 1946 that the U.S.S.R. needed to attain an oil-production of roughly twice the pre-war level in order to be self-sufficient for the increasing mechanization of both her economy and her armed forces; but at present she owns only about 9 per cent. of the world's proven oil reserves, whereas some 86 per cent. is in American, British and Dutch hands.[3] She is therefore impelled to seek new sources of supply, and is naturally attracted to the known deposits in Persia adjacent to her frontiers. Frustrated, at least for the present, in her demand for an oil-

---

[1] Labour party pamphlet, *Cards on the Table*, summarized in *The Times*, 22 May 1947.
[2] A. Wolfers, in *International Affairs*, XXIII (1947), 24.
[3] *Economist*, 3 January 1947.

concession in North Persia, she jealously sees the abundant supplies of South Persia and the Persian Gulf region, estimated to contain 30 per cent. of the total world reserves, in the hands of British and American interests. Britain, on the other hand, clings to her Middle East oil as the one source of supply under her own control; while the U.S.A., with her gigantic domestic consumption of oil and the decreasing reserves of the American continent, is anxious to acquire new sources of supply in the Middle East. The relations obtaining between Russia and the other Powers rule out the possibility of an agreement on the fair allocation between them of the Middle East oil supplies, which would be acceptable to the U.S.A. and Britain only as part of a general settlement of all the points at issue.[1]

To sum up the present situation, while Russia's interest in gaining control of the Straits and the oilfields is obviously strategic, her interest in the rest of the Middle East may be described as tactical, her object being to exploit its political and social instability in order to harass the Western Powers and make it more difficult for them to use the region as a base for the 'capitalist war' which she dreads.

---

[1] At the 1947 Labour party conference Mr. Bevin, recalling a delegate's suggestion that parts of the Middle East should become the responsibility of an international organization, said, 'I am not going to be a party to voluntarily putting British interests in a pool, while everybody else sticks to his own.' (Applause.) (*Times*, 30 May 1947).

CHAPTER X

The Western Powers and the Middle East To-day

IN THE First World War Britain confirmed the dominant position which she had in the nineteenth century established in the Middle East for the purpose of using it as an inert shock-absorber interposed between her European rivals and her Indian Empire. However, immediately after that war nationalism, which the Foreign Office had cautiously encouraged during the war as a tactical instrument against the Ottoman Empire, continued to press its demands for independence so violently and at so many points that Britain could not offer it a total resistance without becoming involved in repressive military operations, for which the war-weary British public were not prepared. Such repression would, moreover, have sharply conflicted with the principle of national self-determination then manifest in the world, to which the rulers of Britain, conscious that the period of her unchallenge-able supremacy in the world had passed, could not entirely run counter.[1] Accordingly, successive British governments sought to compromise with the nationalist forces, conceding a large measure of self-government but striving to retain for Britain strategic bases and some control over their foreign policy designed to prevent the Middle Eastern countries from becoming the allies or instruments of any Power unfriendly to Britain. Com-promises providing temporary satisfaction to both parties were thus reached with Egypt, Iraq, Sa'udi Arabia and Transjordan. In Palestine, while permitting a ten-fold expansion and consolid-ation of the Jewish National Home, Britain made concessions to the growing insistence of Arab nationalism by ever-increasing attention, in her interpretation of the elastically-worded Balfour

---

[1] An important factor in British foreign policy has been the need to ensure that it 'is so directed as to harmonize with the general desires and ideals common to all mankind, and more particularly that it is closely identified with the primary and vital interests of a majority, or as many as possible, of the other nations'. Foreign Office memo. by Sir Eyre Crowe, quoted in *British Security*, by a Chatham House Study Group (1946), 34 f.

Declaration and the Mandate, to the clauses safeguarding Arab rights.

Professor E. H. Carr has remarked that while Britain was able to abandon her formal authority in Egypt and Iraq, and yet maintain her military and economic predominance there by indirect influence and control, France shrank from taking the same step in Syria; and he suggested that this difference in policy was the direct consequence of Britain's superior economic power to that of France.[1] While this is true, it is probably not the whole truth, for there is a fundamental difference between the principles underlying the British and French policies towards dependent peoples. Basically, British principles, while realist and self-interested, have in their working-out usually been ready to consider and be influenced by the salient needs and wishes of those peoples. French colonial policy, on the other hand, has a certain idealist basis; but since that idealism is itself rooted in an excess of self-esteem, it is commonly not prepared to give consideration to conflicting claims and interests. In the French acquisition and retention of the Levant mandate material factors did not bulk very large;[2] a more important factor was the desire to expand the extensive French educational and cultural organizations there, or at least to prevent them from passing under the possibly unsympathetic ægis of any other Power. Since the flower of French genius is essentially intellectual, Frenchmen have persuaded themselves that the intellectual elite of other cultures cannot fail to be so convinced of the transcendent superiority of French culture that they will readily discard for it the essentials of their own culture. They have thus disregarded the fact that the sum of habits and beliefs which is the basis of a culture does not consist of intellectual concepts to be adopted or discarded at will, but is derived from deeply-rooted emotions handed down through successive generations of the culture-group. Consequently, when the centrifugal emotion of nationalism has reasserted itself in those who have acquired French culture, their French mentors have been offended at their perversity; and the reaction of French colonial policy to such rebuffs has been the fostering of minorities and the thwarting of attempts at national unity. Thus her policy of protecting the Lebanese Christians led France on to annex the Syrian

[1] *Twenty Years' Crisis* (1939), 131.
[2] Elizabeth Monroe, *The Mediterranean in Politics*, 77 ff.

hinterland, to whose mainly Muslim culture she was distinctly antipathetic; and once committed, not only were the interests of French concessionaires and officials and the upholding of French prestige obstacles to the handing-over of authority, but she could not lightly contemplate relinquishing her hold in the face of growing Arab nationalism without stimulating the demands of the Arab nationalists and supporters of pan-Islam in those North African dependencies which were so much more essential to her. Consequently, even after the collapse of metropolitan France in 1940, her representatives clung on to her Levantine sphere of influence with a desperation that was probably a direct consequence of their inner awareness of their lack of effective power and ability to attain France's ends by means less crude than force; until at length the *fait accompli* of 1945 compelled Frenchmen reluctantly to abandon much that might have been saved by greater readiness to compromise even as late as the previous year.

It is significant that the only period, in which the British have imagined that their culture might be transmitted to others merely by a process of intellectual education, was when the utilitarian Macaulay was planning to educate the elite of India along exclusively British lines. Since that time, however, Englishmen in close contact with peoples of alien culture have become aware that a culture is deeply rooted in inherited emotions which it is both difficult and dangerous to try to uproot. The more understanding British official, in India or in the colonies, has acquired an understanding of, and a respect for, the culture of those among whom he is living, to a degree that seems much less common in the French colonies. The French insistence on their own language as the almost exclusive medium of instruction has no counterpart in British colonial practice. The Englishman, with his physical concept of 'race', does not, like the Frenchman with his intellectual concept of *civilisation*, imagine that other races can be educated into becoming British or French.[1] While the British colonial administrations have been accused of taking too little interest in education, the French have certainly been too much concerned with *assimilation*. When the dependent peoples have shown themselves self-centred, alien, and hostile to this process, the French have been indignant, if not revengeful; but the British,

[1] Though when uprooted from their traditional homes and shipped across the Atlantic they have become Americans.

while over-sensitive to their lack of gratitude for the material benefits of orderly administration, have more philosophically resigned themselves to the transfer of authority, though with typical realism they have hitherto always retained for themselves a strategic *point d' appui*.

Although the Second World War confirmed beyond any doubt the unchallengeable position of the U.S.A. as the greatest world Power, she did not at first adjust herself in her Middle East relationships. Until the war, while reserving for herself the economic 'open door' and the unrestricted right to criticize, she was content that Britain should bear the full responsibility for this region. The war increased American interests and responsibilities there; but when in 1944 political differences in liberated Greece came to a head, the Americans hastened to withdraw their forces and liaison-officers and left Britain to deal with the problem alone. Similarly, at the beginning of 1946, with Russian pressure on Persia visibly increasing from week to week, the U.S. government precipitately withdrew their troops two months in advance of the agreed date. But the impoverishment of Britain's resources in capital, material, and productive capacity as a result of the war subsequently became evident; early in 1947 she had to ask the U.S.A. to take over and augment her financial commitments to Greece and Turkey; and her abdication of authority in India and Palestine is, in part at least, an index of her diminished power in the world. Already in the first half of 1946 an eminent American student of the Middle East had pointed the moral:

'Whereas Great Britain is no longer capable of preserving a balance of power in this strategic area, the question is whether the United States, in co-operation with Great Britain or alone, is able or willing to restore the balance, and whether from the point of view of global politics the United States can afford now, any more than Great Britain could formerly, to contemplate the entrenchment of the Soviet Union in strategic positions along that vital line extending from the Mediterranean to India.'[1]

Later in 1946 the American government stated that it regarded

---

[1] Dr. H. L. Hoskins, *The New Era of Power-Politics* (Foreign Policy Association, Headline Series, No. 57, New York, May–June 1946). On the other hand E. A. Speiser's apprehensions of America's 'pronounced dependence on Britain . . . amounting to a state of vassalage' in Middle Eastern affairs (*The United States and the Near East*, part III, sec. 10), though expressed later in 1946, were already outdated by events.

the maintenance of the independence of Turkey as an essential part of its foreign policy, and was opposed to the Soviet aim of winning exclusive control over the Straits. Henry Wallace's campaign for the abandoning of American 'support of the British Empire' and its replacement by 'collaboration with Russia in the undisturbed economic development of areas in which we have joint interests, such as the Middle East', was sharply rebuffed by the electorate in the congressional elections of November, 1946. The agreement between American and British oil-interests in the following month for sharing the output of the South Persian oilfield foreshadowed a closer collaboration; and in March 1947 President Truman called on Congress to take over and augment the British commitments to Greece and Turkey. In support of this policy Senator Vandenberg, the leader of the Republican majority in the Senate, told that House:

'If the Middle East falls within the orbit of aggressive Communist expansion, the repercussions will echo from the Dardanelles to the China Sea and westward to the rims of the Atlantic. Indeed, in this foreshortened world, the Middle East is not far enough for safety from our own New York. . . .'[1] The U.S.A. has also given moral support to the Persian government in resisting the Soviet demands for an oil-concession, and is supplying it with arms.

Until the autumn of 1947 it had appeared that the Middle East, with its great contrasts of a self-indulgent and arbitrary plutocracy, an intelligentsia discontented with its economic and social status, and an urban and rural proletariat living in great poverty, provided an admirable breeding-ground for Communist propaganda, even though this had not yet had time to produce far-reaching results. Critics were free with their rebukes to the British, and to a lesser degree the American, governments for their apparent attachment to the 'reactionary ruling cliques' of the Arab League countries, Turkey and Persia, and for their apparent failure to single out for support more deserving 'democratic' and 'progressive' elements in the population.[2]

However, the situation has temporarily, at least, been greatly

[1] 8 April 1947.
[2] The most recent criticism of this kind appeared in *The Fortnightly*, February 1948, 96 ff., by an American, Professor Hans Heymann. On the political inadequacy, at the present stage, of Middle Eastern liberal intellectuals, cf. A. C. Edwards, in *International Affairs* XXIII (1947), 56 f.

changed by the Russians' support of the partition of Palestine and their apparent solicitude for the embryonic Jewish State. The changes of Soviet policy are apt to be so abrupt and radical that the Zionists are liable to be dropped as soon as they have fulfilled their purpose in the devious tactics of Soviet foreign policy. Meanwhile, it is probable that the U.S.S.R. has lost a considerable proportion of its support in Arab left-wing circles, which are in general just as anti-Zionist as the rest of politically-minded Arabs; and even if (or when) Soviet policy is subsequently reversed, it will be some time before the loss of confidence can be repaired. This gives the U.S.A. and Britain a short respite in which to assist and encourage Middle Eastern governments to develop their economies for the benefit of the mass of the population. Not that the financing of ambitious plans is an infallible or short-term instrument of economic and social betterment, since 'sums of money starting on a highroad with a definite journey's end in view have a nimble trick of slipping into by-ways'[1] in the Middle East. The longer-term goal is the orderly and evolutionary extension of economic and political power from the present narrow ruling-class to a much wider cross-section of the population, with the urban and rural masses being fittingly educated to fill a more constructive role in the economic life of their communities, and eventually to assist in shaping their political future also. But the process of social change by evolutionary means is inevitably a slow one: Lewis Mumford likens it to 'a geological process of leaching and displacement'[2]; and to accelerate it by impulsion from outside is liable to produce reactions disadvantageous to the impelling Power. Never perhaps has either the American or the British government been required to display a more delicate combination of sensitive understanding, firmness and suppleness of purpose, and tactful handling of personalities, than the situation in the Middle East will demand in the years to come.

In the longer perspective, however, nothing would be more erroneous than to suppose that the development of an economy, the improvement of a social system, the spread of democracy or of socialism, or any combination of these things, will of itself radically improve the condition of man, in the Middle East or elsewhere. After some three centuries of increasing complacency in

[1] *Times* Tehran correspondent, 11 July 1947.
[2] *The Condition of Man* (1944), 335.

human ingenuity in constructing machines and institutions (culminating simultaneously in the atomic bomb and the United Nations Organization!), experience is at last teaching our generation that the mere changing of economic, or social, or political systems does not extirpate or sublimate the inordinate self-will which lies at the root of most human evils: it only causes it to assume new, and perhaps more virulent, forms. The humanist reformer is working against the relentless gravitational pull of human self-will. Sooner or later, he sees all the hard-won progress of generations of peaceful endeavour dissipated in a decade of passion or panic; and in his despair and humiliation he may then realize that the reform of human institutions is no substitute for the regeneration of the human soul. Only religion, divesting mankind of his conceit in himself and restoring him to a proper sense of his true place, can make him see that his own nature 'impels him to corrupt the very instruments and institutions which he devises for the ordering of his social life', and that civilization can be transformed and politics redeemed only through 'the contact of Eternity with the Historical, and through the acceptance of Divine sovereignty as the source from which the many forms of human sovereignty are derived'.[1]

[1] Canon C. E. Hudson, in *International Affairs*, XXIII (1947), 6; Rev. Geraint Vaughan Jones, *Democracy and Civilization* (1946), 281.

List of Authorities

Ch. I

L. Dudley Stamp: *Asia*. (London, 1946.)

V. Gordon Childe: *What Happened in History*. (London, 1942.)

W. F. Albright: *From Stone Age to Christianity*. (John Hopkins Press, 1946.)

Christopher Dawson: *The Making of Europe*. (London, 1934.)

Ch. II

Ph. Hitti: *History of the Arabs*. (New York, 1937.)

R. A. Nicholson: *Literary History of the Arabs*. (London, 1923.)

De Lacy O'Leary: *Arabic Thought and its Place in History*. (London, 1921.)

Sir Thos. Arnold and A. Guillaume (edit.):   *The Legacy of Islam*. (London, 1931.)

A. Mieli: *La Science Arabe*. (Leiden, 1938.)

D. B. Macdonald: *Muslim Theology, Jurisprudence, and Constitutional Theory*. (London, 1903.)

Ernest Barker: *The Crusades*. (London, 1923.)

J. La Monte: *Crusade and Jihad* (in *The Arab Heritage*, ed. Nabih A. Faris; Princeton, 1944).

S. Lane-Poole: *History of Egypt in the Middle Ages*. (London, 1901.)

J. H. Kramers: *Encyclopaedia of Islam*, art. Turks, B.IV.

Ch. III

Encyclopaedia of Islam, Art. Egypt.

★A. E. Crouchley: *Economic Development of Modern Egypt.*
                            (London, 1938.)
Jacob de Haas: *History of Palestine.*   (New York,
                            1934.)
H. Lammens: *La Syrie.* (Beirut, 1938.)
★S. Longrigg: *Four Centuries of Modern Iraq.* (Lon-
                            don, 1925.)
★Sir A. Wilson: *The Persian Gulf.* (London, 1928.)
★Sir Percy Sykes: *History of Persia.* (London, 1930.)
★D. G. Hogarth: *History of Arabia.* (London, 1922.)
A. C. Wood: *History of the Levant Company.* (Lon-
                            don, 1935.)
Edgar Prestage: *The Portuguese Pioneers.* (London,
                            1933.)
Sir W. Foster: *England's Quest of Eastern Trade.*
                            (London, 1933.)

Ch. IV

J. A. R. Marriott: *The Eastern Question.* (London, 1918.)
E. Driault: *La Question d'Orient.* (Paris, 1898.)
H. Dodwell: *The Founder of Modern Egypt.* (London
                            1931.)
Sir Arnold Wilson: *The Suez Canal.* (London, 1933.)
Ph. Graves: *Life of Sir Percy Cox.* (London, 1941.)
E. M. Earle: *Turkey, the Great Powers, and the
                            Baghdad Railway.* (New York,
                            1923.)

Ch. V

Sir Valentine Chirol: *The Egyptian Problem.* (London,
                            1920.)
Lord Cromer: *Modern Egypt.* (London, 1908.)
★Lord Lloyd: *Egypt since Cromer.* (London, 1933.)
M. Rifaat Bey: *The Awakening of Modern Egypt.* (Lon-
                            don, 1947.)   •
★Geo. Antonius: *The Arab Awakening.* (London, 1938.)

P. W. Ireland: Iraq, A Study in Political Development.
                  (London, 1937.)
L. P. Elwell-Sutton: Modern Iran. (London, 1941.)

Chs. VI, VII

Lord Wavell: *Allenby in Egypt.* (London, 1943.)
Great Britain and Egypt, 1914–36 (Royal Institute of International Affairs: London, 1936).
Sir A. Wilson: *Loyalties,* Vol. II. (1936.)
Royal Commission Report on Palestine, 1937.
Great Britain and Palestine, 1915–45 (Royal Institute of International Affairs: London, 1946).
A. M. Hyamson: *Palestine, A Policy.* (London, 1942.)
James Parkes: *The Emergence of the Jewish Problem.*
                        (London, 1946.)
Nevill Barbour: *Nisi Dominus, a Survey of the Palestine*
                        Controversy. (London, 1946.)
The Political History of Palestine under British Administration.
    (Memo. by H. M. G. presented in July 1947 to The United Nations Special Committee on Palestine.)
A. H. Hourani: *Syria and Lebanon.* (London, 1946.)

Ch. VIII

A. Bonne: *Economic Development of the Middle*
                        East. (London, 1945.)
E. B. Worthington: *Middle East Science.* (London, 1946.)
B. A. Keen: *Agricultural Development of the Middle*
                        East. (London, 1946.)
Charles Issawi: *Egypt: An Economic and Social Analysis.*
                        (London, 1947.)
Doreen Warriner: *Land and Poverty in the Middle East.*
                        (London, 1948.)

Ch. IX

Raymond Lacaste: *La Russie soviétique et la Question*
                        d'Orient.(Paris, 1946.)

Index

U

PRINTED IN GREAT BRITAIN
BY THE ALCUIN PRESS,
WELWYN GARDEN CITY

Lightning Source UK Ltd.
Milton Keynes UK
UKOW051140010212

186466UK00001B/95/A